Women, War, and Violence

Women, War, and Violence

Personal Perspectives and Global Activism

*Edited by Robin M. Chandler,
Lihua Wang, and
Linda K. Fuller*

WOMEN, WAR, AND VIOLENCE
Copyright © Robin M. Chandler, Lihua Wang, and Linda K. Fuller, 2010.

Cover image: original collage entitled "Capoeira", Robin M. Chandler.
Collection: Nynex Corporate Art Collection

All rights reserved.

First published in 2010 by
PALGRAVE MACMILLAN®
in the United States—a division of St. Martin's Press LLC,
175 Fifth Avenue, New York, NY 10010.

Where this book is distributed in the UK, Europe and the rest of the world, this is by Palgrave Macmillan, a division of Macmillan Publishers Limited, registered in England, company number 785998, of Houndmills, Basingstoke, Hampshire RG21 6XS.

Palgrave Macmillan is the global academic imprint of the above companies and has companies and representatives throughout the world.

Palgrave® and Macmillan® are registered trademarks in the United States, the United Kingdom, Europe and other countries.

ISBN: 978–0–230–10371–9

Library of Congress Cataloging-in-Publication Data

    Women, war, and violence : personal perspectives and global activism / edited by Robin M. Chandler, Lihua Wang, and Linda K. Fuller.
      p. cm.
      ISBN 978–0–230–10371–9 (alk. paper)
        1. Women and war. 2. War victims. 3. Women—Violence against. 4. Victims of violence. I. Chandler, Robin M. II. Wang, Lihua. III. Fuller, Linda K.

JZ6405.W66W66 2009
303.6082—dc22
                                                        2009051994

A catalogue record of the book is available from the British Library.

Design by Newgen Imaging Systems (P) Ltd., Chennai, India.

First edition: October 2010

10 9 8 7 6 5 4 3 2 1

Transferred to Digital Printing 2015

Contents

Foreword vii
Cynthia Enloe

Preface and Acknowledgments xi
Lihua Wang

List of Contributors xv

Introduction: Life Blossoms in the Killing Fields 1
Robin M. Chandler

Part I Understanding Gender-Based Violence, Rebuilding Personal Security for Girls and Women, and Peace-Building

1 Not Making Excuses: Functions of Rape as a Tool in Ethno-Nationalist Wars 17
   Natalja Zabeida

2 Speaking with Postwar Liberia: Gender-Based Violence Interventions for Girls and Women 31
   Robin M. Chandler

3 Sexual Violence among Refugees and Asylum Seekers Who Come to the United States 45
   Linda Piwowarczyk

4 Victims, Villains, and Victors: Mediated Wartime Images of Women 59
   Linda K. Fuller

Part II Organizational Reconciliation, Policy Reform, and Postwar Effects on Women

5 Challenging Hegemonic Understandings of Human Rights Violations in the South African Truth and Reconciliation Commission: The Need for a New Narrative 75
   Kiri Gurd and Rashida Manjoo

6	A Gendered Approach for Policy in United Nations Peacekeeping Missions *Colleen Keaney-Mischel*	99
7	Aftermath of U.S. Invasions: The Anguish of Women in Afghanistan and Iraq *Hayat Imam*	117

Part III Reframing Twenty-First Century Feminism with Global Ethnic Struggles

8	Women and Peace in a Divided Society: Peace-Building Potentials of Feminist Struggles and Reform Processes in Bosnia and Herzegovina *Anne Jenichen*	137
9	Peace Is the Name of an Unborn Child in Turkey *Simten Coşar*	155
10	Reconstructing Women in Postconflict Rwanda *Laura Sjoberg*	171

Part IV Confronting the Patriarchy of War as Women Combatants and Noncombatants

11	Relationships of War: Mothers, Soldiers, Knowledge *Steven L. Gardiner and Angie Reed Garner*	189
12	Female Participation in the Iraqi Insurgency: Insights into Nationalist and Religious Warfare *Karla J. Cunningham*	205
13	Agency and Militarization in the Heartland: Noncombatant American Women *Michelle M. Gardner-Morkert*	219
14	Horror to Hope, Tragedy to Triumph: The Women of Rwanda *Tadia Rice*	233

Index   255

Foreword

Cynthia Enloe

Books are written in history. We each read any book in history. Each book grows out of a particular historical context—its distinctive understandings, anxieties, and power dynamics. Some readers' understandings of their own historical moment are transformed by reading a book. *Women, War, and Violence* is going to press in the immediate aftermath of two historic international decisions in the ongoing evolution of global gendered politics. First, on Monday, September 14, the 192 state delegations of the United Nations General Assembly voted in favor of creating a new consolidated UN agency for women. Then, two weeks later, the UN Security Council unanimously adopted resolution 1888. It called on all UN agencies and all UN member states to take specific steps to end sexual violence against women in armed conflict, but went further, creating a new Special Representative to provide leadership and monitoring of the steps taken (or not taken) to carry out SCR1888.

Robin M. Chandler, Lihua Wang, and Linda K. Fuller as this book's editors and the researchers who have contributed these chapters to their volume, together, have played a small but crucial role in both of these historic decisions. As their fortunate readers, we are better able to see where we are located at this moment in gendered international history. For it is has been the burgeoning feminist analyses of women's experiences of prewar, war and postwar that have provided much of the ground work for the energetic lobbying of the UN by feminist civil society groups to take the condition of women seriously. For decades, government officials and international civil servants and their contractors have been comfortable in imagining, first, that the prewar subordination of women both by individual men and by masculinized state institutions had nothing to do with the sorts of militarized thinking and militarized relationships that led to repeated outbreaks of armed conflict. That is, paying close attention to—and systematically documenting—women's relationships to men, to property, to violence, and to states would, they casually assumed, add nothing to the causal explanations of why wars broke out.

Second, for generations, policy makers within states and within international agencies relied on the short-sighted notion that wars were merely conflicts between men, but that no curiosity had to be invested in the investigations of masculinities, nor in how the politics of femininity and masculinity played out in women's lives and on their bodies in wartime. Nor did they believe that it was worth paying any attention to the thinking and the organizing that so many women did in the midst of wars. Third, for all these years, state and international actors (some with policy-making portfolios, others with research grants) imagined that the people to worry about in the postwar era were the demobilized male soldiers. They, it was commonly thought, would either subvert the fragile peace or contribute to the postwar national rebuilding efforts. Women in the post war era? They would, it was commonly imagined, simply return to their proper domestic spheres and grieve over their wartime losses in private.

All three assumptions have produced masculinized ceasefire and peace negotiations. Together, these three assumptions have left allegedly sophisticated political observers surprised at the subsequent outbreak of a new violent conflict. The perpetuation of this trio of assumptions has helped reestablish patriarchal familial and political institutions in postwar societies. These three assumptions also have sustained a UN machinery for women that has been fragmented, toothless and chronically underfunded.

The smart editors and contributors to *Women, War and Violence* underscore here—and add nuance to—the burgeoning evidence that is challenging all three of these deep-seated masculinized international assumptions. In doing so, they are adding force to the argument for taking women's subordination in peacetime seriously in the name of preventing war. They are making wartime violence against women a question of policy and thus of accountability. They are making the militarization of both femininity and of masculinity a topic for peacetime investigation. They are extending our too-short attention spans into postwar eras where widows organize to reform patriarchal inheritance laws, where survivors of wartime rape organize to pursue justice, and where transnational feminist alliances press the United Nations General Assembly and the powerful Security Council to move beyond cheap platitudes to meaningful action for the sake of insuring women's rights.

The relationships between feminist research and feminist action can often seem terribly vague. We rethink old questions, we share research through our teaching, we launch new field investigations, we organize conferences where we can reflect on each other's findings, we publish books and articles that we hope someone will read. But who "out there" listens? Whose understandings—framings, discourses, agendas—are changed by all this feminist work? Well, it turns out, that a lot of people are listening. A lot of minds can be changed. Usually, though, it is not the research and writings of just one person which achieves such a shift. It is the diggings and the public sharing of findings by dozens of people in dozens of countries that manage to unsettle masculinist collective thinking, moving it an inch, sometimes a yard.

Preface and Acknowledgments

Lihua Wang

This book has had quite a history, dating as it does from a conference on "Women, War, and Violence" that we organized in 2006 at Northeastern University under the directorship of Robin M. Chandler, then chair of Women's Studies. Like other programs, ours is perceived of as an academic field linked to radical political politics, with academic feminists continually trying to transform public perceptions. Here, we encouraged public awareness of violence against women and girls, with many mutual partners and initiatives.

Lilly Marceline, then program coordinator of the Boston Area Rape Crisis Center (BARCC), proposed her organization's idea of focusing on war-related violence against women. Other local organizations brought a range of different interests, participants including Amnesty International, the Reebok Human Rights Project, the Refugee Immigration Ministry, the Asian Task Force Against Domestic Violence, the Trafficking Victims Outreach & Services Network, the Funding Exchange, and the Boston Care Network. It was both a challenge and an honor to work with all these diverse organizations.

The process included on and off campus efforts, collaborations, and negotiations. Mainly, the planning stages reflecting feminist activism, included collectivity, advocacy, and action. From the beginning, utilizing the whole groups' efforts was our clear goal; to achieve it, we formed a working committee of more than ten representatives from both internal university programs and local organizations. Beside Women's Studies, internal sponsors included the Brudnick Center on Conflict and Violence; the Middle East Center for Peace, Culture, and Development, and the Dean's office of College of Arts and Sciences. Two student groups—the Black Student Organization and the Feminist Student Organization, also participated.

Planning did not always run smoothly, as might be expected. As members of a working committee, we had to learn how to deal with the group's differences—cultural considerations, academic concerns, and nonacademic organizational distinctions—and to work toward our mutual agenda. Working out our differences was an important part in making progress in the planning stages.

Collective efforts were also reflected in our funding and the accumulation of resources. Our needs for multiple kinds of resources allowed both academic and community organizations to use their strengths. My role, as coordinator, involved performing multiple tasks such as serving as a public relation person, conference organizer, and mentor for feminist students. It worked: Our conference reflected the link between feminist knowledge and real life situations, including a preconference film screening and the introduction of advocacy issues in classrooms. Linking classroom learning and popular culture, Linda K. Fuller, a Senior Fellow in our Women's Studies program, suggested films representing violence against women and the Feminist Student Organization and the Black Student Organization organized the screening of films targeting gender and violence. Ann Loos, president of the Feminist Student Organization, arranged these preconference films:

1. *Calling the Ghosts* (1996), which was based on interviews of survivors raped by Serbian soldiers during the Bosnian war.
2. *The Day My God Died* (2003), which documented women and girls who were trafficked in the sex industry in the brothels of Bombay.
3. *Two Women* (1999), which took place during the early years of the Islamic Republic, deals with two young Iranian architects confined by tradition. Its dealing with the taboo subject of domestic violence was hailed as a breakthrough.
4. *Platoon* (1986) is Oliver Stone's graphic depictions of Americans in Vietnam, where massacres, illegal killings, and a particularly gruesome rape make both the soldiers and the audience struggle psychologically.

Relating her own life experiences, Sima Wali, President and CEO of Refugee Women in Development Inc. (RefWID), gave the keynote for the conference, directing our attention to international women's rights. She began by presenting a bloody picture of global violence that was evidenced by 77 documented conflicts around the world, among which only two showed hope for resolution. Situated in the global violent landscape, it was not a surprise that women and young girls made up 77 percent of war-affected populations experiencing human rights abuse, including sexual violence. Wali claimed that there were 19.2 million people affected by violent situations around the globe, concluding that a humanitarian crisis marked the end of the twentieth century and the beginning of the twenty-first century. Moving away from a global perspective about violence, she detailed Afghanistan war and women, identifying how lack of security for women both at home and in the streets was a Number One issue for them. Situated in unstable national environments and patriarchal culture, there was no question that Afghanistan women and children were subjected to trafficking, forced marriages, and domestic violence. In addition, Wali said that 80 percent of Afghanistan women were illiterate, and female suicide and self-immolation continued to trouble the society.

Following up on Wali's remarks, a panel on "Structures of Militarization and War for Women's Rights and Health" continued the theme of violence and women's rights. Hayat Imam, a feminist activist from Bangladesh whose work appears here, discussed the war in Afghanistan and Iraq in terms of its impact on women both there and for American women. Rashida Manjoo, who is on the law faculty at the University of Cape Town, presented a similar topic regarding violence in South Africa; in a collaboration with Kiri Gurd, she challenges the hegemony embedded in the South African Truth and Reconciliation Commission.

Concerning women's property rights, lawyer Marianne Smith Geula, worried about war widows in sub-Saharan Africa, and Laura Rotella presented her research on war-related rape in Vietnam and Bosnia-Herzegovina. Questioning the role of the United Nations in relation to women's issues were Laura Roskos, a feminist activist-in residence at Suffolk University, who discussed U N Security Council Resolution 1325, and Colleen Keaney-Mischel, who presented her doctoral research on obstacles to gender mainstreaming policy in U. N. peacekeeping missions. The second theme of the conference was related to domestic violence. Melissa Gopnik, activist/director of the Boston Area Rape Crisis Center, explained the need to provide support and services to victims of sexual violence, Meghan Finley presented her dissertation research on the issue of violence against military wives, and the media's role in representing violence was discussed by Linda K. Fuller.

Violence experienced by refugees was our third theme. A psychiatrist and codirector of the Boston Center for Refugee Health and

Human Rights, Lin Piwowarczyk discussed refugees and/or asylum seekers; based on her clinical work, she pointed out that women's experiences of sexual violence are very often based on differences such as race, religion, nationality, and political opinion. Taking personal experience into account, Van Chey from the Asian Task Force Against Domestic Violence talked about her own experiences and hardships trying to raise three children in refugee camps from Cambodia to Vietnam, illustrating the maltreatment of women. Lastly, we took on violence prevention. Lisa Hartwick, director of the Center for Violence Prevention and Recovery, explained three of her programs: Safe Transitions (domestic violence intervention), Rape Crisis Intervention, and Community Violence Intervention; collaborating with Beth Israel Deaconess Medical Center to provide services such as advocacy, psychotherapy, and education, she characterized key elements of the prevention program as victim-based advocacy, accessible services, and secure base of support. Carol Gomez, founder and director of the Trafficking Victims Outreach and Services Network, continued the topic of prevention, telling how her organization offers a range of services such as training, education, and consulting on violence prevention to empower women.

Clearly, our conference pointed out the importance of examining violence against women within complex circumstances, including war, domestic, race, political-, and culture-based situations. It required academic feminists to think about violence beyond a gender-exclusive framework, realizing that racial, political, cultural, ethnic, and/or religious differences should be integrated for future investigations. Providing a bridge between academic feminists and local activists, it laid a foundation for future collaborations.

This volume reflects on these themes, encouraging us to translate advocacy into social awareness. I would like to use this opportunity to thank all those conference organizers and participants, including students, faculty, and administration, as well as the many contributors who responded to our wider Call for publishing research relative to women, war, and violence. A special thanks will give to James Stellar, former Dean of the Collage of Arts and Sciences. We are also grateful that Farideh Koohi-Kamali of Palgrave Macmillan recognized the potential of this collection, and it has been a pleasure to work with both her and her editorial assistant, Robyn Curtis, at our first choice for publisher.

Contributors

Robin M. Chandler, of the Department of African American Studies at Northeastern University and former chair of Women's Studies, is an artist-sociologist and former Fulbright Scholar. Her research specialties include contemporary culture and difference, microenterprise development among artisans, the role of technology and race, and global citizenship and human rights. As a scholar, Chandler lectures, teaches, and publishes in the United States and abroad and conducts applied interdisciplinary research on the arts and politics, and community-building, and culturally specific approaches to multimedia. She is the author of numerous publications and is the recipient of numerous grants and honors including the National Science Foundation.

Simten Coşar (Ph.D., Bilkent University), who teaches in the Department of Political Science and International Relations at Başkent University, is the author of several articles on Turkish politics, feminism in Turkey, and modern Turkish political thought. Currently, she is working on the connection between love, nationalism and patriarchy.

Karla J. Cunningham (Ph.D., University at Buffalo) is the Elsie Hillman Chair in Politics and teaches Political Science at Chatham University. A former Political Scientist at RAND, she is the author of numerous articles on female political violence and political change in the Middle East that have been published in *Studies in Conflict & Terrorism*, the *Oxford Encyclopedia of Women in World History*, and various edited volumes. She is writing a book on Jordanian politics entitled *The King's Dilemma: Revisiting Jordan's Failed Liberalization*.

Cynthia Enloe is a research professor of international development and women's studies at Clark University, and has served as Chair of Clark's Government Department and Director of Women's Studies. She is the recipient of the International Studies Association's Susan Strange Award and the Susan S. Northcutt Award through the Women's Caucus for International Studies. Professor Enloe is a feminist writer whose many publications have contributed to current understanding of gender issues and the circumstances of women throughout the world. Her research has focused on the interplay of women's politics in the national and international arenas, with special attention to how globalization, militarization, and militarism affect gender discourse. Enloe's most recent publications include *The Curious Feminist; Bananas, Beaches, and Bases*; and *Maneuvers: The International Politics of Militarizing Women's Lives.*

Linda K. Fuller (Ph.D., University of Massachusetts), a professor of Communications at Worcester (MA) State College, has been a Senior Fellow at Northeastern University since 2003. The author/ (co)editor of more than 20 books and 250+ professional publications and conference reports, most recently *Sport, Rhetoric, and Gender* (2006), *Community Media: International Perspectives* (2007), and *African Women's Unique Vulnerabilities to HIV/AIDS* (2008), she has had Fulbrights to Singapore (1996) and Senegal (2002), and recently presented a paper on child soldiers at a conference on Media, War, and Conflict at Bowling Green State University.

Michelle M. Gardner-Morkert (Ph.D. Clark University) is faculty coordinator of the Women's and Gender Studies Program at Concordia University Chicago. Her current writing project is an analysis of the militarization of noncombatant American women during the Afghanistan and Iraq wars.

Steven L. Gardiner is a visiting professor of Anthropology at the Lahore University of Management Science (LUMS). His research interests include military masculinity and right-wing American social movements.

Angie Reed Garner is a contemporary artist and writer with longterm interest in issues of gender, power, and war. She lives in Lahore, Pakistan with her partner and research collaborator, Steven L. Gardiner.

Kiri Gurd is a Sociology Ph.D. candidate at Boston University. Her dissertation research analyzes the proliferation/ diffusion of humanitarian institutions through the lens of globalization, neo-institutionalism, and critical gender theory; she focuses specifically on truth commissions. She was a visiting fellow at Goldsmith's College's Unit for Global Justice center in 2008.

Hayat Imam (M. Ed., Antioch University), a Muslim feminist and active member of Dorchester People for Peace, is a long-time proponent of renewable energy. She has worked internationally as a fundraising and development consultant. Former director of the Boston Women's Fund, she is committed to promoting the economic and political capacity of women so they can build sustainable changes in their lives. She is the coauthor of *Watermelons Not War!* (New Society Publishers, 1984).

Anne Jenichen is currently pursuing her Ph.D. research on advocacy processes in the field of women's rights in postwar Bosnia and Herzegovina. She is a Research Fellow at the United Nations Research Institute for Social Development (UNRISD) in Geneva, Switzerland, assisting in a comparative research project on Religion, Politics and Gender Equality.

Colleen Keaney-Mischel (Ph.D., Sociology, Northeastern University) has taught at both Northeastern University and Merrimack College and has worked as a volunteer with the International Rescue Committee's North Star Program for Refugee Women and Children. Her current work includes a focus on peace-building in conflict-affected areas as a consultant with Coexistence International at Brandies University.

Rashida Manjoo is a UN Special Rapporteur on Violence against Women. She holds a professorship in the Department of Public Law at the University of Cape Town, South Africa. She has also served as the Des Lee Distinguished Visiting Professor at Webster University, USA, where she has taught courses in human rights with a particular focus on women's human rights and also transitional justice. She was the Eleanor Roosevelt Fellow with the Human Rights Program at Harvard Law School (2006–7) and also a clinical instructor in the program in 2005–6. She is an Advocate of the High Court of South Africa and a former commissioner of the Commission on Gender Equality (CGE), a constitutional body mandated to oversee the promotion and protection of gender equality. Prior to being appointed to the CGE she was involved in social context training for judges and lawyers, where she has designed both content and methodology during her time at the Law, Race, and Gender Research Unit, University of Cape Town and at the University of Natal, Durban. Manjoo was involved in setting up both a national and a provincial network on violence against women and is the founder of the Gender Unit at the Law Clinic at the University of Natal and the Domestic Violence Assistance Programme at the Durban Magistrates Court (the first such project in a court in South Africa). She has also been involved in the Provincial Executive of the Women's Coalition, a forum that was established pre-democracy to formulate the Women's Charter (a document setting out the demands of women in a new democracy). She is a member of the International Coalition for Women's Human Rights in Conflict Situations and also a member of the Women Living under Muslim Laws Network. She was also an active member of the Women's Caucus for Gender Justice in the International Criminal Court and remains an Advisory Board member of the Women's Initiative for Gender Justice.

Linda Piwowarczyk is cofounder and codirector of the Boston Center for Refugee Health and Human Rights, a hospital-based multidisciplinary program that works with survivors of torture and refugee trauma from over 60 countries. She is also an assistant professor of psychiatry at the Boston University School of Medicine and is a Distinguished Fellow of the American Psychiatric Association.

Tadia Rice is an international business consultant, speaker, and author with expertise in leadership, organizational development, women's empowerment, cultural acuity, and diversity. Rice motivates clients to actualize unsurpassed potential. As author of "Breaking Into the Boys Club," she shares her compelling experiences in all-male business environments. "In the Midst of a Miracle" chronicles Rice's experience as an international election observer in South Africa's first-ever democratic election. Rice founded the Tahirih Association (www.tahirihassociation.org) that has educated 21 women and girls in South Africa, China, Namibia, United States, Honduras, Liberia, and the Lakota/Oglala Nation. Rice also serves on the Board of Directors of the Princess of Africa Foundation (www.princessofafrica.co.za), helping fight malaria on the continent. For her many achievements Rice has been honored by United States Congresswoman Diane Watson, California Senator Barbara Boxer, Los Angeles Mayor Tom Bradley, and Atlanta Mayor Bill Campbell.

Laura Sjoberg (B.A., University of Chicago; Ph.D., University of Southern California, J.D. Boston College) is Assistant Professor of Political Science at The University of Florida. Dr. Sjoberg is author of *Gender, Justice, and the Wars in Iraq* (2006), coauthor of *Mothers, Monsters, Whores: Women's Violence in Global Politics* (2007), and editor of the forthcoming *Gender and International Security: Feminist Perspectives* (2010); and (with Amy Eckert) *Rethinking the 21st Century: New Problems, Old Solutions* (2009). Published in *International Studies Perspectives*, *International Studies Quarterly*, the *International Feminist Journal of Politics*, *International Politics*,

International Relations, and *Politics and Gender*, among others, she has served as president of the International Studies Association-West and chair of their Feminist Theory and Gender Studies Section.

Lihua Wang (Ph.D.) is the coordinator of the Women's Studies Program at Northeastern University in Boston and an associate in research at the Fairbank Center for East Asian Studies at Harvard University. Her research has focused on official economic policy and the global impact on women's lives in China. As a recipient of a Ford Foundation grant, she conducted three years of fieldwork regarding economic development and micro-credits for rural women in China. Her articles about her research have been published in both English and Chinese. She edited *Globalization and its Chinese Discontents: Feminist Critiques* (Peking University Press, 2008), attempting to capture critical debates on globalization. Dr. Wang uses her teaching opportunities to address feminist activism by offering a Service Learning class at Northeastern University.

Natalja Zabeida (Ph.D., Northeastern University) has done research on nationalism, rape in war and sex trafficking. She currently lives in Germany and works at SUANA—a consultation and advocacy center for migrant women victims of domestic violence, and teaches at Hannover University.

Introduction

Life Blossoms in the Killing Fields

Robin M. Chandler

> The world has never yet seen a truly great and virtuous nation because in the degradation of woman the very fountains of life are poisoned at their source.
>
> —Lucretia Mott

This book contains stories from what has come to be known as "the killing fields": an unprecedented pandemic of gender-based violence (GBV) during war and conflict. According the United Nations High Commissioner for Refugees (UNHCR), the term "gender-based violence" is used to distinguish violence that targets individuals or groups of individuals on the basis of their gender from other forms of violence. GBV includes violent acts such as rape, torture, mutilation, sexual slavery, forced impregnation, and murder. When involving women, it is violence that is directed against a woman or girl because she is female, or that affects women disproportionately. The authors address both the troubling and triumphant personal experiences of girls and women in war-related conditions and the activists, both men and women, who are shedding humanitarian floodlights on the epidemic of violence against women in many forms worldwide. According to the World Health Organization, gender-based violence accounts for more death and disability among women between the ages of 15 and 44 than the combined effects of cancer, malaria, traffic injuries, and war.

What unites these essays and their writers is a community of discourse and action on international human rights. Many practitioners, activists as well as those who have experienced violence, are witnessing an expanding and worldwide social justice movement among people whose organizational identities fall beyond conventional notions of citizenship. This new identity of global citizenship emerging over the last century brings together those from state and nongovernmental organizations (NGOs), nonprofit organizations, and the traditional development sector. Devoted to a host of crises affecting human culture all around us, we see the formation of transnational social and political subjectivities, each focused on a revitalization of the notion of the value of human life and inherent nobility. Referred to by some in the policy research and community-based domains as "the third sector," many such alliances of heterogeneous entities and individuals are directed specifically to the rights of girls and women. Utilizing novel mobilization strategies from technology and social networking, to social and economic initiatives, a new form of civic engagement is unfolding across generation, class, and economic status.

Some readers will be aware of numerous texts and reports on this subject from individual scholars and activists, NGOs, the United Nations agencies, research and policy institutes, the public health domain, and some governments. *A problem from Hell: America and the age of genocide* by former Balkan war correspondent, Samantha Powers (2003), covers the overarching realities of genocide in Bosnia and Rwanda. Integrated Regional Information Networks (IRIN) has published *The shame of war: Sexual violence against women and girls in conflict* (2007) as an online report. Vlachova and Biason have documented GBV statistics in their edited volume, *Women in an insecure world: Violence against women: Facts, figures, and analysis* (2005). Women for Women International's director, Zainab Salbi, concurs in the alert entitled *The other side of war: Women's stories of survival and hope* (2006), which comes closer to the advocacy tenor of our book. The array of survey data and media attention given to this critical subject has grown between 1995 and 2004 as reported by the United Nations *World's Women: Progress in Statistics* (2005), yet there is an unfortunate parallel with the pervasive institutionalization of violence against girls and women in many regions of the world, including postwar and peacetime conditions. In order to imagine a conceptual framework in which to understand GBV, we have tipped our hats to a number of development theorists, and have included Amartya Sen's *Development as Freedom* (2000), and partnered with the World Health Organization and PATH, Ellsberg and Heise provide a useful text, *Researching violence against women: A practical guide for researchers and activists* (2005).

Inspired by a conference on *Women, War, and Violence* held in Boston at Northeastern University alluded to in Cynthia Enloe and Lihua Wang's comments, this book will, hopefully, become a consciousness-raising partner in the global advocacy against war and its lifelong assault on the bodies, minds, and spirits of girls, women, and families. In borrowing an iconoclastic term from the unpopular Vietnam War of the second half of the twentieth century—the "killing fields"—we ask the reader to recall the landmark histories of twentieth-century wars and to focus attention on the disquieting and ongoing ravages of conflict well into this new century, particularly the systematic, socialized, and institutionalized silence on this subject. The globalized identity of violence, targeted, relentless, and, in some cases, unmitigated physical terrorism is now an "accepted and normalized" feature of human culture due to the ubiquity of information and communications technologies as well as international activism and citizen journalism. As much as we hear, "never again," GBV continues to escalate, eroding the advancement of global civilization itself. As a collection of personal transnational narratives, eyewitness accounts, professional perspectives, academic research, community activism strategies, clinical reflections, law and policy reform movements, and chilling reports from the field, these essays are not social tourism pruriently exposing the lives of "exotic others": rather, our book presents unique voices both in the scope of national contexts represented and the diversity of our authors.

The women and girls described on these pages have survived multiple traumas of GBV: family loss, the disruption of community, health complications, social stigma, poverty, emotional and psychological abuse, low self-worth, and the near-complete absence of a sense of personal safety. All of their stories are war-related and almost all of these women and girls are heroically rebuilding their lives. While reading these accounts, consider these women as real people, as state citizens entitled to equal rights, and as human beings whose inherent nobility has been denied. This book, and the conference on which it was based, presents both critique and reportage on how women are experiencing war-related violence, before, during, and after, those events. Focused on these intimate journeys through the heart of darkness of women, authors report on how war impacts their sense of humanity, their womanhood, family life, and their remarkable and inspiring resilience. Here, we offer testimonials, reframing lives of dignity, of integrity, of nobility, and the transformations that have occurred in some nations as partnerships between governments and activists redirect policies and interventions to prioritize these crimes against humanity. Many of these interventions, as you will read, fall within the scope of public health pandemics because sexual activity, reproduction and pregnancy, and epidemiology are drawn into interdisciplinary strategies to combat the repercussions of sexually transmitted disease and rape.

Our conference was only the beginning of our institutional and group journey to inform ourselves and others of what we all must do to eliminate terrorism against women wherever it resides at home and abroad. This is neither a task only for feminists, nor women, nor is it a problem that clusters in any one part of the world. From villages to palaces and from ancient times to the present, west and east, developed and developing sites, GBV has prevailed in all of our cultures and societies.

Contributors to Women, War, and Violence

Our contributors represent a vast assembly of cross-disciplinary empirical research, clinical reflections, advocacy, and activist reports from local community-based agencies, national organizations, religious perspectives, and international agencies. Its ultimate value, then, is the combination of academic and practical, real-life applications. Our attention is directed at the international dimensions of GBV in order to clarify that war has a lifelong physical and psychological impact on girls and women in nations with the rule of law, redress, and a human rights philosophy.

To the credit of a growing activist community and the age of information technology, recognition and reactions to GBV are reaching broader communities of interest around the world. Any review of the literature, therefore, must include, not only traditional published research from the social sciences, law, and the international development world, but also those technological devices that reach intergenerational and transnational audiences sooner than later. Live electronic broadcasts can deliver visual electronic data more swiftly than conventional newscasters whose media entities may marginalize, sensationalize, or ignore women's issues (Gallagher 2006). We recognize that many writers, academics, and research scientists in every field have been devoted to this theme since the 1990s but find hope in the fact that both academics and nonacademics are reporting on GBV in greater numbers in the last decade, such as Immaculee Ilibagiza (2007) on the Rwanda holocaust; Jen Marlowe's (2006) documentation of oppression since the Sudan Liberation Army took up arms in Darfur; Marjane Satrapi's (2004) remembrances during a time of upheaval in Iran; and Luong Ung's (2006) stories of Cambodia's genocidal Khmer Rouge. Classified in several areas of research on human sexuality and development, national policy perspectives, public health pandemics, wide-ranging narratives on the struggle against silence on GBV remain relevant. Our editorial view pursued a focus not on the military, but on everyday women, especially poor women in the developing world because these girls and women have limited access to personal voice and frequently live amidst conditions of conflict and war. We are also influenced by a desire to contextualize these narratives by inviting contributors who are either native to the subject country or who have done extensive field work, and/or who have lived abroad. Therefore, our vision is directed toward the present and future; that is, what the current conditions are on the ground, what policies and initiatives are being implemented, and what the dimensions of GBV interventions are, which promise longevity as part of a sustained vision of peace-building that will transform our histories of misogyny and aggression toward a future society founded on the equality of men and women.

At the crossroads of poverty and gender, women and children present some of the most troubling violations involving a range of human development issues from public health pandemics to refugeeism, and social and political instability. There has existed around the world a culture of impunity, disrespect, and contempt for women, which explains in part, the legion examples of vulgar and criminal attacks on their reproductive identity, sexuality, and status as noncitizens and unequal partners to the point where the notion of the female body is devalued through every imaginable assault ranging from female infanticide to sex and drug trafficking rings, which sell children and women. As editors, we choose to highlight positive strides to regain our humane instincts by shedding light on projects and processes that often fall beneath the political radar. We stand shoulder to shoulder with those who press on to oppose the normalization, increase, and frequent dismissal of GBV as a private aberration of individuals and societies dominated by men in patriarchal societies. Our project concerns a reframing of spiritually centered cultures of peace and responsibility. We offer this book as a welcoming partnership with all men and women who understand that peace, equality, and justice for girls and women must be part of our universal consciousness.

PART THEMES OF WOMEN, WAR, AND VIOLENCE

Many of the conference presenters are represented in this volume, joined by national experts and international scholars from many disciplines. The editors have divided the chapters into parts that focus, respectively on (1) Understanding gender-based violence, rebuilding personal security for girls and women, and peace-building; (2) Organizational reconciliation, policy reform, and postwar effects on women; (3) Reframing twenty-first century feminism with global ethnic struggles; and (4) Confronting the patriarchy of war as women combatants and noncombatants.

Part I: Understanding Gender-Based Violence, Rebuilding Personal Security for Girls and Women, and Peace-Building

Natalja Zabeida analyzes the United Nations classification of rape as a "war tactic" in her chapter, "Functions of Rape as a Tool in Ethno-Nationalist Wars." The histories of bloody fighting in the former Yugoslavia and more recently on the African continent—Rwanda, Congo, the Sudan—expose the delayed reaction of the media to this devastating problem.

As pages of international news media broadcast current cases of war-related GBV, Zabeida laments the hardships suffered by former war victims whose perpetrators may never incur legal punishment. She discusses the functions that war-related rape serve in the destruction of forms of identity, from self to national, and as a form of male-to-male communication through retaliation. Zabeida calls for a confrontation with the manipulation of women's greater vulnerability not only as subjects of physical assault, but the ideological propaganda that accompanies patriarchal rationalizations for rape as a tactical appropriation of violence that threatens not only women but their families and communities.

In "Speaking with Postwar Liberia: Gender-Based Violence Intervention for Girls and Women," Robin M. Chandler presents Liberia's struggle to emerge from decades of violence following a fourteen-year civil war in which women's lives were ravaged, leaving more than half of the West African country's girls and women as victims of rape, sexual assault, and exploitation (SEA). Interviewing governmental officials, women's organizations, NGO workers, attorneys, peace movement activists, and university personnel, her chapter highlights the national presence of international governments and agencies that have rushed to reinforce the postwar government of President Ellen Johnson-Sirleaf, the United Nations Military in Liberia (UNMIL) presence, and the vast legal, judicial, police, public health, and civil reforms being undertaken in Liberia. In a nation whose infrastructure was devastated during the war, Chandler briefly examines the role of Liberia's history and the priority given by its new President to eliminate the tragic remnants of GBV through new intergovernmental policies and programs, which support girls and women and focus on poverty-reduction and literacy education by the government and NGO community.

Lin Piwowarczyk's "Sexual Violence among Refugees and Asylum Seekers Who Come to the United States" reports on forced transnational women refugees and asylum seeker emigres and their lives of constant danger at the hands of men who violated them sexually. Discussing issues of public health and human rights among those forced into exile, her chapter sheds light on the psychological and emotional trauma and the vulnerabilities associated with overcoming cultural taboos on speaking publicly about sexual assault and violence against women. Following a media wartime thread that is at the core of this book, Linda K. Fuller's "Victims, Villains, and Victors: Mediated Wartime Images of Women" takes a broad overview of the phenomena, examining gendered violence in media and everyday perspectives, both activist and personal, moving readers to an ethical understanding of how violence against women affects our sisters globally. Because the topic of violence against women is so statistically alarming, so varied both physically and psychologically, and so sensationally depicted, Fuller calls for a critical analysis of its differing definitions as it affects its role in our lives. We are reminded of war-related rape in the Democratic Republic of Congo suffered by Congolese women who transport water under continuing fear of rape by armed militia, choosing this as a more acceptable accommodation than the death that awaits their husbands if they carry out the same rural errand. We ask how this can be a viable choice for family life in the path to equality and freedom, a path that repeatedly places women at the crossroads of impossible sacrifices?

Part II: Organizational Reconciliation, Policy Reform, and Postwar Effects on Women

Kiri Gurd and Rashida Manjoo's "Challenging Hegemonic Understandings of Human Rights Violations in the South African Truth and Reconciliation Commission: The Need for a New Narrative," observes the relationship between truth commissions and hegemony, making visible the way that hegemony functions to assert, reproduce, and maintain unequal power relations, and drawing on analyses, examines women's experiences of apartheid.

Through their focus on women, they expose the taken for granted meaning of human rights violations and of violence as individualistic, solely public, and purely physical, showing how they limit or silence stories of daily systematic inequality and structural violence. As a result, centuries of racialized, gendered oppression were reduced to the traces they left on the corporeal body. The historical and contemporary roots of the conflict remained largely unspoken, and the way individual harm was connected to a broader historical project of global capitalist enterprise, was effaced. Gurd and Manjoo argue that, if truth commissions are to meet their mandated objectives to assist in national reconciliation and the establishment of peace, then a reconceptualization and usage of both human rights and violence needs to take place and a counterhegemonic narrative needs to be established that makes visible local and global systems of inequality that underlie and create overt conflict. In "A Gendered Approach for Policy in United Nations Peacekeeping Missions," Coleen Keaney-Mischel looks back to 1997 when the United Nations began implementing a policy of gender mainstreaming into its peacekeeping missions. The policy requires gender advisers to assist United Nations personnel in fulfilling their mandate of adopting and applying a gender perspective to all aspects of their work within the missions. This chapter examines the strategies used by the gender advisors to achieve those goals. Drawing on in-depth interviews with full-time United Nations advisers, Keaney-Mischel outlines the various approaches advisers take to this task, and how they interpret their role within the missions. It examines how they negotiate their relative lack of power in this setting and the potential for success that their actions have on the gender mainstreaming mandate.

In "Aftermath of U.S. Invasions: The Anguish of Women in Afghanistan and Iraq," Hayat Imam examines the role of masculinity and power in war. Imam suggests that war is a largely male enterprise: The majority of soldiers are men, decisions about launching war and its conduct are made by men, the wounds of the frontlines are experienced mostly by men, and peace is called and settled by men. But war and violence, asserts Imam, impact women and children in very significant ways both short and long term. This chapter focuses on the impact on women as a result of the U.S. invasions of Iraq and Afghanistan, discussing backgrounds and conditions faced by women. In addition, the "sting-back" effects of these invasions on U.S. society on U.S. soldiers, particularly women soldiers, are briefly covered.

Part III: Reframing Twenty-First Century Feminism with Global Ethnic Struggles

From another generation, Anne Jenichen's "Women and Peace in a Divided Society: Peace-Building Potentials of Feminist Struggles and Reform Processes in Bosnia-Herzegovina," analyzes three cases of feminist advocacy and reform processes in postwar Bosnia and Herzegovina in order to discuss their potential contributions to building peace in the politically and socially divided country: A campaign advocating the promotion of women's political representation and participation, the foundation of state institutions for the advancement of gender equality, and a campaign supporting victims of war-related sexual violence. Jenichen argues that such struggles for women's rights entail important potentials for peace-building in divided postwar societies. Women are frequently among the first who cooperate across ethnic divisions established and hardened during ethno-political war, both at the level of society and of the state. Furthermore, the author suggests that feminist policy reforms often strengthen common state structures and their legitimacy, contributing to the overcoming of ethnic divisions. Yet, this chapter highlights the fact that it's not women's participation per se that is the key, but rather their feminist commitment, meaning their efforts to advocate the rights of women, independent of ethnic and political differences. Respective feminist contributions should therefore be, according to Jenichen, much more recognized and promoted in peace-building processes. Given the enduring reluctance of national and international policy makers to systematically integrate women's rights into their postwar reconstruction efforts, this chapter provides arguments that might be useful in mobilizing support for domestic and international decision-makers as well as donors. Simten Cosar analyzes the nature of the feminist struggle against structural violence in Turkey in "Peace Is the Name of an Unborn Child in Turkey," and takes issue with different forms and strategies that have emerged from within the women's movement there, one that emphasizes antimilitarism, and thus, structural peace in thought patterns and in action. Presenting the works of Turkish feminist writer Pinar Selek, Cosar compares these works with other discursive formations in Turkey's political establishment and the women's movement examining antimilitarist feminist politics of women's collectives in Turkey. In addition, until recently there have been no attempts to problematize the connection between violence against women and militarism. The case study in this chapter symbolizes one of the rare and marginal attempts to connect antimilitarism with feminism. Laura Sjoberg's "Reconstructing Women in Postwar Rwanda" offers a further assessment of gender in that country. The state that is now internationally recognized as the possessor of the world's most gender-equal government (the parliament is fully 49 percent women) was, just fifteen years ago, in the midst of one of the bloodiest genocides in human history. That genocide itself was a gender anomaly—from what we can tell, a record number of women were involved in its leadership and perpetration. Still, women's violence then, like women's participation in government now, was framed in both Rwandan and western media sources in different, feminized terms when compared to men's violence and political participation. This chapter provides evidence that, in the face of women's changing behaviors and roles in Rwandan society, many of the dominant narratives of the reconstruction of Rwanda rely heavily on the narrative preservation and revitalization of traditional gender roles.

Part IV: Confronting the Patriarchy of War as Women Combatants and Noncombatants

Rounding off our focus on media, Steven and Angie Reed Garner's, "Relationships of War: Mothers, Soldiers, Knowledge" investigates the ways in which these interactions are negotiated. Focusing on the relationship between a particular mother and her soldier-son, they examine how both military practice and well-established cultural forms shape the capacity to understand war-making. Drawing on life history interviews with soldiers, veterans, and family members, the authors demonstrate ways in which knowledge requires the active integration of information into meaningful contexts, and how access to these contexts is not politically neutral. Mothers, as the iconic representatives of familial interiority, are placed in an untenable position: they must learn about war-making in order to give support to their soldier-children, and yet they must not know too much about the caustic realities of war to which their children are subject, lest they become less able or willing to give support to soldiers fighting wars. Karla Cunningham's "Female Participation in the Iraqi Insurgency: Insights into Nationalistic and Religious Warfare" reflects on the more immediate dangers of the Iraq War and the ways in which women are enticed and threatened into counterinsurgency struggles through nationalist loyalties along with what has been learned about how gender complicates the precarious control women have over their lives. Women's participation in Iraq's violent response to the United States 2003 invasion has evolved from sporadic, limited involvement, to an upsurge in attacks since 2007. Female insurgents have increased their proportion of attacks, and casualty rates have risen significantly. This analysis by Cunningham discusses the evolution of women's participation in the Iraq War, especially within the Sunni insurgency, and both its immediate and broader lessons.

Michelle M. Gardner-Morkert's "Agency and Militarization in the Heartland: Noncombatant American Women," analyzes a Midwestern American community and the militarization of noncombatant women during the Afghanistan and Iraq wars. Responding to interview data collected from 2003 to 2006, Morkert argues that we can recognize patterns in the global gendering of militarization by examining the relationship between patriarchy and militarization. More specifically, the findings presented in this chapter indicate that banal militarization is found wherever patriarchal ideology is advocated and embraced by both women and men.

While screenings of *Hotel Rwanda* (2004) left viewers with the visceral horror of genocide, the rapidity with which the murders took place, and a few brief seconds of film footage that captured sexual slaves corralled like animals outside a storage facility as a truck pulled in, the personal narratives, issues, and present efforts to acknowledge gender-based violence survivors ends our documentation of this subject. Tadia Rice's chapter, "The Raping of Rwanda and How Women Rebuilt and Healed a Nation" examines the nature of transcendence unveiled as rape victims in Rwanda refuse to be defined by their trauma, and reengage their rage and despair through peace-making in a postwar African state. Rwanda's 1994 genocide was the most massive and systematic killing of civilians to occur since the Holocaust of World War II. Rice investigates Rwandan women's lives and the war that left an orphan population infected with HIV/AIDS, and a female population impregnated by Hutu men, tortured, and many suffering from Traumatic Gynecologic Fistula (TGF). Yet, she concentrates her reflections on the postwar scenario, on the women who helped to heal their society and establish a new government free of tribalism, and unified in national pride instead of ethnic divisions. This chapter highlights the courageous and resilient Rwandan women as they fostered a process of reconciliation and justice. Rice recounts her model of conflict resolution called "gacaca" (penance through confession) by revealing how forgiving—but not forgetting—may be the only effective method for rebuilding any shattered nation devastated by genocide.

IMPLICATIONS FOR REFLECTION AND ACTION

To our good fortune, these authors constitute an array of writers, differentiated by age, race and ethnicity, religious affiliation, gender, profession, and politics. Where women suffer disproportionately from poverty and the related patchwork of structural inequalities, societies fail, families are disrupted, and women and children remain "soft targets" of violence, exploitation, and suppression. Three factors stand out as causative in the fight to eliminate GBV, particularly the sexual exploitation and assault associated with civil strife and war. They are (1) Ignorance of rape and sexual assault and rape as a crime; (2) The ensuing conspiracy of silence in addressing these behaviors as criminal, and; (3) The failure of social, governmental, and third sector institutions to transform their own consciousness from cultures of indifference to cultures of conscientious action. Dr. Martin Luther King predicted that, "We will remember not the words of our enemies, but the silence of our friends." The contents of this book reflect the editors' commitment to that truth as well as the complex social, economic, and political realities that render girls and women vulnerable to violence. The intergenerational transmission of poverty is increasingly feminized due to what some refer to as "gender fatigue," a view that renders the recent focus on gender as outmoded, overwhelming, and isolating. Many suggest a more productive tactic, "Menstreaming" (Correla and Bannon, 2006), the inclusion of a more progressive paradigm that considers relationships between men and women and how these interventions function to transform communities. The World Bank report suggests a "crisis of masculinity" in many parts of the world as a result of endemic war and violence as well as the scarcity of economic opportunities. In the developed world (United States, Europe, and Japan), if nations are not directly entrenched in home-based wars, they are deeply entwined and entangled in war and conflict in Third World struggles that are often sparked by the globalization of market economies. The "Second World" or emerging nations (Brazil, South Africa, Indonesia, Turkey, China, India) are also implicated in a web of strategic alliances and networks of cooperation that fuel international arms and drug trade, tourism (and sex-trafficking) industries, war profiteering, and the financial interdependence that characterizes development and humanitarian aid packages. However, while these breath-taking events baffle the mind, individuals and some nations have been taking concerted action against the brand of war-related violence that is deeply rooted in hunger, poverty, poor health, poor sanitation, basic water access, illiteracy, and refugee issues. Just as we have come to understand that women's economic austerity—making do with little—contributes to underestimating the depth of poverty, our task as human beings in the face of GBV is also to crack the fear or hopelessness that crushes womens' capacity to follow through with necessary legal challenges in reporting sex crimes, and the right to safety and security when doing so.

Many of us witness violence against women in our daily lives or have, perhaps, experienced this violation within our families, friends, and communities. We have tried not to play the victim. Yet, as this text is specifically focused on war-related violence, we were interested in focusing attention on the macro manifestations of violence in the forms of rape, indentured sex servitude as transactional, and physical attack only because of their harsher scope. With the socialization of men as primary predators implicated in this crisis, our most successful means for eradicating human rights violations is to draw men into the vortex of antiviolence training and broader times—in campaigns that passionately advocate for violence-free societies, during both peace and war. There have been many conferences, reports, books, laws, policies, and media campaigns addressing the escalation of GBV for more than fifteen years since the United Nations General Assembly adopted the Declaration on the Elimination of Violence Against Women (December 20). Nevertheless, as violence continues, there will be more than enough work for everyone, for several generations to come, to combat this epidemic. We propose a new way of thinking about the spiritual rights of girls, women, and children, and those more vulnerable to exploitation. While the historical feminist discourse on patriarchal domination has been a useful political tool in confronting the structural inequalities that destabilize women, the discourse has widened to expose the conspiracy of poverty and its implication in communities of color in both the developed and the developing world.

We believe, and research demonstrates, that where women and men collaborate to prevent violence and the socioeconomic conditions that breed desperation, the normalization of violence against women will decrease, moving global civilization from depravity to nobility.

References

An assessment of the status of the implementation of United Nations Security Council Resolution 1325 in Liberia (A Case Study). 2006. Geneva: United

National population Fund, Commissioned for the Ministry of Gender and Development.

Andersen, R. 2006. *A century of media, a century of war.* New York: Peter Lang.

Boggs, C. and T. Pollard. 2006. *The Hollywood war machine: US militarism and popular culture.* Boulder, CO: Paradigm.

Ellsberg, M. and L. Heise. 2005. *Researching violence against women: A practical guide for researchers and activists.* PATH.

Elwood-Akers, V. 1988. *Women war correspondents in the Vietnam war.* Lanham, MD: Scarecrow.

"*Ending violence against women-Programming for prevention, protection, and care.*" 2007. New York: United Nations Population Fund.

Gallagher, A. 2006. *Who makes the news? Global media monitoring project.* Toronto: World Association of Christian Communication.

Gioseffi, D., ed. 2003. *Women on war: An international anthology of writings from antiquity to the present.* New York: Feminist Press.

Herdt, G. 2007. Sexual development, social oppression, and local culture. *Sexuality Research & Social Policy*, 1 (1): 39–62.

Ilibagiza, I. 2007. *Left to tell: Discovering God amidst the Rwandan holocaust.* Hay House.

Marlowe, J. 2006. *Darfur diaries: Stories of survival.* New York: Nation Books.

McLaughlin, G. 2002. *The war correspondent.* New York: Pluto Press.

Porter, E. 2007. "*Women's truth narratives: The power of compassionate listening*" Critical Half/Women for Women International. 5 (2, Fall): 21–25.

Powers, S. 2003. *A problem from hell: America and the age of genocide.* New York: Harper Perennial.

"*Programming for violence against women: 10 case studies.*" 2006. New York: United Nations Population Fund.

Salbi, Z. 2006. *The other side of war: Women's stories of survival and hope.* Washington, DC: Women for Women International.

Satrapi, M. 2004. *Persepolis: The story of childhood.* New York: Pantheon.

Sen, A. 2000. *Development as freedom.* New York: Anchor.

"*The shame of war: Sexual violence against women and girls in conflict.*" 2007. New York: United Nations Office for the Coordination of Humanitarian Affairs.

Ung, L. 2006. *First they killed my father: A daughter of Cambodia remembers.* New York: Harper Perennial.

Vlachova, M. and L. Biason. eds. 2005. *Women in an insecure world: Violence against women: Facts, figures and analysis.* Geneva: Geneva Centre for the Democratic Control of Armed Forces (DCAF).

"Will you listen: Voices from conflict zones." 2007. New York: United Nations Population Fund.

Part I

Understanding Gender-Based Violence, Rebuilding Personal Security for Girls and Women, and Peace-Building

1

NOT MAKING EXCUSES: FUNCTIONS OF RAPE AS A TOOL IN ETHNO-NATIONALIST WARS

Natalja Zabeida

In the mid-nineties, when I started working on the issue of rape in time of conflict, today's United Nations (UN) classification of rape as a "war tactic," was sadly and frustratingly a long way away. The world had to go through the bloody fighting in the former Yugoslavia and many regions on the African continent—Rwanda, Congo, Sudan—to finally turn attention to this devastating problem. Now the pages of serious newspapers and magazines sometimes do see reports on the horrible conditions of women in places like the Democratic Republic of Congo and the sexual violence they, along with some victimized men, have to endure. Unfortunately for women in the former Yugoslavia, the latest UN resolution to see rape in war as a weapon and not as a simple side effect has come about a decade too late. I am afraid, too, that unfortunately for women worldwide, the actual will to do something based on this resolution will also come too late. Let us at least hope it will not take another decade.

INTRODUCTION

Any conflict, be it for land or power, has to be conceptualized within the context of identity: Some differences, most often based on a set of ethnic characteristics (language, religion, origin, and the like) lend themselves to manipulation and enticement of extreme actions. This identity does not have to and most often is not the cause of the conflict; it is, however, an integral, if not the most essential part in organizing support for the war. Within this context, women become victims because of the intersection of their gender and ethno-national identities. To fully understand why rape has become such a widespread state-sponsored or at least state-ignored strategy, we must analyze it through the lens of both gender *and* national identities.

This chapter looks at the functions that the use of rape serve during hostile military actions in the eyes of perpetrators. The very notion of finding some logic in this horrible deed is unsettling, giving one fear of somehow justifying the use of this crime in war (and possibly peace) by providing a logical explanation for its occurrence. Let me be explicitly clear: Under no circumstances can rape be excused, justified, or condoned—whether in war or peace, in marriage, or in unknown encounters. Under no circumstances should rape of anyone go unpunished. The international community, state governments, and single individuals have been guilty of the attitudes toward and treatment of cases of rape that provide no possibility for its minimization in the lives of women and some men. However, as a community of supposedly civilized societies, in order to prevent mass rape, we must understand what is used as logical argumentation for the establishment of unwritten policies to rape as a tactic of war, and accept our responsibility to act against it.

While rape occurs in most violent conflicts and is hard to eliminate completely, the case of authority-sponsored (either a state or a well-organized power group fighting for control over a territory) genocidal rape is a specific phenomenon where prevention is possible. In order to have any hope of preventing this crime in the future, understanding of all component parts are essential: what created opportunities for mass rape to occur, what allowed it to continue and what needs to be done in order not to allow it to happen in the future. Understanding and accepting that rape is given a function and is used as a strategically selected means of carrying out hostilities allows for a systematic classification of rape as a war crime and, hopefully, for consistency in prosecution.

No matter what we wish to think about individual rapists, most of them do not start out as evil, bloodthirsty, homicidal maniacs plagued by sexual frustrations. There is no doubt that there are some who are, as some would like to call them, originally evil. I argue that the policy of genocidal rape does not and cannot rely only on the few in the society who are willing to commit such crimes without reservation, motivated solely by their own deviance. Treating rape only as a "single event" perpetrated by a single sick individual separate from the wider culture of violence, militarism, and gender discrimination is, first, failure to understand the complexity of this social rape and the intension of the perpetrating side and, second, failure to accord the women the protection and the victims justice.

Mass rape, genocidal rape, rape as a war tactic, was and is able to exist because it is seen as functional within the broader socially delineated hierarchies: Us versus them, good versus evil, nationally/ ethnically pure and legitimate (i.e., claim to territory and statehood) versus contaminated and illegitimate. Most of all, however, it is able to exist within the social system of simplified dichotomies, especially in the time of violent change, of women versus men with all the idealization, restriction, control, and resulting victimization. Because this type of rape carries certain functions and is supported or condoned by official authoritative structures (either by the political or military leaders or both), it is, therefore, possible to identify the crime, set up rules for the prevention and, ultimately, punish.

Some authors have argued that rape carries no specific political motivations or functions to allow all men to rape any woman. In her early work, Brownmiller (1975) argued that men raped to perpetuate patriarchal power of men over women; however, in time of war, rape is also used to terrorize and demoralize victims and members of ethnic groups. While it is plausible that some individual men have raped women in war because of their "contempt for women" (Ibid: 32) in general, without any political goals in mind, it can be argued that political motivations establish the opportunity and justify rape as a tool of war. Authority guided rhetoric encompassing the negative aspects of patriarchal sexism and radical exclusivist nationalism provide political and moral excuses for rape made convenient through nonpunishment and allow it to reach massive proportions.

In addition to sexist attitudes held by perpetrating sides, perceptions on nationalist ethnic differences play a part in making rape a functional tool for groups and, therefore, acceptable to rapists. Women become victims of rape not only because they are women (although domination of patriarchal social perceptions make it a strong argument), but also because they are *other* women due to their national, ethnic or ideological difference. Carried out for very specific reasons "by *some* men against *certain* women" (MacKinnon, 1994: 188; emphasis in the original), rape in war occurs at a specific time and place. Women become targets of genocidal rape because, as individuals, they belonged to a group designated as the national ethnic enemy. They are dehumanized by perpetrators' nationalist rhetoric, belonging to an enemy group posing an imminent threat to "our" national survival. Additionally, they are sexualized by patriarchal sexist rhetoric as the embodiment of a nation's continuity through reproduction. Whether individual war rapists subscribe fully to the rationalization of nationalist rape or just use it to assuage feelings of guilt, rape in war serves several functions, some of which are different than those of "peace time" rape.

FUNCTIONS OF RAPE IN WAR

For a history of the use of sexual violence as a weapon of war, most will turn to current examples of Africa and the events of the 1990s in the former Yugoslavia. Some may also remember the mass rape of women in Nanking in 1937, as the Japanese invaded China, or the WWII "comfort women" —Chinese and Korean women forced into prostitution to serve the Japanese military. The stolen women of the Indian-Pakistani war of the early 1970s for the independence of Bangladesh is a less known example of women as pawns in an ethnonationalist war.

As outlined in Article 27 of the Fourth Geneva Convention, the International Humanitarian Law, which sets rules of conduct for the parties to a war, considers rape, forced prostitution, or any other physical and emotional sexual mistreatment of women a crime. The International Committee of the Red Cross (ICRC), which attempts to uphold the four Geneva Conventions on the protection of combatants and noncombatants in war and motivate state actors to abide by them, is a strong advocate for the preservation of dignity and honor of people in general, and women in particular. It defines rape as "willfully causing great suffering or serious injury to body or health," in violation of the Geneva Conventions (Human Rights Watch, 1994: 12).

What follows is a discussion of several functions that war rape serves: Destruction of "self"; destruction of the "enemy"; rejection of the right to existence (and claim to territory) of the national group; male-to-male communication; means to dishonor the men of the opposing group; "push" effect; means to increase own group's numbers; retaliation for rape of "our" women now; and retaliation for past rapes and injustices.

DESTRUCTION OF "SELF"

Rape in general, as well as rape in war, strikes at the very center of a human being—her or his feeling of safety, integrity, dignity, and emotional and physical wellbeing. Rape "shatter[s] the fantasy structure of the individual" (Salecl, 1993: 218)—or, what one knows and feels about self. It is the ultimate violation of a person's integrity, of a world once known. By destroying this sense and security of self, the war rapist undermines not only the individual's identity, but also the social structure and cohesion of the group to which the victim belongs. Unlike other forms of torture after which the affected individual could gain new social respect and admiration for having endured the inhumane treatment, a rape victim often must return to a society that sees her as *dirty* because of the patriarchal demand on the purity of women's bodies secured through controlling and limiting their sexual activity. Thus, the internal emotional turmoil of losing the sense of security and wholeness is compounded by social attitudes that see anything connected to sex as uncomfortable or forbidden. The Muslim and other more traditional communities especially pride themselves on the untouchablilty of their women as a source of honor for their families. "[F]or a young Muslim woman, rape thus has the meaning of a symbolic death" (Salecl, 1993: 218), because, made into a fallen woman through sexual contact with a man even against her will, she is often seen as lost not only to herself, but also to her community.

Destruction of the "Enemy" Group

The second function is related to the influence of patriarchy and social status of women based on patriarchal demands on their purity, exacerbated by the time of national conflict. Ruth Seifert (1994: 56–57) disputes the old belief that rape in war is a manifestation of male sexual drive or perversion in conflicts by comparing different societies showing that rape occurs mostly in communities where (1) Male power has become unstable; (2) Women have a subordinate status and low self-esteem; and (3) Rigid definition and hierarchy of values of "masculine" and "feminine" prevail. While under normal circumstances a society can rely on a seemingly more egalitarian treatment of men and women, and propagate both positive and negative gender stereotypes of both, troubling times usually involve a more restrictive dichotomization of gender differences. Hypermasculinity and hyperfemininity of limited socially acceptable roles of men as warriors and women as mothers during anxiety and fear-ridden times of social and political change is intensified and manipulated by calculated nationalist rhetoric. This creates the opportunity for justification and acceptance as normal of women-unfriendly policies and behaviors eventually leading to establishing conditions for sanctioning genocidal rape. In a conflict for power defined within the discourse of national differences, women are allocated the "honor" and responsibility for keeping the nation and, hence, the right to self-rule alive. As a consequence, defining women's role and worth only through the discourse of motherhood and associating the nation with mothers, places them in a position more vulnerable to violence.

This function of rape must be seen from the point of view and social assumptions of the perpetrator. Sexist patriarchy makes women more vulnerable to genocidal rape. Men who rape subscribe to certain ideas of gender and sexual relations in order to find social and personal justifications. While an understanding of the effects rape has on women and their community might provide a logical, rational foundation for the use of rape as a tactic, the war rapist acts as much, if not more, out of his own social understanding of the proper role of women in society as his assumption of women's status in the targeted community, and out of acceptance and internalization of the present conflict defined as the war for national survival against an evil *other*. Cynthia Enloe argues that, in the act of rape, "The male militarized rapist in some way imposes his understanding of 'enemy', 'soldiery', 'victory' and 'defeat' on both the women to be raped and on the sexual assault" (2000: 110). Because women are not seen as individuals, but rather as members of an enemy group, rape is carried out in the name of the victory. As constructed within the discourse of a war for survival, of "us against them," any means of eliminating the national enemy is seen as acceptable. Because rape destroys the general fabric of society, the existing communal relations are, therefore, one part of the policy of genocide.

Rejection of the Right to Existence (and Claim to Territory) of the National Group

The presence of societal patriarchal values explains the assigned functions of war rape. They often derive from the social perception of women as providers of the pure connection between the generations to the "authentic" national past, as the insurance for the survival of the ethnic group that is kept distinctly different through the nonmixing of bloodlines and as the source of honor for the men in their personal lives and community. Women's bodies designated as property of the group to keep its purity become the object of protection and prohibition on the movements and choices of women. This is done to maintain the imaginary border between various ethnic groups. Women become the "signifiers of the 'social body'" (Wobbe, 1995: 91), and "the property of the national collective" (Milić, 1993: 115), because of their reproductive functions and assigned importance in the survival of the ethnic nation. Therefore, rape in war becomes a logical extension of the aggression on the enemy's physical territory. Seen as property of the community and of other men, aggressors treat women's bodies as "a ceremonial battlefield, a parade ground" (Brownmiller 1975:38), staking their claims on all aspects dealing with difference and right to self-determination and territorial and blood-line integrity. Raping other men's women blurs the imaginary border of delineated difference and "denies" the purity of the nation it encapsulates, serving as an indisputable proof of lack of a group's right to statehood and territory.

The danger of nationalist discourse lies in its insistence on seeing women as vessels of ethnic purity, serving as passive untainted repositories for the ethnic genetic material of ancestors, to be passed on to the future generations. This rhetoric (as actually any other male dominated idea of procreation) paints the woman as a passive object, "Accepting male seed without contributing anything original to it, anything of her own" (Nikolić-Ristanović, 1995: 59). This perception and treatment of inheriting ethnic identity, which is seen as innate and not acquired, makes rape a 'natural' element of an 'ethnic' war" (Zarkov, 1995: 113). It is "natural" not because of the innate conditions of maleness, and "ethnic" not because the reasons for war are derived from innate predispositions of any particular ethnicity, but because the nationalist rhetoric, having constructed the right to self-determination through purity and difference based on ethnic characteristics, makes ethnicity and gender of others a target for metaphoric contamination to discredit any such rights.

Male-to-Male Communication

Within the perception of women as property, and an object for delineation between national communities, rape also becomes a form of communication between men of warring sides (Das, 1995; Brownmiller, 1994). Women's bodies thus become a message board for accusations, denials, and symbolic killing. Through rape, the enemy sends a message to the adversary that the claim to purity and integrity is no longer valid. Rape also points to the inability of the protecting male to save his woman and his territory from harm. In the communication between men, this serves as proof of his impotence and his failure as a man and as a soldier. Therefore, in the rape of women, men are seen and see themselves as "actual" targets of this sexual violence.

Means to Dishonor the Men of the Opposing Group

Rape in war also comes as a consequence of social definition of men's honor through the honor and purity of women in their community and family (Das, 1995; Zalihic-Kaurin, 1994; Nikolić-Ristanović, 1995). Especially, but not exclusively, in the Muslim communities women's contact with inappropriate or unapproved men or outside the socially established code of behavior is seen as a dishonorable reflection on the men in the life of that woman. Thus, rape of women, especially of Muslim faith, is supposed to bring disgrace and shame to the woman's male relatives. In a society that demands "death before dishonor" (Zalihic-Kaurin, 1994: 173), it also plays into another form of male violence against women—justifying so-called *honor killings* of women by male family members to wash off the perceived shame with the blood of the offending female, should the woman fail to "show respect" for her family and kill herself first.

"Push" Effect

Rape as a tactic of ethnic cleansing through terror was used in the wars in the former Yugoslavia (Folnegovic-Smalc, 1994; Nikolić-Ristanović, 1995; Salzman, 1998) and is now used in cases like the fighting in the Democratic Republic of Congo or Sudan to force entire families and communities off their land. Rapists are often members of the towns and villages who are familiar to the victims. Rapes are often committed outside of the woman's house, with her family and neighbors being forced to watch. In the former Yugoslavia, for example, some rapes were publicized over the radio (Nikolić-Ristanović, 1995:55) to further humiliate the victim and send panic and terror throughout the community: Women fearing for themselves and, along with men, fearing for their relatives. This way, the very memory and idea of a home in the mind of the woman and her family becomes associated with pain, fear, humiliation, and cruelty of their neighbors or acquaintances. Living in such a place becomes almost impossible. Thus, rape of women serves the purpose of forcing entire families out not only after rape, but also as "secondary victims" (Folnegovic-Smalc, 1994:175) who witness other women's rape and leave the area to escape a similar fate. It is an "economical" tactic to clear the land of the unwanted population, as opposed to fighting directly with men using actual weapons and risking death, the attackers choose weaker and unarmed targets to achieve the same goal.

Means to Increase Own Group's Numbers

Some have suggested that rape carries another function—as a means of increasing the population numbers of the rapist's ethnic group because of the patrilineal line of descent accepted in most societies. There is evidence that women were refused an abortion or kept in captivity until after they passed the stage of pregnancy where termination would be possible (Salzman, 1998). As seen in many personal accounts of women collected in the volume *Molila sam ih da me ubiju* ("I begged them to kill me") (Ajanović, Filipović, and Kisević, 1999), many women rape victims reported that, during rape, men told them that they would give birth to a Serbian/Ustaša/Croatian/Četnik baby, the assumption being that the potential baby would inherit the rapist's ethnicity. *Ustaša* and *Četnik*, it should be pointed out, are terms often used in derogatory ways by opposing sides to identify Croatian and Serbian nationalists, respectively.

While the patriarchal patrilineal logic undoubtedly provides an added reasoning for rape (or, more likely, just a chance to humiliate the woman by telling her she will carry a "foreign" child, an enemy's child), it does not seem to be a well-thought-out strategy. Judging by accounts available in the volume mentioned above as well as by rape statistics of the Medical Center in Bosnia-Hercegovina (Cockburn, 2003), in Yugoslavia many women of pre- and post-childbearing age were also raped. There were no organized attempts made by the rapist, his community's political elites or military commanders to raise children in their own community. The intent of war rape, therefore, seems to be to simply deny the purity of the other ethnic group by impregnating their women and humiliating and psychologically destroying the victim, not necessarily to increase the numbers of one's own group. In the case of nationalist wars, pure (uncontaminated by contact with enemy men) women are endowed with the responsibility and duty to produce ethnically pure offspring. For example, in the wars in the former Yugoslavia, even when the father was a Serb, in the case of rape, the child was still considered impure because of the connection to the non-Serbian mother or simply, ironically, as a result of a rape. Hence, the intent of rape is to destroy the concept of purity of the identity of the other group and normalcy of social family relations in the enemy community as well as to "clear the territory" for a takeover rather than to establish numeric power of the rapist's group.

Retaliation for Rape of "Our" Women Now

Rape has also often been used as a form of retaliation against men who have committed rapes of women whom men considered theirs. Those men, feeling wronged by enemy actions, often felt justified to rape women of opposing sides in the eye-for-an-eye logic of male-to-male communication and retaliation. The horrors carried out by some groups' men for some reason made their women deserve such treatment. The relationship here again was not between men and women, but between men through women, where the rape of women was seen as punishment to their men. For example, discussing the rapes carried out by the Congolese Force Public against the Belgian women during their fight for decolonization, a "black American minister" said, "It is hard on the children and women but the Belgians deserved it. That's hard for a minister to say, isn't it?" (Brownmiller, 1975: 137). Apparently, it is not.

Since men are seen as owners, or at least legitimate claimants, to the land and country, and since women, along with land, are often defined only through their relationship to these men, women then, along with land and country, are seen as property of men. As so taken, the rape or kidnapping of the women is seen as a rational extension of the logic of (re)claiming the recently lost land and country, and as a justified target for tit-for-tat retaliation.

Retaliation for Past Rapes and Injustices

Warring groups and their political and military authorities do not limit themselves to the use of the present injustices as material for inciting militaristic fervor. They often dig into the past and revive stories of rapes of their own women by the current enemy to justify the rape of their women. Granted, this rhetoric of reliving historical rape does not directly serve as a function of present rape; it does so, however, indirectly: Partly normalizing the rape of the enemy women now and partly adding to the image of the enemy as a subhuman, evil entity worthy of elimination by all means. As was the case in the former Yugoslavia, its history of Ottoman rule held stories of Muslim rapes of Slavic women and taking children away to serve in the Ottoman army against their mother's community. More recently, the rapes were also placed in the context of publicized and often exaggerated rapes of Serbian women by Kosovo Albanians where modern nationalism was "Intertwined with sexual phantasmagorias...as the main agent of national sentiment" (Ule and Rener, 1997: 227). Hence, even before the war, rape in the Serbian nationalist discourse was defined as a tool in ethnic conflicts between groups. Within the more global context, for the creation of the myths and stories that authority figures use to build up militaristic sentiments, any stories of real or invented injustices to "us" through "our" women would suffice to do the same.

Means to Prevent Social Contact across Ethnic Lines

The last function of rape discussed here is its ability to terrify women into a paralysis, taking away the chance for self-determination and action as an independent human being. Even before the war, rape or fear of rape by men of other ethnic groups is used as a control mechanism to prevent close group communication between, in that case, Serbian women and Kosovo Albanian men (Meznaric, 1994). This was done not so much to save their own women from the perceived sexual predators of other ethnicity, but to disallow the creation of normal civil interethnic communications that could potentially diminish "us—them" distinctions or the justification for fear and hate of others. Thus, the threat of ethnic rape even before the hostilities serves to further push the two sides apart and to create an atmosphere of distrust and fear with easy escalation to direct violence in the future.

Conclusions

Pressed to comment on the rape of women in war, almost anyone would be able to admit that it has occurred for centuries in war. Some, following a more traditional view of sexual violence against women, would quietly and somberly note the inevitability of such violence in a course of hostilities. Others would passionately argue that rape is used by men to attack their women as a means to undermine a group's viability. For many, rape in war is seen as a crime against the national/ethnic group as a whole, not as a crime whose target is individual women.

The truth about rape in war rests somewhere in the middle of these reactions. While some women are targeted for rape purely because they are women, others are more deliberately systematically isolated for their national, racial, class, or ethnic characteristics. The problem with rape in war is that it is erroneous to attempt to separate it as a crime against women or a crime against their ethnicity. Most often, as was the case in the former Yugoslavia, a victim's national and gender identities were factors in her victimization. Nationalist rhetoric identifies women as the authentic source of connection to the past and security of the group's survival in the future. Along with the insistence on strict nationalistic differentiations and demonization, it set the stage for genocidal rape to occur in the context of the breakup of the Socialist Federal Republic of Yugoslavia. This crime was a crime against ethnicity, but it was first and foremost a victimization of women through their ethnicity: It is a crime against women.

In order to prevent genocidal rape, we have to have an effective system of punishment for the perpetrators; to get there, we must convince the international community to start seeing rape in war as a tactic on a par with, if not more serious than, other war crimes, and then we must act. This is not a radically new thought, but is, however, one that has not yet been incorporated into the mainstream discourse on war.

The plight of women in war has been misunderstood, undervalued, and underanalyzed until very recently. Attempts to classify war rape as a crime, comparable to other war crimes, and to see it as a tool used strategically will hopefully accord this issue more international attention. The UN Resolution is the beginning of the serious attempt to address this problem. To follow in the right direction, we will also have to broaden common understanding of this crime and set up a system of punishment in order to have any hopes of preventing its occurrence in the future. Understanding that rape in war is not a simple side effect, but a planned strategically selected tactic, is a step in the right direction.

References

Ajanović, I., M. Filipovic, and E. Kisevic, eds. 1999. *"Molila sam ih da me Ubiju": Zločin nad ženom Bosne i Hercegovine. ("I begged them to kill Me": Crime against women of Bosnia-and-Herzegovina.*) Bosnia and Herzegovina: Center for Research and Documentation of the Association of the Camp-survivors.

Anderson, B. 1983. *Imagined communities: Reflections on the origin and spread of nationalism.* London: Verso.

Brownmiller, S. 1975. *Against our will: Men, women and rape.* New York: Fawcett Columbine.

———. 1994. Making female bodies the battlefield. In Stiglmayer 1994, 180–182.

Cockburn, C. 2001. 2003. *The space between us: Negotiating gender and national identities in conflict.* London: Zed Books.

Das, V. 1995. National honor and practical kinship: Unwanted women and children. In *Conceiving the world order: The global politics of reproduction*, ed. F. D. Ginsburg and R. Rapp, 212–233. Berkeley: University of California Press.

Enloe, C. 1990. Bananas, bases, and patriarchy. In *Women, militarism and war: Essays in history, politics and social* theory, ed. J. B. Elshtain and S. Tobias, 189–206. Lanham, MD: Rowman and Littlefield.

———. 1994. Afterword: Have the Bosnian rapes opened a new era of feminist consciousness? In Stiglmayer 1994, 219–230.

———. 2000. *Maneuvers: The international politics of militarizing women's lives*. Berkeley: University of California Press.

Folnegovic-Smalc, V. 1994. Psychiatric aspects of rapes in the war against the Republic of Croatia and Bosnia-Herzegovina. In Stiglmayer 1994, 174–179.

Human Rights Watch. 1994. *Bosnia-Herzegovina*. 6 (15). The Open Society Archive, Central European University, Budapest, Hungary, File 304-0-13, Box 1.

MacKinnon, C. A. 1994. Rape, genocide and women's human rights. In Stiglmayer 1994, 183–196.

Meznaric, S. 1994. Gender as an ethno-marker: Rape, war, and identity politics in the former Yugoslavia. In *Identity politics and women: Cultural reassertions and feminisms in international perspectives*, ed. V. M. Moghadam, 76–97. Boulder, CO: Westview Press.

Milić, A. 1993. Women and nationalism in the former Yugoslavia. In *Gender politics and post-communism: Reflections from Eastern Europe and the former Soviet Union*, ed. N. Funk and M. Mueller, 109–122. London: Routledge.

Nikolić-Ristanović, V. 1994. Nasilje nad zenama u uslovima rata i ekonomske krize (Violence against women under the conditions of war and economic crisis). *Socioloski pregled (Sociological Review)* 28 (3): 409–417.

———. 1995. Seksualno nasilje (Sexual violence) In *Žene, nasilje, rat (Women, violence, war)*, ed. V. Nikolić-Ristanović, 34–70. Beograd, Serbia: Institut za kriminološka i sociološka istraživanja (IKSI, Institute for criminal and sociological research).

Salecl, R. 1993, October. The fantasy structure of nationalist discourse. *Praxis International* 13 (3): 213–223.

Salzman, T. A. 1998. Rape camps as a means of ethnic cleansing: Religious, cultural, and ethical responses to rape victims in the former Yugoslavia. *Human Rights Quarterly* 20 (2): 348–378.

Seifert, R. 1994. War and rape: A preliminary analysis. In Stiglmayer 1994, 52–72.

Stiglmayer, A. 1994. The rapes in Bosnia-Herzegovina. In *Mass rape: The war against women in Bosnia-Herzegovina*, ed. A. Stiglmayer, 82–169. Lincoln: University of Nebraska Press.

Ule, M. and T. Rener. 1997. Nationalism and gender in post-socialist societies: Is nationalism female? In *Ana's land: Sisterhood in eastern Europe*, ed. T. Renne, 220–233. Boulder, CO: Westview Press.
Wobbe, T. 1995. The boundaries of community: Gender relations and racial violence. In *Crossfires: Nationalism, racism and gender in Europe*, ed. H. Lutz, A. Phoenix, and N. Yuval-Davis, 88–104. London: Pluto Press.
Zalihic-Kaurin, A. 1994. The Muslim woman. In Stiglmayer 1994, 170–173.
Zarkov, D. 1995. Gender, orientalism and the history of ethnic hatred in the former Yugoslavia. In *Crossfires: Nationalism, racism and gender in Europe*, ed. H. Lutz, A. Phoenix, and N. Yuval-Davis, 105–120. London: Pluto Press.

2

Speaking with Postwar Liberia: Gender-Based Violence Interventions for Girls and Women

Robin M. Chandler

> And weeping, the women let loose.
> —Toni Morrison, *Beloved* (Knopf, 1987)

The barbarism of gender-based violence (GBV) against women in Liberia is still only whispered about in secret moments among women, but those whispers are getting louder since the end of the country's fourteen-year civil war. There is no way to ignore that, despite the gender advancement protocols in the United Nations Millennium Development goals, a "war on women" has occurred during peacetime as well as during war in many countries. This chapter, based upon my recent interviews conducted in Liberia, deals with how violence during the Liberian War normalized and sanctioned what Liberians refer to as sexual exploitation and assault (SEA) and the postwar efforts to assess it with policy commitments, laws, public health interventions, and massive citizen reeducation.

Historically, Liberia's political history and identity are unique, with roots as a colony founded in 1847 by freed slaves from the United States. Between indigenous Africans and repatriated African Americans, the result has been a country of dual warring loyalties to western ideals and African traditions.

Legacies of Slavery and Recolonization

In Toni Morrison's 1987 Pulitzer Prize-winning novel *Beloved*, there is a fictional recreation of a church meeting among the enslaved of the antebellum southern United States in which the "unchurched, unannointed" preacher, Baby Suggs, calls her disenfranchised congregants to the center of "the Clearing." Offering a blessing, she prays, and group by group, calls to the children to play and the men to dance, to share the communal joy of life under hardship. When she gets to the women, she tells them or, rather, gives them spiritual license to weep, and through the character's urging, the women "let loose." In postwar Liberia, the women have let loose—from communities entrenched as subjects of violence and abuse, surviving through a church tradition that concerned healing.

The need for healing in Liberia is ubiquitous. Government statistics confirm that the majority of its girls and women are survivors of war-related sexual violence. Postwar traumatic stress in this predominantly Christian nation, with rates of 80 percent unemployment and 85 percent illiteracy, presents a formidable opportunity for truth-telling. My interviews, running concurrently with the nation's Truth and Reconciliation Hearings (August 2008), revealed the postapocalyptic scale of war-related sexual violence. Community elder and former teacher, Mrs. Mary Brownell, a founder of the Women's Peace Movement, reflected on the days of war:

> We informed the international press because under [Charles] Taylor negative propaganda was not permitted. We contacted the EU, AU (OAU), and the UN to let the world know what was really taking place. Using peaceful demonstrations we visited the warlords offices and met them one on one hand delivering personal letters. As mothers our children were being recruited and forced to take up guns.

Such testimonials highlight the activism and resistance movements unfolding in the country during the war, and the ongoing challenges of sharing information with the media and the outside world.

Liberia under Ellen Johnson-Sirleaf

The war ended in 2003, following a peace accord, which was swiftly followed in 2006 by a presidential campaign, and ultimate inauguration of Liberia's first woman president: Ellen Johnson-Sirleaf. Johnson-Sirleaf campaigned on a dual platform of ending corruption, and confronting GBV; her ministries of gender, justice, labor, and education mobilized to make rape a capital, unbailable offense. The new law contained unfortunate loopholes in implementation that, in the midst of a novice police force, did little to intimidate sexual predators, but a newly rehabilitated Criminal Court at the Temple of Justice established a "fast track" for sexual violence cases. An array of strategic national public media campaigns, from road signage to radio and newspaper promotions, are being organized to educate a population of diverse literacy levels away from a culture of violence.

Persistent headlines in Monrovia's *Daily Observer* lead with such features as "Notorious Rapist on the Run," while recent films on Liberia's political instability, including *Pray the Devil Back to Hell* (2008), focus on the role of human rights. Filmmaker Virginia Rediker reported that, "When women in Kurdistan and Georgia [saw the film, they] wept and then wrote a peace agenda" (cited in Silverstein, 2008).

The United Nations Development Fund for Women (UNIFEM) suggests that the term "gender-based" highlights the context of unequal power relationships distinguishing men from women, a power relation that also includes children and some male victims. Numerous agencies, like Women for Women International, UNICEF, and Amnesty International, keep GBV in the public eye. The late "Mama Africa," Miriam Makeba, visited rape survivors in the Democratic Republic of Congo (DRC) to urge the international community to not forget the continuing crisis there. An all-too-steady stream of personal narratives on the rite of passage from victim to survivor highlight Africa's, and particularly Liberia's, struggle with sexual assault. Such narratives, including Internet blogs, maintain a constant presence—the centerpiece of the push is to increase awareness of the twin concepts of GBV and human rights, and to shed light on the complex psychosocial and age-specific difficulties of understanding consensual versus nonconsensual sex. Deddeh Howard of the Ministry of Foreign Affairs' Girls Empowerment Program revealed her story:

> As a girl I experienced sexual abuse by men in power. If exploitation is not defined in your mind, you don't recognize it, but I went ahead and went to school, yet I saw this pattern among other girls who got stuck. The girls have a fear within and no voice. I worked with Madame Johnson-Sirleaf to make other young women aware and developed the Girls Empowerment Program in October 2007. We have a special need for adolescent policies and projects for youth groups that keep girls grounded. Girls, girls, girls... that's my focus.

Listening and Activism

Traveling to the outskirts of Montserrado County, accompanied by Senior Senator Gbehzohngar, Professor Levi Zangai, and others, I visited orphanages and women who were coming to grips with how to be open about rape and sexual assault, as well as how to safely report abuse cases. Throughout Liberia, the physical presence of the international community is evident in a multisectoral, global approach dedicated to making reconstruction work in a nation overshadowed by a war where "The blood-dimmed tide is loosed.... And everywhere the ceremony of innocence is drowned" (Yeats, 1920). Chinua Achebe's opus, *Things Fall Apart* (1958), which used this Yeats poem, documented the social disruptions of European and African cultures in an Igbo village in Nigeria, setting the literary stage for the ensuing conflicts in west and sub-Saharan Africa.

In Liberia's Grand Bassa County, south of the capital, Monrovia, the Bassa Women's Development Association (BAWODA) gathered together in August 2008 to engage with me in a dialogue concerning endemic incidents of GBV and its impact on their communities. While our team was driven by car on a road full of pot holes, a number of these women had walked many miles—so, they had "walked to talk." During the dialogue, women "let loose" intimate details of systemic and long-standing incidents of sexual exploitation and abuse (SEA) in their county, one articulating the question so many women around the world have asked, "Why do men make violence on we women?"

They revealed the long dark night of a normalized GBV deeply entrenched by a long war that ran the course of the life of an average teenager. The horror stories ran the gamut from prepubescent girls' being preyed upon by 40-year-old men, husbands implicated in wife beating, which frequently manifests itself in marital mortality, spousal murder figures (IPV-intimate partner violence), brutal and often serial rapes committed in public view, and the rape of infants and children. The failed infrastructure resulted in a policing system originally unresponsive even to courageous testimonials. The aftermath of Liberia's war leaves added forms of VAW that take the form of FGM (female genital mutilation), TGF (traumatic gynecologic fistula), and public health pandemics including partially undocumented HIV/AIDS rates. Despite limited infrastructure, there are impressive high schools that manage to graduate 400 high school students per annum. However, graduation rates of girls are compromised by an array of pressures that form a disturbing pattern of socially institutionalized oppression. According to BAWODA women, the pressures of SEA are a combination of traditional and economic factors. First, parental pressure for prostitution to secure money for maintaining the family; second, the pressure on young girls to engage in early sex in order to produce grandchildren; third, pressure from excessive materialism exported by Barber's notion of *McWorld* to acquire "bling bling"— material goods (clothes, jewelry, cell phones) as emblems of social status; and fourth, pressure from older men to engage virgin, prepubescent, and adolescent girls in anal, oral, and vaginal sex.

In some instances, women reported heinous cases of brutal rape, beatings, and murder of both unmarried girls and married women. The difficulties of identifying, detaining, arresting, prosecuting, and jailing perpetrators, even when identified, are well known to international aid workers providing services to nations with ineffective, weak, or gender-unfriendly policing and judicial systems. While traditional practices of early sex, pregnancy, and marriage were common in rural Africa up through the last century, ignorance about existing public health pandemics, myths concerning disease contraction and elimination, absence of sex education, including abstinence, contraception availability and affordability, and even ignorance of basic human anatomy is prevalent. Numerous international agencies, such as the UK-based MERLIN, have been working with the Liberian Ministry of Health for over a decade, and even during the war's escalation in 2001, scaled up their clinical services in training traditional midwives, offering immunization awareness programs and counseling to reduce teenage pregnancy rates and the spread of infectious diseases and, at the height of the fighting, MERLIN provided a city wide ambulance service, latrines, and clean water. With special attention to the context specific conditions of war, MERLIN installed solar panels at more than thirty clinics so women could safely deliver their babies at night during dangerous security conditions. (Interview with Abbey and van Osch, 2008.) The Ministry of Gender collaborated with MERLIN staff to address the conspiracy of silence about reporting GBV, training Liberian staff in five countries in prevention and response techniques. According to MERLIN's Isaac Abbey:

> Although we started out training on reproductive health issues, in the last two years we have introduced gender-based violence into our programs. In our county-wide support groups women speak more openly in groups about their psycho-sexual lives and separate men's groups work to disempower men through awareness that it's not normal to rape returning home with a change of heart.

The agencies' programs, as one of many foreign donor agencies in Liberia, have served an estimated 1.7 million people. In this same interview, outgoing Country Director Sonja van Osch warned that Liberia's National Health Plan "Will have to ensure that everyone has access to health care, including the most vulnerable sections of the population." Within the new climate of the rule of law, policing, judicial, and nongovernmental sectors are being rebuilt through the retraining of these personnel, and raising public awareness among Liberia's citizens. Beyond Liberia, international reports of war-related sexual assaults began to reach public scrutiny as early as the Vietnam War and as recently as the Darfur crisis, two wars decades and continents apart. One of the worst by-products of the civil war in Liberia has been traumatic gynecologic fistula (TGF)—an injury caused by violent sexual assault through the tearing of vaginal tissues with objects such as sticks with nails or guns. In Liberia, and elsewhere, a woman or girl who sustains this injury is rendered incontinent of urine and/ or feces. The length of Liberia's war (1989–2003) created a unique hell for women, one in which sexual violence became the norm, with festering injuries left unattended due to a lack of medical services.

According to USAID, "Together with the horrible physiological consequences of her condition, she must also bear the psychological sequelae of sexual assault, as well as the double social stigmatization due both to her unpleasant incontinent state and to her socially undesirable status as a victim of sexual assault." This USAID report further highlights African nations with high incidences of sexual assault, highlighting the Democratic Republic of Congo as representing the largest reported number of cases, but warns that recent cases being tracked in Rwanda, Sierra Leone, and Sudan have emerged. Given the gaps between the end of wars, the gradual reestablishment of the rule of law, and the often slow pace of collecting statistical data on women's health in postconflict settings, it is not difficult to imagine that Liberia's cases of TGF may tragically rise considering that 40–50 percent of Liberia's girls and women were sexually assaulted or raped during and after the war. The lag in reporting would not be unusual for Liberia because their war-torn counterparts in all parts of the world also reflect the shame women have internalized. Recently, family, community, and national shame is being reported in Mozambique, Bosnia Herzegovina, Pakistan, Haiti, Peru, Kosovo, and too many other places. However, Liberia's history as an African nation stands apart as a unique rapprochement between itself and the United States, and bears on the political forces that shaped the inevitable war that only ended in 2003. Its national history, governance, and geopolitical position over the past two centuries deserve brief mention here in order to contextualize the status of women in this West African nation.

LIBERIA THEN AND NOW

For more than 100 years, African American expatriate freed slaves ruled Liberia, a population who, as a tribal group, contended with indigenous Africans over power and governance since the founding of the country. As in many of Africa's nations encountering political strife, this polarization produced what some Liberians refer to as "inxiles" and "exiles." The eruption of the recent war created such instability that many families found themselves crossing borders back and forth between the neighboring nations of Guinea, Ivory Coast, and Sierra Leone seeking to avoid the relentless armed militia of the Charles Taylor regime—the former president, now being indicted by The Hague for crimes against humanity. Religion, especially Christian sectarianism, dominates Liberia's social landscape. With churches aplenty, the role of Christian religious and missionary organizations constitutes an adaptive institutionalization of the older, more traditional men and women's societies of Africa's past.

For demographic realities of a nation in transition from war to peace, consider that the median age of Liberia's population is eighteen for males and females, and the population growth rate will soon reach 4 percent (2008/CIA). Life expectancy rates are 41 years, with female rates slightly higher than males. While infectious diseases carry a very high risk for most of the population, beyond HIV/AIDS, other threats include food or waterborne diseases (bacterial and protozoa diarrhea, hepatitis A, and typhoid fever), vector borne diseases (malaria and yellow fever), water contact diseases (schisosmiasis), aerosolized dust or soil contact diseases (lassa fever), and animal contact diseases.

In Liberia, the difficulty of identifying, detaining, arresting, prosecuting, and jailing perpetrators, even when identified, is immense. Despite the widespread nature of SEA and the apprehension of pathologically violent men, the police and court systems are often threatened by perpetrators who are bailed out of jail, thereby defying police, and, subsequently, continue to engage in sex crimes with impunity. Human rights attorney and Minister of Labor, Samuel Kofi Woods, in our interview, reflected on the wartime mentality, "The people were afraid of a government that had no love for human rights." Having grown up in the slums of Liberia, he described the historical status and conditions of women as complicated by legal, constitutional, cultural, and customary barriers, "Inheritance laws and cultural practices limited the advancement of women and were unenforceable. [Today] awareness and [the] education of ordinary people and traditional leaders in rural areas are needed...and women themselves need to know the evident and practical manifestations of the new law...that it has implications for traditional marriage and will be affected by judges." The judicial courts, as they undergo reform, exist in parallel with traditional courts in Liberia and Woods asserts that, "These laws need to be in harmony with the main body of laws because traditional courts can undermine the creation of one system." In light of the universal frailties of corruption, deceit, and a lack of respect for women's human rights, Liberia stands as only one of many nations combating violence against women through education and legal reform.

Not only has Liberia's new Congress passed an antirape law, lawyers and legislators are deliberating on making rape an unbailable offense to offset inadequate sentencing. Johnson-Sirleaf, addressing a UNFPA Symposium, asserted, "We will, furthermore, enforce the Rape Law—which came into effect the day after my inauguration—without fear or favor." The narratives of postwar atrocities are clearly connected to, and driven by poverty, a disproportionately high unemployment rate, and by high rates of illiteracy. Liberia's gender-based *Violence National Action Plan* (2008) states that over half of Liberian women are survivors of GBV, so it has a multisectoral strategy for combating the pandemic that carries with it "harmful traditional and cultural practices that perpetuate violence against women."

Listening to the women of BAWODA, individuals revealed they had taken initiatives against both perpetrators and their families to expose the violators and remind them that their activities are being watched. Some have also revived the traditional practice of intervening for girls preyed upon by older men. In the circle of our conversation, the BAWODA women confided about long years and deep pain. The group was composed of a mix of adolescent, middle-aged, and elder women who, one by one, unburdened themselves of story after story of brutalities against women in their communities and the conspiracy of silence that prevented vetting these crimes. According to them, in traditional societies, clan and traditional leaders, families, and even other women have conspired to silence these crimes to preserve a façade of honor behind a veil of fear.

The 2005 UN Progress in Statistics report, *Slow Progress in Official Statistics Bringing Violence Against Women to Public*

Scrutiny, cites sixty-eight geographic regions of the world have constructed at least one survey on VAW; in Africa, thirteen countries conducted such surveys from 1995 to 2004, only four with national coverage. As the HIV/AIDS rate for Liberia is 1.5 percent, based upon the 2007 LDHS (Liberia Demographic Health Survey)—a suspiciously low rate for which there may be varied explanations (war mortality, underreporting, low/no access to health care, a very low rate of the routing screening, social welfare gaps, poverty, and other potential explanations), Dr. Abdelhadi Eltahadi, Chief of Party for Africare's *Improved Community Health Project*, remarked, "Within this context, 1.8 percent of women (aged 15–49 years) are HIV-infected versus 1.2 percent of men in the same age group. The highest age group of women (35–39 years) showed 2.5 percent, and 25 to 29 years showed 2.1 percent." Considering the long-term effects of GBV and the gestation of the HIV virus, Liberia could rival Swaziland for the highest HIV/AIDS rate in Africa, and there is growing qualitative and quantitative evidence supporting the GBV connection.

Riding the well-traveled Tubman Boulevard in Monrovia, road signs and billboards installed by the government's varied national awareness campaigns are astutely designed. In one sign, we see an act of rape occurring with a giant "X" over the image. Another portrays a crouching man defecating in a stream, again with a giant "X" over the image, in an effort to discourage contamination of drinking water, and to encourage positive hygiene practices. In a society with an 80 percent illiteracy rate, it has been in the new Liberia's interest to promote stay-in-school, antirape, basic hygiene, clean water, voting, and immunization messages to people who may not be literate in the formal sense but who are visually literate. The signage conforms to the hopeful convergence of capacity building from both internal and external stakeholders.

In achieving ways and means for a nation traumatized by a fourteen-year civil war, Chancellor Angela Merkel of Germany has advocated cancellation of all Liberia's debt at the International Monetary Fund (IMF), and Germany has provided aid to the tune of more than 18 million Euros along with 300,000 mosquito nets to combat malaria. The civil war has left emotional and psychological scars, two of every three Liberian women being victims of rape during the bloody conflicts. Johnson-Sirleaf has announced "zero tolerance" for such violence—but she must first bring about changes in awareness, such as in the training of police officers, judges, and the general population.

Institutionalized Testifying and GBV

The Truth and Reconciliation Commission (TRC) hearings in Liberia pursued the path of their predecessors in other African countries (South Africa, Rwanda, Ghana, Sierra Leone, and Morocco) and beyond the continent, in Argentina, Canada, Guatemala, the Solomon Islands, East Timor, and other nations. Testimonials offered by individual women, supported by the Ministry of Gender and the Association of Female Lawyers of Liberia (AFELL), have given public voice. Integrated Regional Information Networks (IRIN) has reported accounts of kidnappings, sex enslavement, and trafficking of women in settlement camps during the war, and there is a continuation of VAW acknowledged by NGO's working in Liberia. AFELL director and attorney Deweh Gray told us, "In the hinterlands violations of constitutional law exposed a dual legal system. Women were seen as property and traditional areas women's marriage rights were being threatened." Under the previous head of state, Charles Taylor, she continued:

> It took us eight years to pass the inheritance laws and AFELL was seen as interfering with customary laws. Women could not sit on tribal councils and yet, during the war women had helped to build and run farms. There were forms of violence against women and children but we only started hearing about GBV after the war...violent acts that needed advocacy and awareness.

Throughout the conduct of this research in Liberia, endless stories of the victimization of Liberian girls, women, and children were almost always countered with others of unimaginable courage and industriousness on the part of women who maintained families and small farms and businesses, and who took their food to market to feed their families in the midst of chaos. Women learned house building skills, such as carpentry and masonry, kept small vegetable gardens and sold produce, and helped one another. "Women were playing the roles of men during the war," stated Deweh Gray, and "Once they had this new capacity, there was no turning them back." Relative to interventions on redefining crime and punishment, she told of legal persistence, in one case, "When we sought the death penalty for the rape of a young child...it was regarded as too harsh by international agencies."

AFELL has plans to decentralize transportation and is working with the Ministry of Justice regarding sex offenders and legal aid clinics. If one thing is apparent in both urban and rural Liberia, many nations are helping; besides Germany, add Denmark for justice; Chinese contractors are rebuilding roads; Lebanese monopolize the small hotel and restaurant businesses; and the United Nations Military in Liberia (UNMIL) is the largest troop deployment in the world. *Africare* has funded the development of antirape committees.

Currently, GBV International Rescue Committee (IRC) staff provide case management services for survivors in Liberia's Montserrado, Lofa, and Nimba counties, and work to enhance local capacity to prevent and respond to GBV through raising awareness, training, male involvement and coordination of all actors in close collaboration with the Ministry of Gender.

> We are the trash they leave behind in their wars
> —*Our Bodies, Their Battleground* (IRIN, 2004)

In October 2007, a *New York Times* front page photograph of a 53-year-old woman who had been raped by militia near Bukavu (Congo) documented yet another "epicenter of a rape epidemic." We rarely see photographs of male perpetrators. Such photographs force women to relive the "shame game" of sexual assault. Liberia's small population has suffered, but having ended its civil war, is focused on healing the survivors of rape, implementing criminalization of sexual assault, and providing comprehensive interventions.

Statistical comparisons do little to increase humanitarian awareness and response unless and until the scope of such violence spreads to the developed world. Then will we care or, will it be too late to care? It is not necessarily only that conflict and war are increasing, but also that electronic media journalists, filmmakers, and YouTube or Face Book producers and citizen journalists have become more adept at producing projects on social and political commentary. Memoirs from women and child soldiers have become common, from the Sudanese Halifax Bashir's, *Tears of the Desert* (2008) to Cambodian Somaly Mam's memoir, *The Road of Lost Innocence* (2008) a continent away to *The Day My God Died* (2003), a film recounting the rescue of New Delhi's brothel girls. Liberia needs more safe houses for girls and women brutalized by sexual exploitation and violence. With support from UNMIL and UNICEF, one opened in June 2008, where on-site clients receive counseling, literacy and numeracy skills, vocational training, and information on reproductive health and HIV/AIDS awareness.

Conclusions

As a society, Liberia is facing a daunting climb back into civility and the legal requirements that will help women feel safe as citizens in the new democracy. The presence of UNMIL and hundreds of international agencies and governments are resounding messages of support. Geared especially toward peacekeeping, the UN film, *To Serve with Pride* (2006) "helps men and women to see that sexual abuse is part of gender-based violence on the bottom-up approach" said Merlin's Isaac Abbey, adding that, "To kill a tree you have to pull it out by its roots." And here are some other bright spots:

- The government's *National Policy on Girls' Education/Plans to Make Girls' Education Better* (2008) is a strong policy pledge from the Ministry of Education.
- The Ministry of Gender has partnered with other ministries to craft strategic approaches to gender equity.
- The World Health Organization (WHO) and PATH have developed guides for activists in violence reduction and public health technologies that intervene in the cycles of poverty.
- Perhaps the most long-lasting transformations, yet to be measured, are the human rights training of lawyers, judges, and the national police. The Association of Female Lawyers of Liberia is handling seven to eight victim cases per day, but is also engaged in the retraining of lawyers and judges, all of whom must be retrained to recognize rape and sexual violence not only as crimes but as human rights violations.

Yet, the intransigence of a male-dominated military, police force, and judiciary has, over the decades, created one of the most serious deadlocks against the societies' transformation to a new consciousness of the oneness of humanity and the equality of men and women. This will be a long, but invaluable walk toward sustaining a civil society in Liberia. There is no question that the reduction and elimination of violence, sexual assault and exploitation, prostitution, child trafficking, marital violence, and war-related rape rests in the hands of decent men, women, and nations throughout the world. The conspiracy of silence around these issues, or the dismissal of aggressive acts against children and women as "cultural ways" or "the way things are," are tired rationalizations.

Women and the organized movements they launch against SEA will remain the infantry of this public health pandemic for as long as it lasts—until they are joined by mens' conviction that aggression and violence are unethical and immoral. There is no single response to the attitudinal and behavioral impact of war-related rape and SEA in Liberia. A multipronged approach, including congressional awareness, active law and policymaking, social welfare program interventions, creative media reporting and campaigns, activism, judicial training and reform, police training, reform, enforcement of laws, reduction of corruption, community awareness, and medical and public health campaigns in the hinterlands, must all be promoted. The hope is that Liberia's shame may one day transform the country into a haven of social justice.

Note

The field research for this chapter was conducted in August 2008 and included interviews with survivors of war-related GBV, government officials regarding policy and law-related efforts to prevent ongoing violence against girls and women, interviews with and by NGO projects, and radio and press outlets. The research was funded under a grant from the Office of the Provost, Northeastern University.

Author Interviews, Listed as Presented in Chapter

Interview a: Mary Brownell. August 20, 2008.
Interview b: Deddeh Howard. August 20, 2008.
Interview c: BAWODA Women's Association. August 23, 2008, accompanied by Senator Gbehzohngar Findley, Ms. Fredrica Perkins (Paramount Young Women's Initiative), and Dr. Levi Zangai of the Ministry of Education and World Bank.
Interview d: Isaac Abbey and Sonja van Osch/ MERLIN, August 22, 2008.
Interview e: Minister S. Kofi Woods, August 21, 2008.
Interview f: Dr. Adelhadi Eltahir, August 22, 2008.
Interview g: Attorney Deweh Gray, August 26, 2008.

Filmography

2001 *Women Facing War.* Producers: Urban Films and ICRC.
2004 *Our Bodies, Their battleground-DRC and Liberia.* Producer: IRIN.
2005 *Women in an Insecure World.* Producer: Geneva Centre for the Democratic Control of the Armed Forces (DCAF)

2006 *Liberia: An Uncivil War.* Producer/Director: Jonathan Stack
2006 *Liberia: Hope at last.* Producer: ICRC.
2006 *To Serve with Pride: Zero Tolerance for Sexual Exploitation and Abuse.* Producers: ECHA/ECPS UN and NGO Task Force on Sexual Exploitation and Abuse.
2007 *Iron Ladies of Liberia.* Directors: Daniel Junge and Siatta Scott Johnson
2007 *Liberia: Homecoming in Gorlu.* Producer: ICRC
2007 *Women Fleeing War.* Producer: ICRC.
2008 *Pray the Devil Back to Hell.* Director: Virginia Reticker.
2008 *The Road to Redemption.* Directors: Jonathan Stack and Lila Place

References

Achebe, C. 1958. *Things fall apart.* New York: Anchor.
An assessment of the status of the implementation of UN Security Council Resolution 1325 in Liberia. 2006. United Nations Population Fund.
CIA–Central Intelligence Agency World Fact book, 2008.
Gettleman, J. 2007. Rape epidemic raises trauma of Congo war. *New York Times* (October 7). Available at http://www.nytimes.com/2007/10/07/world/africa/07congo.html.
A letter from Monrovia: Violence against women during the Liberian civil conflict. 1998. *Journal of American Medical Association* 279 (8).
National policy on girls' education: Plans to make girls' education better. 2008. Ministry of Education, Liberia and UNICEF.
Our bodies, their battleground: Gender-based violence in conflict zones. 2004. *IRIN.* Available at http://www.irinnews.org/IndepthMain.aspx?IndepthId=20&ReportId=62814.
Silverstein, M. 2008. Pray the devil back to hell. *Huffington Post* (September 4). Available at http://www.huffingtonpost.com/melissa-silverstein/ipray-the-devil-back-to-h_b_99848.html.
Sirleaf-Johnson, E. 2009. *This child will be great: Memoir of a remarkable life by Africa's first woman president.* New York: Harper Collins.
Traumatic gynecologic fistula as a consequence of sexual violence in conflict settings: A literature review. 2005. USAID/ACQUIRE.
Yeats, W. B. 1920. "The second coming" [poem].

3

SEXUAL VIOLENCE AMONG REFUGEES AND ASYLUM SEEKERS WHO COME TO THE UNITED STATES

Linda Piwowarczyk

Each year, thousands of people flee to the United States and other countries as they are forced into exile, many having experienced sexual violence or torture. At the end of 2008, there were 34.4 million people of concern to the United Nations High Commissioner for Refugees (UNHCR) , which include refugees, asylum seekers, returned refugees, internally displaced, and stateless persons (UNHCR, 2009). A refugee is someone who has crossed his or her national border, and is petitioning a third country to accept them (United Nations, 1951), whereas an asylum seeker has already arrived in the host country when she/he requests protection (United Nations, 1967; U.S. Citizenship and Immigration Services).

Persecution often takes the form of sexual violence in the context of warfare, ethnic conflict, political turmoil, and/or torture. The perpetrators are often those who society entrusts to protect its citizens including police, army, military, and secret police. The victims of sexual violence can be men or women. Names have been changed, and here are some of their stories:

> Mary was helping villagers acquire a living wage. As part of her work, she taught literacy and encouraged women to organize. She was particularly sensitive to the needs of women who she felt the government did not support. After criticizing the government, she was arrested, beaten, and repeatedly raped. She didn't expect that something like this could happen to her, as no one she knew who had been imprisoned ever talked about it.

Martha's husband had a government job. There was increasing turmoil in the country and rebel fighting. She noticed that late at night he would use a short wave radio. She didn't know with whom he spoke, but it worried her and she asked him to stop. One night, government soldiers entered their home accusing him of collaborating with the rebels. They brutally raped Martha and her daughters, and set her husband on fire, and he died. The soldiers took the children and put Martha in jail from where she was able to escape with the help of some people from her church. After several years, she has finally been reunited with her children.

John was active politically for as long as he can remember as his father told him it was the way to change the country. He did not agree with the practices of the ruling party. As the presidential elections were approaching, John vocally supported an opposition candidate. Before the elections, he and many others were arrested. During his detainment he was raped, beaten, given electric shocks, and told that the next time he is vocal in his opposition he will not be so lucky. He was eventually released and fled the country, leaving his family behind as he is now trying to get asylum in the United States.

The Boston Center for Refugee Health and Human Rights is a multidisciplinary program at Boston Medical Center in Massachusetts that works with survivors of torture and refugee trauma from over 60 countries. At any given time, approximately 55 percent of its clients are women. Over one-half are asylum seekers, and about 40 percent are survivors of sexual violence—defined here as intentional sexual humiliation, physical trauma to the genitalia, and rape or attempted rape. My goals are to describe the contexts in which sexual trauma can occur, to describe its potential effects, and to share clinical implications gleaned through our work with this population.

The Context in Which Sexual Violence Occurs

Sexual violence in the context of wartime has been characterized as associated with politics. It can be part of the experience of torture for women and men, punishment to women who do not follow cultural norms, an act of revenge on a subsegment of the population, exploitation of women in protected circumstances, and a means of information gathering (De Neef and De Ruiter, 1986). The United Nations (1984) defines torture as acts "By which severe pain or suffering, whether physical or mental, is intentionally inflicted on a person for such purposes as obtaining from him [her], or a third person information or a confession, punishing him [her] for an act he [she] or a third person has committed or is suspected of having committed, or intimidating or coercing him [her] or a third person, or for any reason based on discrimination of any kind, when such pain or suffering is inflicted by or at the instigation of or with the consent or acquiescence of a public official or any other person acting in an official capacity."

Women are often targeted for sexual violence, as they are believed to be the "bearers of cultural identity" (WHO, 1997). As such, they are at risk for mass rape [as in ethnic cleansing], military sexual slavery, forced prostitution, forced "marriages," and forced pregnancy (Schmuel and Schenker, 1998). According to the United Nations High Commissioner for Refugees (UNHCR, 1995), during armed conflict there are multiple factors heightening the incidence of sexual violence, including the breakdown of social structures. There may also be a lack of security with resultant lawlessness. Certain groups in power, or pushing for power, often try to exert authority and control. Sexual violence may also arise out of accentuated ethnic differences or socioeconomic discrimination. All too often, refugee camps are unsafe places due to the social structures of some camps and their design, camp leadership (typically male), lack of protection, and at times, hostility of the local population (UNHCR, 1995; Hirschfeld et al., 2009).

Sexual violence in the context of war happens worldwide, and there are countless examples. In a study done by Physicians for Human Rights in 2002, of 991 random households interviewed in Sierra Leone, approximately one-eighth reported one or more incidents of war related sexual violence. Gang rape was reported by one-third of the women who reported sexual violence. In the war in the Congo, sexual assault victims are three times more prevalent than gunshot casualties and five times more common than wounded soldiers. In the words of Dr. Denis Mukwege, director and founder of Panzi General Hospital, "It is sexual terrorism that seeks to destroy the identity of the individuals and their communities" (cited in Goodspeed, 2008). In a sample of Rwandan genocidal survivors, 39 percent of interviewees reported that they had been raped during the genocide, and 72 percent said they knew someone who had been raped (Avega Agahozo, 1999). By 1993, the Zenica Centre for the Registration of War and Genocide Crime in Bosnia-Herzegovina had documented 40,000 cases for war-related rape (Ward et al., 2005). Notwithstanding reports of sexual violence among women who fled Darfur to camps in Chad, it was also suggested by Amnesty International (2004) that some women did not flee the country for fear of being stigmatized—which says that, for some, stigmatization by one's community could have greater bearing on a decision to flee than the risk of ongoing violence.

One cannot separate sexual violence from the risk of contracting HIV, particularly in areas where the disease is endemic. Factors shown to increase its risk during conflict include the following: increased interaction among military and civilians, increased levels of commercial or casual sex, decreased availability of reproductive health and other health services, decreased utilization of reproductive health and other health services, increased levels of malnutrition, decreased use of means and information to prevent HIV transmission, increased population mixing following large internal or regional movements, the emergence of norms of sexual predation and violence, and/or the fragmentation of families and resultant vulnerable households. On the contrary, there may also be an increase in protective factors against contracting HIV during conflict due to the increased isolation of communities, increased death rates among high risk groups, decreased casual sex associated with trauma and depression, and disruption of sexual networks following conscription or displacement (Mock et al., 2004). Let me tell about one of my clients:

> Seraphine was active in the political process in her country. She saw the conditions they were living under, and decided to get politically active so that her children might have more opportunities. She was arrested three times, and each time she went back to her fight for independence for her people. Her final arrest was the most brutal. She was gang-raped and left for dead. After arriving in the United States, she had a medical evaluation that included HIV testing. She had been negative in her own country. Although she was granted asylum, she fears that people in her community will find out that she is HIV positive, and ostracize her.

Rape has not always been identified as a crime against humanity. During the Nuremberg War Crimes Trials, evidence of rape by soldiers was first presented, but not included in the final decision. At the Tokyo War Crimes Trials after World War II, sexual violence was proclaimed a war crime (Swiss and Giller, 1993). It was not until the advent of ethnic wars in Bosnia and Rwanda, when thousands of women were raped in sweeps across their countries, that the International Criminal Court recognized mass rape as not only a violation of the practice of war, but also as a crime against humanity that was punishable (Hargreaves, 2001). Women have long been the spoils of war, but these intracountry conflicts were unprecedented in their brutality. In this context, the Secretary General of the U. N. defined rape as a crime against humanity as, "Any acts of rape which are committed as part of widespread or systematic attack against a civilian population on national, political, ethnic, racial, or religious grounds (1993). More recently, it has been publicly recognized that sexual violence affects not only the health and safety of women, but also the economic and social stability of nations with untold safety implications, making it an issue to be addressed by the Security Council (Farley, 2008).

UNHCR (1995) has long recognized that refugees who appear to be at greatest risk for sexual violence include unaccompanied women, unaccompanied children, lone female heads of household, children in foster care arrangements, and those in detention or detentionlike conditions. Often, sexual violence goes unreported or under-reported, which may relate to the stigma and shame pinned to a victim who is still, in many cultures, considered to blame. Husbands, families, and communities may ostracize survivors of rape should they be exposed. In addition, survivors may not be considered desirable or even allowed to marry. Coming forward can risk additional attacks, particularly in the face of impunity, and emotional and physical impacts may be so great that the trauma may remain a hidden wound, too risky to disclose and/or to seek support.

THE REFUGEE PROCESS

When thinking about refugees and other uprooted people, it can be helpful to have a chronological perspective; for example: What was their life like before a war or persecution? Why did they flee their home or homeland? What happened to them in the course of flight, and when they arrived in the country of first asylum? What is their life like having come, if to the United States, before and after September 11, 2001? The conceptualization of the refugee experience has shifted from one that historically addressed issues of acculturation to one that looks through the lens of trauma exposure due to massive refugee flows in different parts of the world (Brody, 1994). Most recently, more effort is placed on recognizing qualities of resilience (Betancourt and Khan, 2008; Grigg-Saito et al., 2008, Ghosh, Mohit, and Murthy, 2004; Hsu, Davies, and Hansen, 2004; Hosin, 2001).

UNHCR (1995) has recognized that sexual violence can occur at many places along the journey, as depicted in this adapted table: *Sexual trauma as a threat during the migration process.*

Table 3.1 Sexual trauma as a threat during the migration process

A. PRIOR TO FLIGHT	By police and military, rebels, ethnic cleansing, for bartering, during interrogation
B. DURING FLIGHT	By pirates, bandits, security forces, border guards, and smugglers
C. COUNTRY OF ASYLUM	By local populations officials, border guards, police military, international refugee workers, fellow refugees, camp attacks, coercive prostitution

When comparing events during wartime and during peacetime, the World Health Organization (1997) reminds us that gender-based violence (GBV), including sexual violence, is often not an either/or phenomenon but is, rather, a continuum. It further suggests that, as societal mores collapse during conflict, underlying attitudes about violence against women become more overtly acceptable. Having said that, it is also important to remember that one may also have been a victim of sexual violence before a conflict began, or it may have occurred after one arrived in a country of asylum or resettlement.

Seeking Asylum

Asylum seekers flee their countries in search of safety due to persecution at home and well-founded fears of persecution on the basis of race, religion, nationality, membership in a social group, and/or political opinion. Unlike refugees who do so abroad, asylum seekers petition for protection after arriving in their host country, where they hope to be allowed to remain and ultimately be reunited with their families (United Nations Conference on Plenipotentiaries on the Status of Refugees, 1951; United Nations Declaration on Territorial Asylum, 1967). Once arriving in the United States, asylum seekers have one year to apply for asylum (INA§208(a), 1999). In a clinic-based sample of asylum seekers seeking mental health services (n=134), one-half had experienced rape or attempted rape. At the time of entry, an asylum seeker is required to present a case for credible fear in front of a uniformed official. In this clinical population, 69 percent of the females (61/88) and 13 percent of the males (6/46) experienced rape or attempted rape. This raises issues relevant to disclosure to immigration officials, and the need for having the option to choose the gender of the immigration officer (Piwowarczyk, 2007). In another sample of asylum seekers, sexual violence was found in three-quarters of the women—anal and vaginal rape, often multiple times, and by different persons (Edston and Olsson, 2007).

Credibility can be questioned if someone does not disclose information at the beginning of the immigration process but does so later—even though sexual violence is often very difficult to talk about. In a study from London (Bogner, Herlihy, and Brewin, 2007), asylum seekers who suffered sexual violence experienced greater Post Traumatic Stress Disorder (PTSD), more dissociative symptoms, greater feelings of shame, and more difficulty disclosing information. Those with higher shame also had higher PTSD scores and increased avoidance and arousal symptoms, whereas those with dissociation, had higher levels of shame and greater PTSD avoidant symptoms. Shame appears to mediate between sexual violence and PTSD avoidance (ibid). In the case of sexual violence, then, psychological factors such as dissociation, numbing, and the triggering of PTSD symptoms need to be taken into account when assessing the veracity of someone's claim if they were unable to disclose their sexual trauma history when first meeting immigration officials, but then do so later.

Consequences of Sexual Violence

It can be helpful to look at the consequences of sexual violence on four levels: potential health consequences, emotional impact, social and community consequences, and existential issues. As we know, sexual violence can result in injury, disability, death, and sexually transmitted diseases, including HIV/AIDS. Unwanted pregnancy and unsafe abortions may also result. Moreover, survivors of sexual violence may also be at risk for reproductive health disorders, miscarriage (UNHCR, 1995; UNHCR, 2003), and/or chronic infections, and excessive bleeding (Mollica and Son, 1989). Significant trauma at the time of rape can result in long-term damage to the vaginal wall, causing fistulas requiring surgical intervention that, for many, is prohibitively expensive (Longombe, Claude, and Ruminjo, 2008; The Acquire Project, 2005).

Sexual violence does not exist in a vacuum; the emotional impact can be devastating. Feelings after sexual violence may range from anger, fear, self-hate, and resentment, to shame, insecurity, decreased concentration, loss of function, difficulty sleeping, and/or eating disorders. Survivors may be also at risk for the development of post-traumatic stress disorder as well as major depression, and even suicide (UNHCR, 2003). Victims of sexual trauma may feel very numb and go on to have difficulties with intimacy into the future (UNHCR,

1995; Mollica and Son, 1989). Other common responses to assault, as summarized by Foa and Rothbaum (1998) include dissociative reactions and anger, in addition to potential social problems. In a study of women (41/130) who had accessed emergency room services at a general hospital in the previous one to two and one-half years due to sexual assault, one-half still felt alone and three-fourths felt suspicious of others. Many felt that their lives were restricted (Nadelson et al., 1982).

Many factors have been shown to mediate the traumatic effects of sexual violence, influencing the nature and intensity of traumatic responses. In the case of torture, they include the circumstances of torture, including its perception and interpretation, social context before, during, and after the torture, community and peer resources, values and attitudes about trauma, political and cultural practices, severity and duration of the traumatic events, genetic and biological vulnerabilities, developmental age, age of the victim prior to the history of trauma, and preexisting personality characteristics (Iacopino, Ozkalipici, and Schlar, 1999).

Their own families or communities may marginalize survivors if information about their GBV becomes known. They may be blamed for what happened, even rejected for polluting their family honor. Families may unequivocally disown them, as they are believed to be unclean—making it difficult to find a marriage partner (Mollica and Son, 1989). As a result of isolation from the community, one may not be able to get necessary resources for survival and support, and there can also be the risk of further violence (UNHCR, 1995).

As with any traumatic event, our assumptions about the world as a benevolent and meaningful place and the self as worthy are challenged (Janoff-Bullman, 1992). Aside from the emotional, social, and physical effects of sexual violence, survivors of sexual trauma may face significant existential questions in their efforts to make meaning out of what has happened to them. It is often the intentionality of cruelty, which is most difficult to grapple with as sexual violence happens in the context of an unequal power dynamic.

Barriers to Treatment

There are a range of barriers making it difficult for uprooted peoples to get medical treatment in a new country. Language is often a major issue in accessing and utilizing health services. There may be fears related to insurance, which for many is a new concept. Many newcomers have fears related to their immigration status and seeking services.

Poverty and focusing on survival may preclude leaving the home, and religious beliefs may dictate particular solutions to problems. In addition, new arrivals may not be aware of services available to them, or they may lack a means of transportation to access these services. The situation becomes increasingly complex when we begin to think about differing explanatory models of health and illness. Communities themselves may have solutions embedded in the culture, which are the preferred practices. Sometimes, the duration of symptoms can be so great that a concrete connection is not made between the symptoms and the original traumatic events. There may also be a lack of awareness of existing methods to alleviate the symptoms from which one is suffering. The topic of rape is often so taboo that community resources cannot be mobilized.

Relative to potential emotional consequences of sexual violence, specific challenges exist in the mental health arena. There can be a stigma in the community related to having an emotional problem, or of being thought of as crazy, or even being seen in a psychiatric clinic. Sometimes the frame of reference for mental disorders is limited to knowledge of interventions available back home. Across cultures around the world there are different explanatory models of illness and health such that the nature and the cause of distress can vary from culture to culture. Distress can also be expressed through bodily symptoms such as chronic pelvic pain. The idea of talking to a stranger about private information can be unthinkable. In addition, getting help for oneself can be delayed due to pressing issues related to survival and adjustment of oneself and one's family, such that the sexual issues are relegated to a lower priority apropos of Maslow's (1943) hierarchy of needs.

CLINICAL CONSIDERATIONS

Within the context of the patient/client provider dyad, cultural issues can come into play, which influence the meaning of nonverbal signals, as well as differing ways of coping and communicating (Gorman, 1986). Some cultures do not stress emotional abreaction. Self-disclosure may mean different things to different communities (Sue and Sue, 1990). Other factors that must also be taken into account include power and role differentials as well as gender and age factors. Cultures also differ as to how they receive and give help, and how they perceive problems (Gorman, 1986).

The meaning of sexual trauma and torture is embedded in historical and cultural traditions (Mollica and Son, 1989). It is very important to understand the cultural meaning of the experience of sexual trauma, as it may range from thoughts such as the rape of a woman is also considered the rape of her husband or family. To rape is a crime. Some communities believe that the rape experience should be hidden and quickly forgotten, emphasizing the future not the traumatic past. If one is unmarried and becomes pregnant, there may be an expectation that the victim marry the perpetrator. Survivors may worry about the impact on one's ancestors, questioning whether it is even worth living anymore. Treating someone who is traumatized often means working with them to understand the meaning of their experiences on both cultural and existential levels.

It is equally important to understand how communities have dealt with trauma in their own countries. Are solutions found in the family more than with the individual? What traditional methods are available to the population, and what do they mean to us or to them? What are the traditional ways of coping with systemic violence in their community? Are there spiritual networks and rituals that could become part of the healing process? What practices and traditions are transferable to a new country? The spiritual/existential issues that arise when one is exposed to intentional cruelty can be the most challenging, particularly when the conflict involves neighbor versus neighbor. Effective treatment often requires engaging clients in conversation about suffering from the vantage point of their belief system (Piwowarczyk, 2005).

Summary

It is critical for providers working with these communities and friends and family to create a place or environment in which victims of sexual violence can feel safe. By understanding the cultural implications of their experiences, we can help to create more meaningful connections. Understanding the barriers to treatment and concerns around confidentiality are critical. Less direct approaches may at times be preferable as disclosure, itself, may result in the triggering of memories. Creating a safe place and acknowledging one's needs from a holistic perspective can help to reframe experiences. Working in groups can be potentially useful as survivors learn from others, and are less isolated.

Women supporting women who have been victimized by sexual violence is essential in beginning to change social mores that often dictate that survivors should be marginalized. Moving beyond a moralistic frame of reference to one acknowledging rape as a crime and a human rights violation is necessary to shift the onus of responsibility from the survivor to the perpetrator or perpetrators. It is here that general society has a role to play in the healing of its members. The U. N. Resolution 1325 is an effort to protect women during conflict. With the pandemic of HIV/AIDS, clear efforts need to be made to prosecute these war crimes. At the same time, efforts are necessary to destigmatize the experience of rape as it stands in the way of reaching out for help and recovery. We know that social support is a helpful mediator for the impact of trauma. If communities see sexual violence through the lens of a crime or human rights violation rather than as a loss of honor by the individual/family, there is an opportunity for a reduction in suffering and an opportunity to heal.

Note

A version of this paper was presented at Northeastern University's 2006 "Women, War, and Violence" conference.

References

Amnesty International. 2004. *Sudan: Darfur: Rape as a weapon of war: Sexual violence and its consequences.* New York: AFR/54/076/2004.
Avega Agahozo. 1999. Association of Widows of the Genocide. Survey on violence against women in Rwanda. Kigali.
Betancourt, T. S. and K. T. Khan. 2008. The mental health of children affected by armed conflict: Protective processes and pathways to resilience. *International Review of Psychiatry* 20 (3): 317–328.
Bogner, D., J. Herlihy, and C. R. Brewin. 2007. Impact of sexual violence on disclosure during home office interviews. *British Journal of Psychiatry* (191): 75– 81.
Brody, E. 1994. The mental health and well-being of refugees: Issues and directions. In *Amidst peril and pain*, ed. A. J. Marsella, T. Bornemann, S. Ekblad, J. Orley, 57–68. Washington, DC: American Psychological Association.
De Neef, C. E. J. and S. J. De Ruiter. 1984, July. *Sexual violence against refugee women: Report on the nature and consequences of sexual violence suffered elsewhere.* Netherlands: Ministry of Social Affairs and Labour.
Edston, E. and C. Olsson. 2007. Female victims of torture. *Journal of Forensic and Legal Medicine* 14 (6): 368–373.
Farley, M. 2008. U. N. Security Council says sexual violence akin to war crimes. *Los Angeles Times* (June 20).
Foa, E. B. and B. O. Rothbaum. 1998. *Treating the trauma of rape: Cognitive behavioral therapy for PTSD.* New York: The Guilford Press.

Ghosh, N., A. Mohit, and R. S. Murthy. 2004. Mental health promotion in post-conflict countries. *Journal of the Royal Society of Health* 124 (6): 268–70.

Goodspeed, P. 2008. Rape new war strategy in Congo, doctor says: Sexual terrorism. *National Post* (December 1).

Gorman, W. 1998. Refugee survivors of torture: Trauma and treatment. 106th meeting of the American Psychological Association, San Francisco, CA.

Grigg-Saito, D., S. Och, S. Liang, R. Toof, and L. Silka. 2008. Building on the strengths of a Cambodian refugee community through community-based outreach. *Health Promotion Practice* 9 (4): 415–425.

Hargreaves, S. 2001. Rape as a war crime: putting policy into practice. *The Lancet* 357: 737.

Hirschfeld, K., J. Leaning, S. Crosby, L. Piwowarczyk, J. VanRooyen, G. Greenough, S. Bartels, A. Fricke, S. Sirkin, L. Black, V. Iacopino, K. Lanigan. *Nowhere to Turn: Failure to Protect, Support, and Assure Justice for Darfuri Women*. A Report by Physicians for Human Rights in partnership with the Harvard Humanitarian Initiative. www.darfuriwomen.org.

Hosin, A. A. 2001. Children of traumatized and exiled refugee families: Resilience and vulnerability: A case study report. *Medicine, Conflict and Survival* 17 (2): 137–145.

Hsu, E., C. A. Davies, and D. J. Hansen. 2004. Understanding mental health needs of Southeast Asian refugees: Historical, cultural, and contextual challenges. *Clinical Psychology Review* 24 (2): 193–213.

Iacopino, V., O. Ozkalipici, and Schlar, C. 1999. *The manual on effective investigation and documentation of torture and other cruel, inhuman or degrading treatment or punishment*. The Istanbul Protocol, presented to UNHCR.

Janoff-Bullman, R. 1992. *Shattered assumptions towards a new psychology of trauma*. New York: Free Press.

Longombe, A. O., K. M. Claude, and J. Ruminjo. 2008. Fistula and traumatic genital injury from sexual violence in a conflict setting in eastern Congo: Case studies. *Reproductive Health Matters* 16 (31): 132–141.

Maslow, A. H. 1943. A theory of human motivation. *Psychological Review* 50 (4): 370–396.

Mock, N. B., S. Duale, L.F. Brown, E. Mathys, H. C. O'Maonaigh, N. K. L. Abul-Husn, and S. Elliott. 2004. Conflict and HIV: A framework for risk assessment to prevent HIV in conflict-affected settings in Africa. *Emerging Themes in Epidemiology*. 1(1): 6.

Mollica, R. F. and L. M. Son. 1989. Cultural dimensions in the evaluation and treatment of sexual trauma: An overview. Treatment of victims of sexual abuse. *Psychiatric Clinics of North America* 12 (2): 363–379.

Nadelson, C. C., M. T. Notman, H. Zackson, and J. A. Gornick. 1982. A follow-up study of rape victims. *American Journal of Psychiatry* 139 (10): 1266–1270.

Piwowarczyk, L. 2005. Torture and spirituality: Engaging the sacred in treatment. *Torture* 15 (1): 1–8.

———. 2007. Asylum seekers seeking mental health services in the United States: Clinical and legal implications. *Journal of Nervous and Mental Disease* 195 (9): 715–722.

Schmuel, E. and J. G. Schenker. 1998. Violence against women: The physician's role. *European Journal of Obstetrics and Gynecology and Reproductive Biology* (80): 239–245.

Sue, D. W. and S. Sue. 1990. *Counseling the culturally different* (2nd edition). New York: Wiley.

Swiss, S. and J. E. Giller. 1993. Rape as a crime of war. *JAMA* 270 (5): 612–615.

The Acquire Project. 2005. *Traumatic gynecologic fistula as a consequence of sexual violence in conflict settings: A literature review.* Available at http://www.acquireproject.org/fileadmin/user_upload/ACQUIRE/traumatic_fistula_review—final.pdf.

United Nations Conference of Plenipotentiaries on the Status of Refugees and Stateless Persons. 1951, July 2–25. Geneva, Switzerland. Available at http://www.unhcr.org.

United Nations Convention Against Torture and Other Cruel, Inhuman or Degrading Treatment or Punishment. 1984. General Assembly Resolution 39/46.

United Nations Declaration on Territorial Asylum. 1967, December 14. Adopted by General Assembly resolution 2312 (XXII).

United Nations High Commissioner for Refugees (UNHCR). 1995. Sexual violence against refugees: Guidelines on Prevention and Response.

———. 2003. Sexual and gender-based violence against refugees, returnees and internally displaced persons: Guidelines for Prevention and Response. Available at http://www.unhcr.org.

United Nations Security Council Resolution 1325 on Women, Peace and Security. 2000, October 31.

U.S. Citizenship and Immigration Services (previously Immigration and Naturalization Services). Available at http: //www.uscis.gov/graphics/shared/aboutus/statistics/publist.htm.

Ward, J., J. Kirk, L. Ernst, and Integrated Regional Information Networks. 2005. *Broken bodies, broken dreams: Violence against women exposed.* Geneva: United Nations Office for the Coordination of Humanitarian Affairs.

War-Related Sexual Violence in Sierra Leone: A Population-Based Assessment. 2002. Physicians for Human Rights and UNAMSIL.

World Health Organization. 1997. *Violence against women.* Geneva: WHO.

4

VICTIMS, VILLAINS, AND VICTORS: MEDIATED WARTIME IMAGES OF WOMEN

Linda K. Fuller

A century ago, 90% of war casualties were male soldiers. There have been 250 major conflicts since World War II, with 23 million acknowledged casualties. Today an estimated 90% of these casualties are civilians, and 75% of these are estimated to be women and children.
—Zainab Salbi (2006: 14), Women for Women International

In the home, in refugee camps, and/or on battlefields, women might be depicted in the media along a spectrum of gender-based to gender-perpetrated violence. As you examine the various chapters included in this volume, it is critical to keep in mind what (re)sources have been available and used by the media—both violence against women (VAW) and violence by women (VBW), what messages are interpreted, and what effects might be anticipated. Beginning with the notion of media mediation, this chapter offers an overview of varying gendered wartime representations, examining mediated images of women in general, women and war, and then offering areas of activism and personal, individual means of understanding and caring about how it affects us and our sisters personally, professionally, and globally.

MEDIA MEDIATION

Between competing red/black states, liberal/conservative "news," and other polarizing concepts, it is almost easy to choose reports and representations to support our already formed, prejudiced views. As Gow and Michalski (2008) remind us, images affect war and our understanding of it—just as media scholars of violence (e.g., George Gerbner's Cultural Indicators project) outline how heavy television consumers develop patterns fearing victimization and vulnerability. There is a kind of catechism of statistically alarming data that those of us who study media violence (Gerbner and Fuller, forthcoming) tend to chant to any audience we can, whether in classrooms, PTA groups, family and friends, and/or boardrooms:

- More than 99 percent of households in the United States have televisions, and according to Nielsen ratings, the average TV is on for more than seven hours per day.
- By the age of five, the typical American child has logged over 200 hours of violent images (typically five acts/hour during prime time, and twenty–thirty acts/hour on children's programming, such as Saturday morning cartoons). And this doesn't account for the fact that we know that some one million kids under the age of five are watching television after midnight.
- The average 14-year-old has witnessed the killing of 13,000 human beings—of course without seeing anyone's grief, or any repercussions (except maybe in *The Sopranos*, for revenge). The average 18-year-old will have spent 11,000 hours in school, and yet will have spent double that amount of time (more than 22,000 hours) watching TV—more than anything else except sleeping. During those 22,000 hours, he or she will have seen some 350,000 commercials and 18,000 murders.
- According to Amnesty International (2001), a woman in the United States is battered every fifteen seconds, raped every six minutes, while each day in North Africa some 6,000 women are genitally mutilated, 15,000 Chinese women are sold into sexual slavery annually, and 7,000 Indian women are murdered over dowry disputes. Reporting on a 10-country study on women's health and domestic violence, in 2008 the World Health Organization (WHO) found that, with some 5,000 annual honor-related murders, widespread trafficking, forced and child marriages, and global sexual abuse of children, some 15 to 71 percent of women reported physical or sexual violence by a husband or partner; further, many said their first sexual experience was nonconsensual, and 4 to 12 percent were physically abused during pregnancy.

The topic of violence and the media is intricately tied to issues of gender, class, ethnicity, and religion; by default, it includes considerations about children, the horror film genre and psychological thrillers, the rhetoric of violence, domestic violence, sports, hate crimes, news, music and violence, comics and cartoons, gender and gender orientation, the Internet, popular cultural interpretations of violence, and censorship. Above all, patriarchal power offers images of women cringing, crying, and basically being victims. At its most extreme, it forces us to reframe topics of VAW such as "femicide" (Russell and Radford, 1992) or "gendercide," sex trafficking, mass rapes, forced pregnancies, acid burning, bioterrorist acts, and other insidious, misogynous acts.

Whether in print, electronic, or film, media violence involves storytelling from major conglomerates aiming to encourage us, as consumers, to want more media—the overall result being desensitization and acceptance of the media world as the "real world." Drew Humphries (2009) contends that media, through television networks such as Court TV, the Lifetime Channel, and WE (Women's Entertainment), along with popular programs like *Crime Scene Investigation* (CSI), *America's Most Wanted*, *Law & Order*, and *Prime Suspect* and *Crimewatch* in the UK, encourage victim blaming. "Male criminality is portrayed primarily as an ambiguous, lurking threat from unknown strangers who attach from outside the family," Cuklanz and Moorti (2006: 318–319) contend about prime time victimization, while, "Female criminality is primarily depicted as an insidious interpersonal dysfunction that destroys the family and society from within."

Through longitudinal research such as content analysis, we also learn that violence is increasingly recognized as performed not just to, but also *by* women, who are "equally likely to hurt or kill as to be hurt or killed" (Signorelli, 2005: 35). The year 2007 saw the publication of McKelvey's *One of the Guys: Women as Aggressors and Torturers*, Owen, Stein, and Vande Berg's *Bad Girls*, Tannen's *The Female Trickster*, and White's *Violent Femmes*, while headlines and "breaking news" bring us stories of female suicide bombers, abusive prison guards (think Lynndie England at Abu Ghraib), "girls with guns" (West, 2005), and other examples of villainous females that Sjoberg and Gentry (2008) argue act consciously. And so, we must include VBW.

Media Images of Women

"The ways in which women are represented in news media send important messages to the viewing, listening, and reading publics about women's place, women's role, and women's lives," Byerly and

Ross (2006: 40) remind us. We read newspapers, watch television, go to the movies, listen to music, flip through magazines, log onto the Web. Yet, do we consume pornographic materials, buy violent comics, listen to sexist rap lyrics, subscribe to dirty tabloids, and/or participate in videogames like *Mortal Kombat*? Writing about exclusion and marginality relative to female portrayals in Israeli media, Dafna Lemish (2004: 44) states,

> The preference of the media for dealing with women as victims (overcreative or active women, for example) is a double-edged sword. On the one hand, the media create public awareness of violence against women, thus advancing social debate and remedies. On the other hand, the media's tendency to eroticize, trivialize, and sensationalize...depicts the phenomenon as the private battles of passive, unfortunate women, rather than a structural, inherent, social problem arising from power relations and inequality.

Mediated images of women and violence best begin with Amazons; recall its derivation from the Greek "a" meaning *without*, "mazo," *breast*—for women warriors who cut off one of their breasts to facilitate archery. Popular imagery includes numerous similar examples of VBW (Inness, 1999, 2004; Mainon, 2006; McCaughey and King, 2001), such as Buffy the Vampire Slayer, Mulan, Xena, Warrior Princess, Lara Croft, and many other Wonder Women. When we talk about the feminization of poverty and images of women in degraded circumstances, we also need to address the feminization of violent media. Recognizing that gendered violence is a social construction is the first step (Boyle, 2005; Oliver, 2007).

Media Images of Women and War

> Around the world, women and girls are victims of countless acts of violence. In a great many of these instances, the violence is not random—women and girls are victims because they are female. The range of gender-based acts of violence in conflict is devastating, occurring, quite literally, from womb to tomb. Among other abuses, violence against women includes: rape, sexual mutilation, purposeful infection with HIV/AIDS and other sexually transmitted infections, forced impregnation, forced abortion, female genital mutilation, sexual harassment, trafficking, forced prostitution, dowry-related violence, domestic violence, battering, and marital rape. Violence against women and girls occurs in every segment of society—regardless of class, ethnicity, culture, country, or whether the country is at peace or war.—Introduction, UNIFEM (WomenWarPeace.org)

Filmic and Televised Portrayals

Military women, according to mainstream movies, have ranged from Goldie Hawn as *Private Benjamin* (1980) to Demi Moore as *G.I. Jane* (1997); Meg Ryan serving with *Courage Under Fire* (1996) in the Persian Gulf War; or Kate Beckinsale as a nurse in *Pearl Harbor* (2001). Glenn Close braved being the lead in *Serving in Silence: The Margarethe Cammermeyer Story*, a 1995 biopic about the highest-ranking woman in the Armed Forces, outed as a lesbian. *She Stood Alone: The Tailhook Scandal* (1995) took on sexual harassment in the military, while *The General's Daughter* (1999), who was found dead, staked and strangled and presumably raped, takes the phenomenon of gender-based violence (GBV) to its extremes. Then too, there is the female gun-toting VBW subgenre, launched in 1973 in *Cleopatra Jones*, with Tamara Dobson and Shelley Winters pitted against one another as good/evil characters, like Uma Thurman in *Kill Bill* (2003, 2004) revenge dramas, along with some scifi, animated action films and anime where the strong female protagonist demonstrates martial arts, gunplay, and various stunts.

Fortunately, there are some powerful documentaries about women, war, and violence—notably, Kylie Grey's *My Home, Your War* (2006), on the Iraq War through the eyes of an Iraqi woman; Beate Arnestad and Morten Daae's *My Daughter the Terrorist* (2007), a member of Sri Lanka's Tamil Tigers (LTTE); Tamar Yarom's *To See If I'm Smiling* (2007), which explores the Israeli/Palestinian conflict through testimonies of six female soldiers fulfilling their compulsory military service in the Occupied Territories; and Lisa F. Jackson's *The Greatest Silence: Rape in the Congo* (2008), which shatters the silence surrounding the plight of women and girls being systematically kidnapped, raped, mutilated, and tortured by soldiers in the DRC, and many more.

No doubt you are familiar with televised typecasting in *M*A*S*H* (1972–1983), *China Beach* (1988–1991), *J*A*G* (Judge Advocate General, 1995–2005), or *NCIS* (the Naval Criminal Investigative Service, 2003–). Mostly, though, women in the military play secondary characters, complimenting men—or, more likely—being violated by them. Fortunately, there are other than mainstream media representations. A key example is *Through Our Eyes*, a 2006 project begun in a refugee camp for Liberians in Guinea; jointly sponsored by American Refugee Committee International (ARC) and Communication for Change. It produces local videos on such tough topics as rape, forced marriage, and wife beating.

Mediated Rape

Of all the mediated images relative to GBV and war, probably none are more horrific than those involving war and rape (Barstow, 2000; Bourke, 2007; Ensler, 2001; Frederick and the Aware Committee on Rape, 2001; Rehn and Sirleaf, 2002; Amnesty International, 2004; Fuller, 2005; *The war within the war*, 2002). "Rape, enslaved prostitution, and other sexual violence against women have been a part of war for all of recorded history—across *all* cultures, and in all kinds of wars," states Kathryn Farr (2005: 165), "be they religious, colonizing, or revolutionary."

While we may know that rape has been a product of war since ancient times, when it was considered something of a reward to the victors, its more recent use in a systematic, almost expected manner as part of terrorism is particularly unsettling. Women and children as casualties may have been part of Greek and Roman battles, the American Civil War, the European slave trade, Native American genocide, and World Wars I and II. Consider how Japanese soldiers abducted hundreds of thousands of Asian (mostly Korean, but also Chinese, Filipina, and Indonesians) women and forced them into sexual slavery. Today rape warfare tends to be genocidal, manifesting itself in civil wars in Bangladesh, Ethiopia, Liberia, Sierra Leone, Kashmir, Sri Lanka, East Timor, Turkey, Peru, Uganda, the former Yugoslavia, Kenya, the Democratic Republic of Congo (DRC), Cote d'Ivoire, Angola, Algeria, Chechnya, Myanmar, Rwanda, and too many other places. It has claimed innumerable victims, with more recent atrocities such as those still ongoing in Somalia, the Sudan, and Iraq demanding our attention beyond media reportage.

Wartime rape, we know, is a deliberate assault not only on the woman; it involves her whole family, her whole community (*Glossary of Violence Against Women*, 2004). Nicholas D. Kristof (2008) considers its increase, "First, mass rape is very effective militarily...it's preferable to terrorize civilians sympathetic to a rival group and drive them away, depriving the rivals of support. Second, mass rape attracts less international scrutiny than piles of bodies do, because the issue is indelicate and the victims are usually too shamed to speak up." As we know all too well, rape might take the form of humiliation, torture, demoralization, or all of the above. Nearly always, it leads to both stigma and ostracism, to medical and/or mental problems, and women considered as "damaged goods." Always, rape is a human rights violation. During times of either war or peace, against women or by women, it is a crime—criminal in any perspective.

Sexual politics, while always playing a part in the socioeconomic background, seems to escalate during times of war. Even if they have been "protected" by their respective societies by means of dress codes, religious rights, educational activities, and/or any number of other male-subscribed rules, girls and women become fair game in times of war. Consider its role in the issue of "ethnic cleansing," a frightening phenomenon aimed at eliminating whole communities of people, many captured women consciously impregnated with "preferred" genes for new clans or ethnicities (Žarkov, 2007, 2008). These rapes, often performed in front of families and neighbors, leave women not only traumatized but also abused and abandoned beyond repair. Outcasts, they face further victimizations, such as survivor guilt, stigma, accusations of collaboration and complicity, even having feelings for various militia members.

Yet, even when rapes are practiced at a mass level, such as the 200,000 "comfort women" subjected to sexual slavery by the Japanese military during World War II, or when Serb troops raped some 20,000 women during the 1992–1995 war, we still need to remember that they are performed on *real* people—even if they might seem invisible to their perpetrators. Perversely, we have the Bosnian and Rwandan conflicts to thank for raising our awareness, hopefully making us sensitive to atrocities occurring today in places like the Sudan. "Because of the devastating effect sex crimes has on communities, we are noticing that wartime rape crimes are increasingly either encouraged or included as official military strategies," according to Kelly Askin, author of the 1997 book *War Crimes Against Women* (cited in Vo, 2000). Also, while we think we know all about the Holocaust, only recently are we getting reports about some 100,000 German women raped by Russian forces as other atrocities were highlighted. Employing the theory of "power over" an "other," Lucinda Marshall (2004: 1), founder of the Feminist Peace Network claims that VAW is exacerbated by militarism:

> Since the beginning of patriarchy, women have been considered the spoils of war, made invisible today under the euphemistic phrase, "collateral damage." Military training frequently encourages the hatred and belittling of women. The use of gender slurs motivate men to act aggressively, both toward women within their own culture and women of the "other" culture. Pornography and prostitution have always been unofficially sanctioned forms of entertainment for soldiers.

In its century-old history, movies have often depicted images of war—albeit typically from the male perspective. War movies as a genre have always been good box office draws, easy visuals letting us know heroic good guys versus enemies. When rape becomes part of the plot, however, it becomes much stickier—for ratings, promotion, visual imagery, and for us viewers. Like advertisements for sanitary products, early examples of cinematic wartime rape were presented vaguely, forcing us as audiences to fill in the blanks. Looked at chronologically for the last quarter-century, we see how rape as a control mechanism has both evolved and remained the same. My review of forty-two films from some thirty-three countries (Fuller, 2005) represents depictions of wartime rape allowing us to see patterns of geographic displacement around the world, even if basic themes remain. At the least, we can take some consolation from the fact that media has gone from breaking taboos to dealing with them at deeper levels.

Conclusions

Framed as a gender issue, related to discrimination and human rights, the subjects of VAW and VBW have typically received media attention in sensationalistic, tabloid-type form (Meyers, 1997; United Nations, 2007). Media, we realize, is a social institution aimed at both shaping and reflecting our worldviews; yet, we need to seek alternative perspectives if we seek truthful answers. Once we recognize that GBV results from a pervasive ideology of sexism assuming and alleging women's inferiority, we can begin considering policies and practices.

The United Nations has made it very clear that it wants to eliminate gender disparity at all levels by 2015, particularly VAW—an extension of the 1993 Vienna World Conference on Human Rights and expansion of the 1995 Beijing Platform for Action. Additionally, we owe enormous debts to organizations like Amnesty International, Human Rights Watch (HRW), Medecins Sans Frontieres (MSF, or Doctors Without Borders), the United Nations Development Fund for Women (UNIFEM), Refugees International, PeaceWomen, the WHO Task Force on Violence and Health, the Geneva Centre for the Democratic Control of Armed Forces (DCAF), World Watch, the National Sexual Violence Resource Center (NSVRC), the 16 Days of Activism Against Gender Violence campaign, and many NGOs and people working in this area. We owe them attention, support, and promises of our own activism. In particular, we owe a debt of gratitude to playwright Eve Ensler for founding V-Day, which highlights VAW and underscores the fact that too much systematic rape and sexual violence continues today, and to Jackson Katz, cofounder of the Mentors in Violence Prevention program and subject of Media Education Foundation's documentary *Tough Guise: Violence, Media & the Crisis in Masculinity*. These actions need to top our advocacy and policy agendas, as too many people still equate women with peace, and men with war.

In 2005, the Radcliffe Institute for Advanced Study sponsored a conference examining gender roles in "The War Zone." "Gender fallout is part and parcel of the business of war," declared Jacqueline Bhabha, executive director of the University Committee on Human Rights Studies, pointing out that women have always been involved in war—supporting husbands and sons, suffering loneliness and loss, experiencing atrocities such as systematic rape and other forms of sexual violence, mourning and burying the dead, rebuilding devastated societies, sometimes even acting as combatants themselves. Yet, women living in war conditions are clearly not always victims. We all know many strong women, many strong voices, and many strong stories. "War has a paradoxical impact on feminism," Alyson M. Cole (2008: 22) has noted, "It forecloses feminism by reinforcing patriarchal structures, yet at the same time it often requires women to act without men, which can catalyze feminism." Luckily, the media is introducing us to female combatants in training and traumas (Black, 2008), serving as soldiers (Alvarez, 2009; Bragg, 2004) or suicide bombers (Rubin, 2009), and evolving in what has traditionally been an all-male bastion. Meg McLagan, co-filmmaker with Daria Sommers of the documentary *Lioness* (2008), about female troops attached to all-male combat units in the Army and Marines ostensibly to interact with Muslim women who held their own when fighting broke out, explained that, "We need to talk about and recognize what women are doing. The gap between the policy and the reality needs to be closed" (cited in Lee, 2008).

As media consumers and students of media criticism, it behooves us to analyze mediated messages about women as victims and villains, both domestically and internationally, from sociopolitical/economic viewpoints—considering the roles of historical context, definitions of war and definitions of rape, forms of violence against the oppressed, psychological tactics, constructions of filmic "reality," commercial or capitalistic opportunities, implications for HIV/AIDS and/or reproduction, human rights and inhumanities, militaristic terminology, actors, viewer/audience perceptions, and gendered perspectives. Yet too, we realize, those of us who have been part of the feminist movement through its many incantations have the luxury of making these examinations. With Alexander and Hawkesworth (2008), Cockburn (2007), Copelon (1995), and others, we condemn domination and humiliation and demand accountability.

Let me conclude on a positive note. For starters, there are a number of media-related people and organizations working to dispel negative images of women—notably the following: *About-Face* works to combat "negative and distorted images of women in the media"; *Adios Barbie!*, a body image Web site; *African American Women in Cinema* (AAWiC) supports minority women filmmakers; *The Asian-American Justice Center* focuses on television diversity; New York University's interdisciplinary *Center for Media, Culture and History* addresses issues of representation, social change, and identity construction embedded in the development of film, television, video and new media worldwide; the *Center for Media Literacy* (CML) uses a Media Lit Kit curricula; *The Center for New Words* supports diversity "from literacy to blogging to literary writing to opinion-making in the media and other domains of influence"; *The Geena Davis Institute on Gender in Media* operates within the entertainment industry; the *Gay & Lesbian Alliance Against Defamation* (GLAAD) aims at accurate, inclusive representations of gender identities and sexual orientations; Zimbabwe's *Information Campaign on Domestic Violence* uses mobile cinema, community dialogue, and print to educate; the *International Women's Media Foundation* (IWMF) works with women in the news media around the world; the *Media Education Foundation* provides invaluable video resources on gender roles, race, and sexism in the media; *Mind on the Media* raises awareness of negative media images; *National Hispanic Media Coalition* deals with many media-related issues; *Network of Women in Media, India* (NWMI) is a forum for women in media professions; *New York Women in Film and Television* (NYWIFT) helps women in those industries; *Racialicious*, a "blog about the intersection of race and pop culture," critiques questionable media representations; *Reel Grrls* trains teenage girls (ages 13–19) in video technology skills; *SheSource.org* is an online database for female journalists; South Africa's *Media Monitoring Project* (MMP), human rights driven, aims to advance a "fair, free, diverse and ethical" media culture; *Women at the Forefront* (www.womenattheforefront.com) produces documentaries through women's eyes; *Women in Film* (WIF) is based on mentoring; *Women in the Director's Chair* is an international media arts/activist center; *Women Make Movies*, a "multicultural, multiracial, nonprofit media arts organization," encourages filmmakers and videographers; *Women's eNews* offers important perspectives on public policy; and the *Women's Media Center* makes media accountable.

Recalling that most of the world's 960 million illiterate people are women, the role of radio cannot be overstressed for women wanting to keep in touch about wartime activities. For example, *Elles Parlent, Elles Ecoutent* ("She Speaks, She Listens") reaches refugees in Chad and Sudan, hoping to help those who have been traumatized by events they have witnessed; *Kamanga Zulu* is a radio drama aimed at GBV in Malawi; and FIRE (Feminist International Radio Endeavor) from Costa Rica amplifies women's voices worldwide recounting experiences of armed conflict (Thompson, Toro, and Goacutemez, 2007). More than a decade after the Beijing World Conference on Women, we still need to increase networking, given the empowering possibilities of the fourth estate in the twenty-first century. "Whether it is domestic abuse, the use of rape as a weapon of war, or forms of culturally sanctioned violence such as sati [widow immolation on a husband's funeral pyre], foot-binding, genital mutilation, honour killings," D'Cruze and Rao (2005: 1) reminds us, "violence bears an inverse relationship to ideas of full humanity and sexed personhood." Ditto for VBW.

United Nations Secretary General Ban Ki-moon issued a statement in February 2008 declaring that violence against women is, "Never acceptable, never excusable, never tolerable." The question is, though: How much of the media covered this comment? Violence, we know, makes "good copy"; add women and wartime statistics, and consumers capitulate. Mediating, interpreting, critiquing, and/or facilitating images, we continue to realize how powerful a role media plays in warfare.

Note

A version of this chapter was presented at the Women, War, and Violence conference held at Northeastern University.

References

Alexander, K. and M. E. Hawkesworth, eds. 2008. *War and terror: Feminist perspectives*. Chicago: University of Chicago Press.

Alvarez, L. 2009. G. I. Jane stealthily breaks the combat barrier. *New York Times* (August 12): 1, 20–21.

Amnesty International 2001. *Broken bodies, shattered minds: Torture and ill treatment of women*. New York: Amnesty International.

———. 2004. *Darfur: Rape as a weapon of war: Sexual violence and its consequences*. New York: Amnesty International.

Barstow, A. L., ed. 2000. *War's dirty secret: Rape, prostitution, and other crimes against women.* Cleveland, OH: Pilgrim Press.
Black, D. D. 2008. *The holy war: Women in combat.* Frederick, MD: PublishAmerica.
Bourke, J. 2007. *Rape: Sex, violence, history.* Berkeley, CA: Shoemaker and Hoard.
Boyle, K. 2005. *Media and violence: Gendering the debates.* Thousand Oaks, CA: Sage.
Bragg, R. 2004. *I am a soldier too: The Jessica Lynch story.* New York: Vintage.
Byerly, C. M. and K. Ross. 2006. *Women and media: A critical introduction.* Malden, MA: Blackwell.
Cockburn, C. 2007. *From where we stand: War, women's activism and feminist analysis.* London: Zed Books.
Cole, A. M. 2008. The postfeminist dilemma. *Women's Review of Books* 25 (4) (July/August): 21–22.
Copelon, R. 1995. Gendered war crimes: Reconceptualizing rape in time of war. In *Women's rights, human rights: International feminist perspectives,* ed. J. Peters, 116–124. New York: Routledge.
Cuklanz, L. M. and S. Moorti. 2006. Television's "new" feminism: Prime-time representations of women and victimization. *Critical Studies in Communication* 23 (4) (October): 302–321.
D'Cruze, S. and A. Rao, eds. 2005. *Violence, vulnerability and embodiment: Gender and history.* Oxford, UK: Blackwell.
Ensler, E. 2001. *Necessary targets: A story of women and war.* New York: Villard.
Frederick, S. and the Aware Committee on Rape. 2001. *Rape: Weapon of terror.* River Edge, NJ: Association of Women for Action & Research.
Fuller, L. K. 2005. Wartime rape: A filmic chronology. Brown Bag Lunch, Northeastern University.
Gerbner, G. and L. K. Fuller. Forthcoming. Media-mediated violence. *Glossary of Violence against Women.* 2004. Harrisburg, PA: VAWnet.
Gow, J. and M. Michalski. 2008. War, image, and legitimacy: Viewing contemporary conflict. London: Routledge.
Humphries, D., ed. 2009. *Women, violence, and the media: Readings in feminist criminology.* Boston, MA: Northeastern University Press.
Inness, S. A. 1999. *Tough girls: Women warriors and Wonder Women in popular culture.* Philadelphia: University of Pennsylvania Press.
———., ed. 2004. *Action chicks: New images of tough women in popular culture.* New York: Palgrave Macmillan.
Kristof, N. D. 2008. The weapon of rape. *New York Times* (June 15): WK 14.
Lee, F. R. 2008. Battleground: Female soldiers in the line of fire. *New York Times* (November 5). Available at http://www.nytimes.com/2008/11/05/arts/television/05lion.html.

Lemish, D. 2004. Exclusion and marginality: Portrayals of women in Israeli media. In *Women and media: International perspectives*, ed. K. Ross and C. M. Byerly, 39–59. Malden, MA: Blackwell.
Marshall, L. 2004. *Militarism and violence against women*. Available at http://zmagsite.zmag.org/Apr2004/marshall0404.html.
Mainon, D. 2006. *The modern amazons: Warrior women on screen*. Pompton Plains, NJ: Limelight Editions.
McCaughey, M. and N. King, eds. 2001. *Reel knockouts: Violent women in the movies*. Austin: University of Texas Press.
McKelvey, T., ed. 2007. *One of the guys: Women as aggressors and torturers*. Emeryville, CA: Seal Press.
Meyers, M. 1997. *News coverage of violence against women: Engendering blame*. Thousand Oaks, CA: Sage.
Oliver, K. 2007. *Women as weapons of war: Iraq, sex, and the media*. New York: Columbia University Press.
Owen, A. S., S. R.Stein, and L. R. Vande Berg. 2007. *Bad girls: Cultural politics and media representations of transgressive women*. New York: Peter Lang.
Rehn, E. and E. J. Sirleaf. 2002. *Women, war, peace: The independent experts' assessment of the impact of armed conflict on women and women's role in peace-building*. New York: UNIFEM.
Rubin, A. J. 2009. How Baida wanted to die. *New York Times Magazine* (August 16): 38–43.
Russell, D. E. H. and J. Radford. 1992. *Femicide: The politics of woman killing*. Buckingham, UK: Open University Press.
Salbi, Z. 2006. *The other side of war: Women's stories of survival and hope*. Washington, DC: National Geographic.
Signorelli, N. 2005. *Violence in media: A reference handbook*. Santa Barbara, CA: ABC-Clio.
Sjorberg, L. and C. E. Gentry. 2008. Reduced to bad sex: Narratives of violent women from the Bible to the war on terror. *International Relations* 22 (1): 5–23.
Tannen, R. S. 2007. *The female trickster: The mask that reveals*. London: Routledge.
Thompson, M. E., M. Suaacuterez Toro, and K. Anfossi Goacutemez. 2007. Feminist media coverage of women in war: "You are our eyes and ears to the world." *Gender & Development* 15 (3) (November): 435–450.
United Nations. 2007. *Ending violence against women: From words to action: Study of the Secretary-General*. New York: United Nations Publications.
Vo, M. T. 2000. Ending rape as a weapon of war. *Christian Science Monitor*, April 25. Available at http://www.csmonitor.com/atcsmonitor/specials/women/world/world042500.htm.
The war within the war: Sexual violence against women and girls in Eastern Congo. 2002. New York: Human Rights Watch.
West, H. G. 2005. Girls with guns: Narrating the experience of war of FRELIMO's "female detachment." In *Children and youth on the front*

line: *Ethnography, armed conflict and displacement*, ed. J. Boyden and J. De Berry, 105–129. New York: Berghahn Books.
White, R. 2007. *Violent femmes: Women as spies in popular culture*. London: Routledge.
World Health Organization. 2008. Violence against women. *Fact sheet #239*. Available at http://www.who.int.mediacentre/factsheet/fs239/en/print.html.
Žarkov, D. 2007. *The body of war: Media, ethnicity, and gender in the break-up of Yugoslavia*. Durham, NC: Duke University Press.
———, ed. 2008. Gender, violent conflict and development. New Delhi: Zubaan.

Part II

Organizational Reconciliation, Policy Reform, and Postwar Effects on Women

5

Challenging Hegemonic Understandings of Human Rights Violations in the South African Truth and Reconciliation Commission: The Need for a New Narrative

Kiri Gurd and Rashida Manjoo

Introduction

As feminist critical social scholars, we understand our primary task is to make visible the way that hegemony functions to assert, reproduce, and maintain unequal power relations. We understand hegemony to refer to circumstances where meanings are so embedded in social relations and the social structure that representational and institutionalized power becomes naturalized, taken for granted and, therefore, almost invisible so that it goes uncontested (Silbey, 1998). This chapter focuses on the relationship between truth commissions and hegemony. We use the South African Truth and Reconciliation Commission as a case study (hereafter the TRC).

We have focused on truth commissions, and the TRC specifically, because despite an enormous quantity of academic writing in this area, there has been little interrogation of the discursive and epistemological assumptions relative to violence and human rights violations—the meanings of which underpinned, and governed, the TRC. Since the TRC has been heralded as a "best practice model" for truth commissions in general and since the establishment of truth commissions has proliferated practically exponentially since the TRC, such an interrogation seems all the more necessary and relevant.

Moreover, truth commissions are internationally understood and endorsed as a legitimate and effective method, or body, for transitioning a nation from war to peace specifically due to its narrative feature. More specifically, the understanding is that the open, nonjudicial format of truth commissions provides an opportunity for victims and perpetrators to tell their story and speak their truth without the legal requirements of wartime tribunals. Through these stories of "truth," human rights violations committed under the previous regime are made known, a collective, national memory is formed, and the past atrocity is put to rest so that individuals and communities can heal and a new, liberal government can establish democracy and peace (Hayner, 1994). However, much feminist and poststructural critique (Ross, 2002; Nesiah, 2006; Mamdani, 2000) have argued that the distinction between war and peace is often superficial for those who are continually marginalized within a society, that is, structural violence, or systemic oppression, creates a situation of perpetual war for the disenfranchised. In addition, critique has been lodged against the positive effects and transformative capacity of narratives (Ewick and Silbey, 1995); specifically, the commissions "transitional narrative of truth" (Ross, 2002; Orford, 2006).

The critiques makes clear that the "narrative of truth" is not a transparent disclosure of human right violations but rather a political discourse where meanings are contested and power relations determined, and the ability to control this meaning and knowledge is the key to exercising power in society (Foucault, 1980). In other words, the ability to name what counts as truth is an effect of power, and the search for truth often signals the likelihood of injustice being done to those without power (Orford, 2006). In this way, narratives are social acts performed within specific contexts that organize their meanings and consequences and thus rather than initiating transformative action, as stated in truth commission mandates, may actually be complicit in constructing and sustaining the very patterns of oppression they seek to subvert (Ewick and Silbey, 1995). The narrative of truth thus becomes a hegemonic tale (Ewick and Silbey, 1995) that reinscribes and even revitalizes unequal power relations.

In terms of truth commissions specifically, the result is a liberation process that recognizes individuals but fails to recognize structural power arrangements and thus does little to redistribute power and establish substantive equality. The current social and economic inequality experienced by the majority of black South Africans (despite a small but growing middle class), and particularly for black South African women, in the postapartheid state is a case in point. The critiques made clear to us that truth commissions as a "a transitional narrative of truth" that help move a country from war to peace are a salient site to examine how hegemony maintains systems of inequality.

To do this examination, we have drawn on feminist analyses that have analyzed women's experiences of apartheid and how these experiences were absorbed within the TRC. We focus on women because we believe, along with other critical social feminists (Mohanty, 2003; Narayan et al., 2000; Grewal and Kaplan, 1994) that anchoring analyses in the lives of marginalized communities of women provides the most are not inclusive paradigm for thinking about social justice. This particularized viewing allows a more concrete and expansive vision of universal and transformative justice.

We do not claim that all marginalized locations yield crucial knowledge about power and inequity but that there are causal links between marginalized social locations and experiences, the global capitalist order, racism, sexism, and the functioning of hegemony (Mohanty, 2003). By focusing on specific experiences and placing them within a larger global framework we hope to begin to map the way hegemony not only affects women cross-culturally in particular locations around the world but how it undermines efforts of social justice and peace. The outcome draws out points of commonality of how the "logic of capitalism in the contemporary global arena exploits both third and first world women" (Mohanty, 1996: 28) and subverts social transformation.

In the context of this chapter, by drawing on feminist analyses of women's experiences and stories within the TRC, we were able to expose the taken for granted meaning of human rights violations and violence as individualistic, solely public, and purely physical, or "body bound." Such a meaning construction worked to limit and/or silence the stories of the functioning and impact of the apartheid system and, in particular women's stories of daily systematic inequality and structural violence, as opposed to the public and physical violence, which was predominantly experienced by men. Hence, black women's experiences under apartheid were omitted from the "narrative of truth" since it was not predominantly characterized by physical violence but by structural violence.

In addition, and critically, these taken for granted meanings worked to reduce centuries of racialized, gendered oppression in

South Africa to the traces it left on the corporeal body and the historical and contemporary roots of apartheid went largely unspoken, namely the enslavement and exploitation of black South Africans in the service of white imperialism. As a result, the way individual harms were (are) connected to a broader, and historical, project of global capitalist enterprising was effaced and the systemic power relations of inequality—the long-term, latent impetus to the manifest physical violence of the "apartheid civil war"—went unaddressed, unchallenged, and unchanged.

In this way, within a tightly integrated capitalist system, drawing on the particular standpoint of poor indigenous and Third World women enabled an analysis that, we think, provided the most inclusive viewing of systemic power and of the way hegemony functions. We believe that it is this viewing that allows those committed to global justice to think more deeply and act more transformatively. We hope to offer a way of thinking through the connections between "Women" "War" and "Violence" within a larger, global framework of hegemonic functioning by taking a particular case study, an experience that happened on the "ground" to real women, and placing it within a broader, historical, and more macro perspective.

We make four main arguments relative to truth commissions and their ability to assist in a liberation process and the establishment of peace. First, we argue that a reconceptualization of violence and human rights is required so that their politically relevant definitions are not limited to the individual, public, physical realm but defined in terms of power arrangements. Second, we argue that in the post-socialist century, it appears that one of the ways that imperialism has operated is by focusing on, and exploiting the attention to, "recognition" at the expense of a focus on the "redistribution" part of the justice equation (Fraser, 1998). In other words, by focusing on recognition of violence and individual harms, state and nonstate actors interested in maintaining their power through the revolution or liberation process are able to ignore the redistribution of material resources and power (Fraser, 1998). Our position is clear that recognition is critical to justice and equality, but we are arguing for an increase in recognition of the different forms of structural violence. Third, we argue that, in general, we need to be wary of narratives as a tool for postconflict reconstruction, as they can contribute to hegemony by functioning as a means of social control, colonizing consciousness, and by often effacing the connection between particular persons and events and social organizations and arrangements (Ewick and Silbey, 1995). Our last and overall argument is that one of the goals of truth commissions should be to create a counter hegemonic narrative that aims to make visible local and global systems of inequality and which subverts unequal power arrangements, through a focus on the underlying systemic inequalities that most often is a causal factor in conflicts. Therefore, we conclude that if truth commissions are to meet their mandated objectives to assist in national reconciliation and the establishment of peace, then a reconceptualization and usage of both human rights and violence needs to take place so that structural inequality is recognized and comprehensively addressed through the redistribution of resources, economic and social rights, and access to power. It is in this way that hegemony can be subverted and substantive equality established.

SOUTH AFRICAN HISTORY

State-Sanctioned Discrimination and Oppression

Until the advent of democracy in 1994, the history of South Africa from 1652 is characterized by conflict, discrimination, oppression, exclusion, and exploitation of black people. Dutch colonization was followed by British colonization, white minority rule and then by the apartheid system. The systematic entrenchment of discrimination and disadvantage, based both on race and gender, defined the relationship between the colonizers and the colonized. An ideology of separation of black and white people, practices such as the importation of slaves, systematic hunting and killing of indigenous nomadic people, and the dispossession of land from indigenous people, among other atrocities, were the norm during these periods. This resulted in black people being denied citizenship rights including most civil, economic, and political rights. The formal foundations for the system of apartheid were laid in policies outlined by a committee set up in 1905 by the British High Commission in South Africa. The policy which related to indigenous peoples (called "natives" by the colonizers) proposed racial segregation broadly, and more specifically, the creation of separate "locations" on the fringes of cities and towns, for black people living in urban areas. After the Anglo-Boer war, between the British and the Boers (who were of Dutch descent), the Union of South Africa was founded in 1910. This led to a period of white minority rule, with governmental policies including a progressive realization of the exclusion of blacks from political life, and also, a denial of citizenship rights for the majority of black people.

In addition to other laws and policies, which generally led to the exclusion of blacks from political, economic, and social life, the colonial state was also responsible for the enactment of the Native Administration Act in 1927. This legislation effectively created a dual legal system by recognizing African Customary Law and also establishing special courts that would settle disputes between African people. The formal codification of customary law resulted in many distortions and errors that impacted negatively on this racial group. Its impact on women is evident in many areas, including the perpetual minority status conferred on them, the lack of equal status and equal capacity, the designation of black males as heads of households (despite evidence of many women-headed households), the allocation and distribution of land to men only, the lack of any legal enforceable rights against a spouse for people married under customary law and so on.

The culmination of such discriminatory policies led to the creation of a legalized apartheid system after a successful electoral victory in 1948 by the Afrikaaner political party, the Nationalist Party. Beginning in 1948, laws were enacted that legalized racial and gender discrimination, thereby compounding the many disadvantageous consequences of a long history of oppression and discrimination for black people (TRC Report, Vol. 1:25). Laws and policies effectively created a situation of black people becoming foreigners in their own country and being denied the basics of citizenship, including equality and participation rights. The Nationalist Party government ruled from 1948 until 1993. White supremacy was the principle on which the apartheid laws and policies were based and implemented. Racial segregation became the official state policy. The maintenance of a system of rigid political, social, and economic segregation of the four official racial groups (i.e., African, colored, Indian, and white) was the norm. The ideology of the state was based on the need to create separate societies in one country, based on both racial hierarchy and the imposition of an inferior status on all black people. State sponsored discrimination resulted in the enactment of laws that impacted civil, political, social, economic, and cultural rights. In practical terms this included laws and policies pertaining to franchise rights, land, housing, education, employment, health, governance and judicial institutions, freedom of political activity, freedom of movement and family life. Some of the laws and policies included the following: (1) *Population Registration Act,* which classified all South Africans into one of four official racial groups; thereby impacting all forms of human rights, and also dictating levels of benefits and entitlements based on racial hierarchy. (2) *Separate Amenities Act and the Prohibition of Mixed Marriages Act*—laws that generally enforced the total separation of different race groups in public and private places. (3) *Group Areas Act*—created a system of geographic separation for each race group. The consequence of this included forced and also mass removals of black communities from their residences and the relocation to areas that were vastly inferior; the demolition of homes and other amenities; and the creation of "locations" in urban areas for African people. In most instances, very little or no compensation was paid to such communities. Also the areas that people were relocated to, had very little infrastructure and amenities, thereby affecting negatively on educational, employment, family life, and health issues. (4) *Promotion of Bantu Self-Government Act*—established eight black "nations" in different rural geographic areas (based on tribal/ethnic groupings). This was the precursor to the setting up of the independent "homeland" system in the 1970s. (5) *Bantu Homeland Citizenship Act*—forced all black South Africans of African descent to become citizens of a "homeland" according to their culture and language. Political and legal systems based on customary law were set up and administered by traditional leaders who were appointed as civil servants (with control vesting in the central government). In the urban areas "townships" were created for black people. (6) *Black Education Act*—created a system designed to provide an inferior education to black children, so that they could become the providers of menial labor. Factors such as curriculum design; funding; inadequately trained teachers; substandard facilities etc all assisted in making this goal a reality. Consequently, the low number of black students entering institutions of higher education ensured that there was always a large pool of black people to fulfill menial labor roles for the industrial sector. The impact on black women of this state sponsored discrimination was compounded by the "patriarchal" system of traditional communities regarding the education of the black girl child. The influx control laws further exacerbated women's movement, thereby rendering them unable to access educational and training opportunities in urban areas. (7) *Numerous "influx control" laws* and the *"pass" laws* ensured the curtailment of movement of black people. This impacted particularly in economic and educational exclusion, with black people only being allowed to be in urban areas if they had a job and the necessary documents (e.g., a pass). For black women, the restrictions were worse as they were not seen as providers of cheap labor for the industrial sector, hence forcing them to live separately from their spouses and partners. The domestic service sector, which was a source of employment for black women, also had many restrictions that curtailed both freedom of movement and also the right to a family life. In most instances, black women and men worked in the industrial and domestic sectors in urban areas and went "home" to the rural areas once a year. Children were raised by the extended family and community in the rural areas. The ideology underpinning the restriction of women's freedom of travel and confining them to the native reserves was premised on the belief that such reserves were the true "homelands" of the Africans (Walker, 1991:7). Both black and white men also feared that wage labor would erode control over African women and would also affect negatively on the subsistence agricultural sector, which was the second most common form of employment for women in the reserves (Walker, 1991:14). (8) The *creation of "reserves"* for black people ensured that land allocation for blacks was limited to 13 percent of South African land by laws such as the Land Act of 1913. As a result, men were forced to leave the reserves in search of jobs, which provided cheap labor to fuel industrial development (Walker, 1991:6). Since women could only visit their migrant-laborer husband for a maximum of ninety days a year (seventy-two hours at a time), they were effectively confined to the reserves. Isolating women from urbanization and industrialization drastically restricted their employment and educational opportunities (Walker, 1991:7). Women, who comprised two-thirds of the reserves' inhabitants, were able to spend only 10 percent of their time farming; the remainder of the time was occupied with retrieving water and wood, pounding mealies, child-rearing, and other household work (Walker, 1991:147).

In terms of opportunities and access to employment, numerous labor laws were passed, which included *job reservation laws* that reserved jobs for white people. Other laws provided for safety standards, minimum wage, and compensation funds that was restricted for the benefit of white people. Also, legislation such as the Urban Areas Act provided for the exclusion of the "idle and undesirable" from cities, thereby disproportionately affecting black women whose employment prospects in the formal sector were limited in urban areas. This resulted in most black women either working illegally near towns, working informally as domestic workers, or waiting in rural areas for their migrant-worker husbands to send money home. Inadequate health facilities, lack of piped water, and lack of sanitation system in areas that blacks occupied also led to many illnesses and diseases. This also impacted women's right of access to reproductive services, thereby impacting negatively on their educational and economic activities.

The Liberation Struggle

Despite the white minority exercising control through the political and economic instruments of the state, the black majority population resisted. The oppression and use of force against opponents of the system was also the norm during this period. Oppressive political measures included banning all political activities, banning liberation movements, detaining persons without trial, creating a repressive security system, state-sanctioned murder, and the imposition of successive states of emergency. From the 1960s onward, in response to civil disobedience and unrest, numerous states of emergency were declared and all antiapartheid organizations and liberation movements were banned. Laws were also passed to silence and subdue individuals and organizations that were involved in the liberation struggle. Some of these laws included: Suppression of Communism Act, Public Safety Act, Criminal Laws Amendment Act, and the Unlawful Organizations Act. Detention without trial and mass arrests for acts of treason became the norm. Through legislation, the state also set up a special bureau of state security that had vast powers and the task of protecting the country. This bureau was responsible for many violations of human rights including killings, rapes, assaults, and other forms of torture.

Both the apartheid state and the liberation movements used sex and gender-based violence and discrimination in ways that reflected and exploited the norms in society regarding women and gender. The lives, the risks, and the impact of political activism of women are reflected by numerous authors (see generally Walker (1991), Cock (1991) and Russell (1989). Jacklyn Cock and Diana Russell interviewed women who were involved in the liberation struggle and both of their books reflect the realities and the differential impact of detention, torture, and other kinds of oppression (Russell: 1989:15). Russell states that approximately 12 percent of detainees held during the 1986–1987 state of emergency were women and there were several reports of miscarriages in detention, torture using electric shock on pregnant women, allegations of rape by soldiers, and other forms of abuse.

Changes and events in the global geopolitical sphere, for example, the collapse of the Soviet Union and the end of the cold war, seemingly served as a catalyst for the apartheid South African state adopting a much more serious stance of negotiation with the liberation movements in the late 1980s. The unbanning of political organizations was followed by tentative talks between political and civil society leaders. The political negotiation design and process undertaken by South Africa's current political leaders in the Nationalist Party, and future leaders from the liberation movements in general, and with the African National Congress (ANC) in particular, resulted in the ruling party adopting a strategy to force power sharing and the protection of white minority rights in their constitutional negotiation with an inexperienced future ruling party.

A post-amble to the 1993 Interim Constitution, committing postapartheid South Africa to a policy of reconciliation and understanding, as opposed to vengeance, was agreed to in the negotiation process. It also mandated establishing a body to address human rights violations and delineate "the truth in relation to past events as well as the motives for and circumstances in which gross violations of human rights had occurred, and to make the findings known in order to prevent a repetition of such acts in future" (Promotion of National Unity and Reconciliation Act). Thus, the TRC was created.

The Truth and Reconciliation Commission

Structure and Methodology

As indicated earlier, the Interim Constitution mandated establishing a TRC to deal with past human rights violations. The influence of the African concept of "ubuntu" (the recognition of the humanity of the other) underpinned the negotiation of a suitable process and structure to deal with the past so the that the recognition of the humanity of both the perpetrator and the victim became central to the commission as did the understanding that what was needed was healing, forgiveness, reconciliation, and rehabilitation rather than retribution. Ultimately, these negotiations culminated in the creation of a body with a mandate to document "gross violations of human rights," which were defined as specific acts that resulted in severe physical and/or mental injury in the course of the specified period in which the political conflict took place, namely the period from 1960 to 1994 (TRC Report, Vol 1: 60).

More specifically, the Promotion of National Unity and Reconciliation Act 34 of 1995 (hereinafter the TRC Act)—the enabling legislation that spells out the functions and powers of the TRC—had as its principal goals the establishment of a complete picture of the causes, nature, and extent of gross violation of human rights committed during the specified period, the discovery of truth regarding these violations and the political conflict in general, the promotion of reconciliation, the granting of amnesty to obtain full disclosure and the making of recommendations in respect of reparations for the victims/survivors as well as for measures to prevent the violation of human rights. The act also required the holding of public hearings, unless such a hearing was likely to lead to a miscarriage of justice.

The Committee on Human Rights Violations was tasked with investigating and documenting gross violations of human rights and it gathered a total of 21,296 statements of complaints for investigation (TRC Report, Vol 3:3). Approximately 10 percent of these testimonies were aired publicly, while the rest were gathered in written statements (Posel and Simpson, 2002:3). In addition to individual testimonies, special investigations and hearings on sectors of society complicit in maintaining apartheid also occurred. The sectors included business, legal, health, faith, prisons, women, trade unions, media, and so on. The motivation for the institutional hearings was to "seek to explore the broader institutional and social environment and provide the opportunity for self examination by the various sectors, as well as discussion of their possible role in the future" (TRC, Vol 1: 148). Hence, the political, economic, and social environment that gave rise to or allowed for gross violations of human rights, was also publicly on trial to a limited degree. Unfortunately, the TRC report reflects that these hearings were of limited value in terms of relevant information. This was due to many factors including the reluctance of relevant sectors to participate, the fact that the information that *was* shared did not address and acknowledge how the systemic and structural functioning of these sectors impacted black people in general and black women in particular, and because of the narrow terms and interpretation of the mandate.

The Amnesty Committee's role was to consider approximately 7,000 applications for amnesty that were received. Their role allowed an investigative component, if needed. The amnesty clause provided indemnity from both civil and criminal prosecution in exchange for full disclosure of unlawful acts committed in the pursuit of a political objective within the stipulated time frame, and subject to a proportionality test. Referrals of victims to the Reparation Committee were made on granting of amnesty, or on a finding of gross violations of human rights (in cases of refusal). A refusal of amnesty resulted in a referral to the Director of Public Prosecutions for possible prosecution.

The Reparation Committee received cases from both the Human Rights Violation and Amnesty Committees, and also directly from individuals "who are of the opinion that they have suffered harm as a result of gross violations of human rights" (TRC, Vol 1:285). Victims included direct victims, intervening victims as well as relatives and dependants. The reparation and rehabilitation policy includes the following recommendations: individual reparation grants in the form of monetary payment; symbolic reparation (e.g., memorials, proper burials); community rehabilitation programs (e.g., counselling services, housing); institutional reform (proposals on measures to prevent the recurrence of human rights abuses). Between 1998 and 2003, urgent interim relief was granted to 19,000 victims by the government. On April 15, 2003 (after a four year wait), an announcement was made in parliament that the government had decided to pay a one time sum of R30,000 (approximately US$3,000) to the 22,000 victims officially identified by the TRC. This sum is well below the amount recommended for individual reparations, by the TRC in the 1998 report. This has resulted in widespread criticism and also litigation by victims and victims' groups. Foreign civil lawsuits against multinational companies and banks have also been brought by four separate groups of victims' representatives in courts in the United States using the American Alien Tort Claims Act.

Functioning of the TRC with Regard to Women

The TRC Act is "gender-neutral," with no specific reference to women, gender, or to gender-based violence. In March 1996, when the commission began its work, the issue of gender and the TRC was raised in a workshop hosted by the Centre for Applied Legal Studies. Gender activists were both critical of and concerned over potential gender bias in the TRC process. A submission from this conference was coordinated by the CALS and submitted to the TRC, pointing out the injustices that arise from gender-neutral approaches and laws (hereinafter the CALS submission). The commission subsequently organized two workshops with representatives of women's organizations and the media to address the issue. This resulted in awareness that although half of the testifiers were women, the majority of the women testifying spoke of violence pertaining to relatives and dependants (primarily males) who had suffered human rights violations; hence women spoke as secondary victims. Men, on the other hand, spoke of their experiences as direct victims.

As a result, the commission agreed to hold special women's hearings. These hearings excluded men (including male commissioners) from attending or participating. The issues of confidentiality and protective measures, such as on-camera hearings, were also factored in. The commission also made some procedural changes to encourage women to come forward and speak of their experiences as victims of gross human rights abuse, as opposed to only testifying about acts relating to family members or friends. The hearings provided both evidence of women's involvement in the struggle in the three decades under review; as well as evidence of women as direct victims, for example, through detention, torture, and such. Following the definition of "gross human rights violations" stipulated by the TRC mandate, the special women's hearings focused on revelations of women's experiences of physical violence, which was predominantly characterized by sexual violence and torture. The perpetrators of violence against women included both state and nonstate actors and included liberation fighters. However, because of the patriarchal nature of South African society and the entrenched public/private divide, women were seen as less of a threat to the apartheid state, and thus the TRC statistics show that women were less often the victims of murder, abduction, and torture by the state but were more often victims of structural violence, yet this was not included in the either hearings as will be discussed below.

Analysis of the Functioning of the TRC

In the following analysis, we focus specifically on the way the taken for granted meanings of human rights violations and violence were used within the TRC and the epistemological biases they are founded upon as well as the implications these definitions had on women specifically and on the ability of TRC to redress these violations and meet its mandate of reconciliation and assisting in establishing peace. Furthermore, in exposing the implications of these taken for granted definition we hope to make clear that their continued, uninterrogated use can be understood as part of the functioning of hegemony within an ongoing imperial project.

Feminist research examining the TRC has made clear that the commission's definition of violence and human rights violations worked to limit the stories women could tell and as a result, obfuscated from the narrative of truth the structural violence that characterized apartheid and underpinned the physical violence. To recall, the TRC defined apartheid as "gross violations of human rights" and gross violations of human rights were defined as specific acts that resulted in severe physical and/or mental injury in the course of the past political conflict. The past political conflict was understood by the TRC as the period of time from 1960 to 1994 in which the "civil war" took place. In this construction, violence is understood in combative terms: a discrete harm that caused bodily injury to an individual within the context of a local conflict. In addition, this understanding of violence constructed a particular "subject" of apartheid— "the one who has suffered these injuries, the one who had these rights to bodily integrity violated" (Nesiah, 2006:6) and thus the subject of truth, the "iconic victim" of the narrative, was determined to be the individual soldier, or "the dissident, the subversive militant" (Nesiah, 2006:6). This construction reflects the common, taken for granted understanding of violence in which violence is understood, more or less, in physical and, more recently, psychological terms but not in terms of the violence of structural inequality and disadvantage and how this violence is racialized, gendered, historical, global, and strategic. Thus, the victim of "gross human rights violations" is an individual in which all effects of power were "stripped away" except those that left traces on the body (Ross, 2003).

The focus on bodily violence had particular implications for women. More concretely, while women were part of the liberation struggle and did experience physical, combative violence, the majority of the combat related violations perpetrated during the apartheid civil war period (considered, as mentioned earlier, as between 1960 and 1994) were done by men to men, and as a result women's experiences within the commission were primarily reduced to two categories: either "relative/dependent"—mother, daughter, sister, wife—or "sexual victim." In the first category, these women were not understood as primary victims since it was not them who were directly injured and so they were considered to have suffered less. More than half the testimony of the TRC came from women, yet most testimony from women centered on violations of others in their lives, and not their own experiences of torture and other violations (Goldblatt, 2006). The second category consisted of women who had suffered sexual violations such as "assaults to breasts and genitals, rape, beating leading to miscarriage and sexual abuse." These sexual violations were included only later on in the commission into the listed definitions of torture and severe ill treatment. However, although the acknowledgment of sexual violence as a human rights violation was critical and monumental, and part of an effort to be "gender-sensitive," it ultimately restricted the experiences of suffering women could speak about (Ross, 2003).

For example, Fiona Ross, in her anthropological study of women and the TRC, discusses how women's experiences of diverse and complex harms were ignored, or silenced, in deference to what was "presumed the traumatic event and the primary violence"—sexual violation (Ross, 2003). For example, one woman, Mrs. Khutwane, in her initial written testimony described the collusion between state, police and certain medical and legal institutions in her ill treatment, the "fragile and fraught nature of community relationships during violence," and the "widening spiral of violence that once again impinged on the space of the domestic in the damage of her home" (Ross, 2003:87). And yet, during the public hearing, her narrative was "marked and shaped by intervention and questions" (Ross, 2003: 87) regarding her experiences of sexual violation. Ultimately, the commissioners disallowed Mrs. Khutwane's personal narrative to be told and forced her to tell a different story than the one she had originally written. She was made to tell a story of harm in which the defining feature was of her sexual abuse, despite the fact that this was not the way Mrs. Khutwane defined her experience. As a result, Mrs. Khutwane's narrative became widely known, with the help of the media, as a "truth" of sexual violence; The South African Press Association reported her story as: "Woman Tells Truth Body of Sexual Abuse" (Ross, 2003).

However, Mrs. Khutwane's experience within the commission and story of structural violence is not isolated. Ross and other feminist analyses (Franke 2006; Nesiah 2006) of the commission have noted the many different ways that women experienced suffering as result of apartheid laws and policies, as was noted earlier: the difficulty of influx control and pass laws; the heavy burden of being made "breadwinner" within the family because their husbands had been killed; the hardship of the break up of families through the migrant labor system; the denial of rights to employment and housing and as a result having to work as domestic laborers in white households; and the difficulty of obtaining proper medical/reproductive care, particularly after having been forced to move off their land (Nesiah, 2006). However, despite the fact that the majority of women's stories articulated these forms of suffering, they were not understood as "violence" because they did not fit the commission's definition closely enough and were therefore either changed and appropriated, like Mrs. Khutwane's experience, or simply not "accepted" by the commission and thus omitted from the narrative of truth. As a result, these stories of harm were effaced in lieu of stories of rape, other sexual harms, or their stories of their male relatives in combat.

Critically, it is these stories that expose the way the imperial agenda has exercised power through structural and ideological violence within apartheid, colonialism, and, currently, neoliberalism; in this way, the omission of this violence from the narrative reflects the way hegemony is reproduced and reified. More specifically, the women's stories that were omitted as a result of the narrow definition of violence were stories of structural violence. Structural violence refers to any constrain on human potential due to social structures or institutions (Galtung, 1969). Structural violence denotes a form of violence that corresponds with the systematic ways in which a given social structure or social institution kills people by preventing them from meeting their basic needs. It is structural violence that constituted the state supported system of racial apartheid and yet it was this violence that was effaced by the limited definition of human rights violations, which only recognized physical violence, as Fullard notes:

> Whereas tens of thousands were affected by violent physical repression, millions endured the machinations of apartheid from birth to death through the system of racial classification, the "pass laws" and their associated systems of migrant labour, the creation of far flung artificial homelands, and the loss of land and citizenship...While perhaps some 25000 people died between 1960 and 1994 in political violence, millions more were condemned to short brutal lives as victims of racially defined poverty—the human lives withered away. (2004: 9)

The above statement makes clear that the majority of violence that occurred was not physical violence, as a result of the "undeclared war," but rather a consequence of racialized structural inequality and "the absence of value placed on black life by the state" (Fullard, 2004:10). In this way, "the TRC focused on torture, murder and rape, all outside the law, ignoring everything that was distinctive about apartheid and its machinery of violence" (Mamdani, 2000: 181). Furthermore, the historical roots of the apartheid state were established during colonialism, as was noted earlier. However, this legacy of structural violence that precipitated the 1960–1994 conflict was also left out of the narrative. In this way, the commission's definition of violence worked to abstract violence from any social, historical, racial, or political context:

> Understanding violence in terms of gross violation of human rights flattens the complex social terrain instituted by colonialism, apartheid and various resistances and eliminates an investigation of the subjects produced by these processes. In effect then, the Commission's work effaced certain of power's historical dimensions. (Ross, 2003: 16)

Ross highlights here how the commission's focus on "gross violations of human rights" obliterated the protracted effects of power created by the imperialist project. As a result, human rights abuses were understood as a local problem rather than connected to a global agenda. However, the binary construction of local/global is a discursive oppositional staging that masks the way the two are interconnected and interdependent (Grewal and Kaplan, 1994). Therefore, understanding mass human rights violations as an internal conflict within a particular type of nation-state, works to exclude the broader context of international imperialism from the narrative so that "the international community is absent from the scene of violence and suffering until it intervenes as heroic savior" (Orford 2006: 6) to transition the country from "apartheid" to social justice, liberal democracy, and peace.

In our contemporary "era of humanitarianism" (Slim, 1997), the Western model of modernization, namely neoliberalism, has become synonymous with prosperity, democracy, and peace and the West becomes the guarantor of human rights and humanitarian values (Orford, 2006). In this way, the imperialist agenda has been increasingly obscured through humanitarian rhetoric, in which human rights language has been co-opted to disguise subjugating economic policies or, as Peter Uvin has argued, to allow the international community to take the "moral high road" as it pursues the same old imperial agenda. Nesiah argues:

> In the current international context, human rights have become the passport to empire. Human Rights' ostensible innocence of power becomes the Trojan horse of naturalized imperial hubris. From Baghdad to Beirut, it is invoked alongside interventions that speak of the rule of law and the export of good governance from North to South. (2006: 13)

Nesiah attempts to expose the way the Northern liberal agenda has hijacked human rights language to naturalize its imperial agenda. For these reasons, recent arguments have been made that human rights should be understood as concrete social and economic claims on the state rather than the implementation of programs that only reinforce the liberal capitalist ordering (Nesiah, 2006). The analyses problematize the relationship between liberalism and peace.

Furthermore, the analyses highlight the way the narrative produced by the commission is less a narrative truth and more accurately a political discourse that organizes power relations. More specifically, the exclusion of structural violence is not simply, or apolitically, an oversight but rather is a reflection of how the capacity to erase large parts of the story and to control the plot through discursive and epistemological means is to exercise power. This insight raises concern as to the role equality plays within the commission and the future state, as Orford makes clear:

> The ability to name what counts as truth is an effect of power, and the search for truth thus signals the likelihood of injustice being done to those without such power. (2006: 860)

Understanding the narrative in terms of power thus calls in to question the ways in which the particular story told benefits some and disadvantages others. In this way, the discursive decisions made can be considered political decisions that are part of larger hegemonic functioning. More specifically, the initial decisions made in establishing the terms of reference for an official inquiry—decisions about what kinds of actors, what time period, and form of behavior—will always frame and influence the truth produced, the subject produced in the commission, and the citizen produced for the postconflict state, and thus must be understood in political terms (Orford, 2006).

In highlighting the way women's experiences were appropriated, manipulated, and excluded within the commission as a result of the taken for granted definitions used within the commission, the analysis above works to expose the way hegemony reconstitutes itself and thus the way systems of inequality are reproduced even during liberation processes and postconflict reconstruction. The analyses makes clear that the commission's understanding of "gross violations of human rights" and the subsequent focus on bodily injury, constructed violence as a discrete act of isolated, physical harm, done to an individual—not a social group—by another individual, within a local context of political conflict. As a result, the system of oppression that subordinated and subjugated black South Africans because of the color of their skin and black South African women because of their skin color and their gender was made absent from the narrative leaving racism and sexism, and the way they confound each other, unchallenged. In this way, the epistemological and discursive decisions within the truth commissions worked to reproduce and reify the ideology and structure of hegemony and thus the conditions that caused the conflict. In so much that truth commissions are a mechanism meant to redress human rights violations with the purpose of transitioning a nation from war to peace, the above analysis has important implications.

Conclusion

The focus on what was excluded from the South African Truth Commission's narrative helps to place the TRC within a larger discourse of organizational power and global ordering. In this way, the analysis helps to highlight the potential for truth commissions in general, and their narratives, to be used to reinforce hegemonic structures and racist and sexist ideologies. In this light, drawing out what has been excluded works to challenge the presumed transparency and authenticity of the narrative of "truth" and to show how the truth of the narrative works to legitimize a political system of structural violence. As a result, the transformative potential of the narrative and its ability to promote democracy and peace are made questionable. The current social, political, and economic context of the South African postapartheid state may be considered a case in point in terms of the failure of the narrative to be transformative.

On the individual level, women were particularly neglected from adequate reparations. Reparations were awarded to victims of "gross human rights violations" as well as "dependents/relatives of victims." However, the TRC determined that the "dependents/relatives of victims" were only entitled to grants if the "primary" victim had died (Goldblatt, 2006) and thus "the system did not recognize harms suffered by women independently whose sons and husbands were tortured, imprisoned, etc. and who suffered loss of income and status, pain and stress" (Goldblatt 2006: 7). In addition, because harms suffered by the systemic crimes of apartheid were excluded in the definition of "gross human rights violations," reparations for these purposes were not covered. Therefore, the suffering endured due to forced removal of communities from their homes and land, the institution of inferior education for blacks, and laws that restricted the freedom of movement for blacks (Goldblatt, 2006), were not only unrecognized within the narrative but were therein not compensated.

The failure to recognize the structural violence of apartheid has also had far reaching ramifications relating to community reconciliation. In the years since the hearings, race and racism have become a central issue in public discourse and debates within civil society and within governments (Fullard, 2004). It is suggested (Fullard, 2004; Mamdani, 2000; Wilson, 2001) that these heated national debates were a direct result of the lack of attention to race and racism or, in other words, the underpinnings of the apartheid system, in the TRC and that this lack of attention ultimately removed any accountability by those who committed crimes of structural violence so that white

South Africans, in general, who benefited from apartheid were not made to make any public acknowledgment of this system of privilege and inequality (Mamdani, 2000). Such a lack of recognition and distancing creates much social discord and, as a result, a public discourse emerged to bring to the surface this problem and discontent.

In terms of the new nation state, the liberal-democratic capitalist constitution that was seamlessly endorsed and instituted only reflected, and further entrenched, the social inequalities established in the apartheid state. The minimalist definition of democracy—free, regular elections, freedom of the press, freedom of association and basic rights—including the right to private property meant that those who owned and controlled land, factories, and money under apartheid would continue to do so in the New South Africa (Hjort and Ramadiro, 2004). As a result, hardly any change has taken place in the relations of economic power so that the sources of economic power remain in the hands of those who controlled them under apartheid. As a result, access to the basic resources that provide equality have been, once again denied to the majority of black South Africans:

> Instead of expanding social welfare and access to basic services like water, electricity and housing for the black the poor and the working class, the state has bought into the globalized concepts and strategies of cost recovery, privatization and market liberalization. (Hjort and Ramadiro, 2004)

Therefore, the structural violence that was perpetrated by the state under apartheid still exists today in many ways so that the majority of black people remain impoverished and degraded. As a result, South Africa has one of the largest income disparities in the world. While an in depth look of the current political, social, and economic context of South Africa cannot be given here, the point in the above outline is to highlight how the current "peace" prevailing in South Africa, is clearly not peaceful for all of its citizens. In other words, many South Africans could be considered as still living in a state of war and experience severe violence, even if not physical violence.

In this light, if the narrative of truth only retells the same hegemonic tale of social inequality, omitting structural violence and the broader context of global imperialist ordering, it is likely to only naturalize, legitimize, and reinstate the same systems of injustice that created the conflict in the first place, therein planting the seed for further violence and precluding real peace. A transformative narrative thus requires a challenge to dominant ideologies and structures of organized power. Therefore, it is critical that truth commissions understand "gross violations of human rights" as not only bodily injuries but as the ways in which hegemonic ideology and organizational power constrains people's lives and creates injustice and conflict. Human rights should thus be viewed in terms of their potential for "containing (and redirecting) the employment of social power by the state and other powerful institutions bent on undermining human dignity in a systematic manner" (Sjoberg, Gill, and Williams, 2001: 42). In this way, human rights are placed within a political and economic realm so that they are not isolated, individualized, a-historical notions but rather "social claims upon social power arrangements" (Sjoberg et al., 2001: 43) that aim to mediate the effect of hegemony on individual well-being. It is from this understanding of human rights that truth commissions may be able to create a transformative narrative that challenges hegemonic organizations and constructs new social relationships and structures. In this way, truth commissions could fulfill their goals of redress and reconciliation and could assist in transitioning the nation from war to peace.

Bibliography

Butler, Judith. (1990). *Gender trouble*. New York: Routledge.
Buvinic, Mayra. (2006). Gender, justice, and truth commissions. *World Bank*.
Centre for Applied Legal Studies. (1996). "Gender and the TRC"—a submission to the TRC, co-ordinated by Goldblatt B and Meintjies S, University of the Witwatersrand http://www.truth.org.za/submit/gender.htm
Cock, Jacklyn. (1991). Colonels & cadres: War & gender in South Africa. Cape Town: Oxford University Press.
The Constitution of the Republic of South Africa, Act 108 of 1996.
Duffield, Mark. (1994). Complex emergencies and the crisis of developmentalism. *IDS Bulletin* 25:37–45.
———. (2001). Global governance and the new wars. London and New York: Zed Books.
Ewick, Patricia and Susan S. Silbey. (1995). Subversive stories and hegemonic tales: Toward a sociology of narrative. *Law & Society Review* 29, 2: 197–226.
Foucault, Michel. (1980). Power/knowledge: Selected interviews and other writings 1972–1977, Edited by Colin Gordon. Translated by Colin Gordon. Great Britain: Harverster Press and New York: Pantheon Books.
Franke, Katherine M. (2006). Gendered subjects of transitional justice. *Columbia Journal of Gender and Law* 15: 813–828.

Fraser, N. (1998). "Social Justice in the Age of Identity Politics: Redistribution, Recognition and Participation," *The Tanner Lectures on Human Values*, Ed. Grethe B. Peterson, Salt Lake City, Vol 19: 1-67.

Fullard, Madeleine. (2004). Dis-placing race: The South African Truth and Reconciliation Commission and interpretations of violence. *Race and Citizenship in Transition Series* http://www.csvr.org.za/docs/racism/displacingrace.pdf

Galtung, Johan. (1969). Violence, peace, and peace research. *Journal of Peace Research* 6: 167–191.

Goldblatt, Beth. (2006). Gender and reparations in South Africa. http://idl-bnc.idrc.ca/dspace/handle/123456789/35891. New York: The International Center for Transitional Justice.

Grewal, Inderpal and Caren Kaplan. (1994). "Introduction: Transnational feminist practices and questions of postmodernity." In *Scattered hegemonies: Postmodernity and transnational feminist practices*, edited by C. Kaplan and I. Grewal, 1–36. Minneapolis: University of Minnesota Press.

Hay, Mark. (1999). Grappling with the past: The Truth and Reconciliation Commission of South Africa. *Africa Journal in Conflict Resolution* 1, 1: 29–51.

Hayner, Prescilla. (1994). Fifteen truth commissions—1974 to 1994: A comparative study. *Human Rights Quarterly* 16: 597–655.

———. (2001). Unspeakable truths: Confronting state terror and atrocity. New york: Routledge.

Hjort, Linn and Brian Ramadiro. (2004). A long walk to nowhere—ten years of democracy in South Africa. Retrieved December 8, 2006 (http://www.aidc.org.za/?q=book/view/585)

Mamdani, Manhood. (2000). "The truth according to the TRC." In *The politics of memory: Truth, healing and social justice*, edited by I. Abdullahi An-Naim, 176–183. London: Zed Books.

Marchand, Marianne and Jane Parpart. (1995). "Exploding the canon: An introduction/ conclusion." In *Feminism postmodernism development*, edited by M. Marchand and J. Parpart, 1–22. London: Routledge.

Mohanty, C. (2003). Feminism Without Borders: Decolonizing Theory, Practicing Solidarity.

Mohanty, C. and Alexnder, M. J., Eds. (1996). *Feminist Genealogies, Colonial Legacies, Democratic Futures*. New York: Routledge.

Narayan, U. and Harding, S. (2000). *Decentering the Center: Philosophy for a Multicultural, Postcolonial, and Feminist World*. Bloomington: Indiana University Press.

Nesiah, Vasuki. (2006). "Feminism and transitional justice: Towards a critically reflective practice." Conference Paper presented at Globalization, Law and Justice: University of Toronto.

Orford, Anne. (2006). "Commissioning the truth". *Columbia Journal of Gender and Law* 15 (Fall) : 851–883.

Posel Deborah and Simpson Graeme, (eds.). (2002). Commissioning the past: Understanding South Africa's Truth and Reconciliation Commission. Johannesburg :Witwatersrand University Press.

Rehn E. and Sirleaf E. (2003) Women, war and peace: The independent experts' assessment on the impact of armed conflict on women and women's role in peace-building. New York: UNIFEM.

Ross, Fiona. (2002). Bearing witness: Women and the truth commission in South Africa. London and Sterling, VA: Pluto Press.

Russell, Diana. (1989). Lives of courage: Women for a new South Africa. New York: Basic Books.

Silbey, Susan. (1998). Ideology, power, and justice. In *Justice and power in law and society research*, edited by Bryant Garth and Austin Sarat, 272–308. Evanston, IL: Northwestern University Press.

Sjoberg, Gideon, Elizabeth A. Gill, and Normal Williams. (2001). A sociology of human rights. *Social Problems* 48 (1): 11–47.

Slim, Hugo. (1997). Doing the right thing: Relief agencies, moral dilemmas and moral responsibility in political emergencies and war. *Disasters* 21 (3): 244–257.

Teitel, Ruti. (2002). Transitional justice as liberal narrative. In *Transnational legal processes: Globalisation and power disparities*, edited by Michael Likowsky, 316–324. Cambridge: Cambridge University Press.

Tutu D. (1999). *No future without forgiveness*. London: Rider.

Truth and Reconciliation Commission (1998). Special Hearings: Women. Vol 4, Ch 10 http://www.polity.org.za/govdocs/commissions/1998/trc/4chap10.htm

———. (1998). Truth and Reconciliation Commission of South Africa Report, Vol. One to Five http://www.truth.org.za/submit/gender.htm

———. (2003). Truth & Reconciliation Commission of South Africa Report, Vol. Six and Seven

Uvin, Peter. (2000). Rwanda: The Social Roots of Genocide. In *War, hunger, and displacement: The origins of humanitarian emergencies*, vol. 2. edited by Wayne Nafziger, Frances Stewart, and Raimo Vayrynen, 159–186. Oxford: Oxford University Press.

———. (2002) On moral high ground: The incorporation of human rights by the development enterprise. *PRAXIS—The Fletcher Journal of Development Studies* 17: 1–11.

Walker, Cheryl. (1991). *Women and resistance in South Africa*. Cape Town: David Philip.

Wilson, Richard. (2001). *The politics of truth and reconciliation*. Cambridge: Cambridge University Press.

6

A GENDERED APPROACH FOR POLICY IN UNITED NATIONS PEACEKEEPING MISSIONS

Colleen Keaney-Mischel

Feminist sociologists and international relations scholars have advocated for the adoption of a gender perspective in our understanding of international conflicts and the unique postconflict environments accompanying them, problematizing the idea that "conflict" and "postconflict," or "war" and "postwar" periods, actually make up distinct stages (Niarchos 1995, Enloe 2000, 2002, Nikolić-Ristanović 2000, Cockburn 2001, Cockburn and Žarkov 2002). Using the term "postconflict" highlights a continuum of conflict that women experience through which a process of engendering humanitarian agencies, supranational institutions, and other development partners are able to assess specific needs of a population and to implement policies and provide services accordingly. While United Nations (UN) agencies and other international organizations struggle to provide services to those in need, they typically conceive of them in a decidedly "ungendered" way, leading to misguided and often inappropriate services, programs, and activities. The typical refugee, internally displaced person (IDP), or conflict-affected individual is approached as a generic "masculine" individual, devoid of gendered identity that may influence his or her response to and experience of the postconflict situation and, therefore, services required.

As one of the main international institutions charged with intervening in global conflict and assisting communities affected by it, the UN has acknowledged the positive impact a gendered perspective may have on its efforts in this regard. Recently, it has developed a gender mainstreaming policy to be implemented throughout its agencies, departments, and funds. Specifically, the UN Department of Peacekeeping Operations (DPKO) has been an area where this policy has been sorely needed and exceptionally challenged. The policy requires UN personnel within missions to adopt and apply a gender perspective to all aspects, including security, human rights, political affairs, public outreach and information, disarmament, demobilization, and reconstruction (UN General Assembly 2003). In order to satisfy this requirement, the DPKO has hired gender advisers to work in UN peacekeeping missions in advisory capacities to other units and sectors to assist them in consistently mainstreaming gender within their specific initiatives and activities. However, despite research that finds gender mainstreaming increases the success of UN peacekeeping missions and helps conflict-affected communities sustain the peace, the UN is still experiencing limited success in putting the gender mainstreaming mandate into practice in its peacekeeping missions.

This chapter examines strategies used by UN gender advisers to change that reality. It is based on data collected through eighteen in-depth interviews conducted by this author from July 2005 through February 2006. Nine of the ten, full-time senior gender advisers in UN peacekeeping missions, all of whom are women, were interviewed. These conversations allowed for comparison of the individual experiences, perceptions, and opinions regarding challenges and successes of mainstreaming gender in peacekeeping missions. The interviews were supplemented with nine additional in-depth interviews with other UN mission staff, staff from the UN DPKO, and employees from nongovernmental organizations (NGOs) working alongside the UN missions in the field. Drawing on the data, I outline various approaches the advisers take to their gender mainstreaming responsibilities and how they interpret their role within the missions, examining how they negotiate their relative lack of power in this setting and how their actions fit in with the larger UN agenda on mainstreaming gender in its peacekeeping missions. In particular, I highlight the creativity and determination that define their strategies and the potential for a broader application of their various experiences to those efforts at engendering international security and conflict in general.

Official Role of the Gender Advisers

Gender advisers have been slowly incorporated into UN peacekeeping missions since 2000, beginning their work in such missions as those in East Timor (UNTAET), Bosnia and Herzegovina (UNMIBIH),

Kosovo (UNMIK), and the Democratic Republic of the Congo (MONUC). However, they were initially engaged on an ad hoc basis and were not routinely deployed in every mission until more recently. Gender advisers take a two-pronged approach to their jobs: First, they work internally in a supportive and advisory capacity with all members of the peacekeeping mission in order to assist in the application of a gender perspective in all functional areas of peacekeeping. Secondly, they act externally as liaisons with governmental partners, local organizations, NGO partners in countries, and relevant UN agencies, funds, and programs to promote national gender initiatives, increase the involvement of local women in the peace process, and address sexual and gender-based violence (GBV) within the community.

More specifically, the DPKO has developed a Model Terms of Reference (TOR) for a Senior Gender Adviser as part of its "Gender Resource Package for Peacekeeping Operations," created in July 2004 by the Peacekeeping Best Practices Unit. While the individual tasks of each gender adviser vary by their particular mission, country context, or individual personality, the TOR attempts to standardize the role and functions they may typically perform. However, in reality gender advisers' regular duties include much more than the TOR outlines and, in fact, they end up responsible for everything "women" (Personal interview, August 3, 2005), so are stretched beyond their capacities. The confusion as to exactly what role gender advisers play is evident within the mission and is certainly a stumbling block to those on the outside of the mission. NGO workers whom I interviewed explained the difficulties in making the role of the gender advisers clear to not only NGO partners of the UN, but to members of the local community as well. They lamented the fact that if they, as relatively empowered NGO employees, are uncertain about these jobs, then the average refugee or IDP certainly has less of a chance of understanding how to use them as a resource (Personal interviews, August 4 and 16, 2005). While the UN has worked to include a description of the official role of the gender advisers in its documentation, it appears that a more thorough and practical explanation may be needed in order for those within the mission and outside of the mission to benefit from the efforts and services of this crucial position.

Gender Advisers' Perceptions of Their Role

Having briefly outlined the official role of gender advisers, now it is appropriate to consider their *own* perceptions of their role within peacekeeping missions—often at odds with official understandings of their work, and evidence of the nearly impossible nature of their task. Either way, their thoughts about how they—and others—perceive their work and roles within the mission offer insight into how the UN may be able to improve its efforts at mainstreaming gender within its peacekeeping missions.

First and foremost, all the gender advisers interviewed felt that they were doing very important, very beneficial work. In our conversations, I could detect a distinct sense of pride and accomplishment as they told me about their activities and hard work—even if this pride was tempered by their collective opinion that they spent most of their time trying to convince the rest of the mission of the importance of their work. This was especially true if the gender adviser had arrived after the start of a mission, when her efforts were belated from the start. However, even those advisers who were deployed at the outset of the mission still cited difficulties in raising awareness of the value of their job. For instance, one gender adviser had contacted the Electoral Division within her mission for gender disaggregated data so she could determine how many women had registered to vote for the upcoming elections. She was discouraged, but not surprised, when the director told her he did not have the data available because, "It's a question of priority of priorities" (Personal interview, July 22, 2005); in other words, issues pertaining to gender had not ranked on his priority list.

The gender advisers lamented their struggle to promote gender issues in an environment "built on a kind of hypermasculinity" (Personal interview, August 18, 2005), and expressed that they felt the only activities perceived to be of importance were those having to do with military components. One summed up the internal perception of gender mainstreaming this way, "So it's like, it's a little thing; it hasn't got to do with troops, it hasn't got to do with the military, it hasn't got to do with the fighting, and therefore, it's not important" (Personal interview July 22, 2005).

Not surprisingly, many of the gender advisers reported feeling isolated within missions. Despite recommendations to situate gender units within the Office of the Special Representative of the Secretary General (SRSG), or the head of the mission, which has taken place several times, gender advisers still felt that it was difficult to be heard even in prime locations. Although, many noted to me that the level of effectiveness they were able to achieve was very dependent upon the individual gender sensitivity of the SRSG himself or, in the sole case where there is a female SRSG in the Liberian mission, herself. One adviser explained to me how she was excluded from management meetings, even though she herself was the head of the gender unit, and how this kept her from advising the senior managers on how to integrate gender into their activities:

> At the very beginning, I had a very reluctant head of mission to this approach. I mean, he didn't support me absolutely at all. I was isolated physically because I had my, um, office very far from the headquarters, so I didn't meet any of the heads of the units or substantive personnel and I didn't participate in any meetings. Also I am a head of unit, and in fact, senior management didn't advise me of any management meetings, so it was very bad. (Personal interview, January 18, 2006)

Fortunately, she also related how her situation had improved with the arrival of a much more gender sensitive SRSG. Many gender advisers mentioned that mission personnel only sought their advice if the issue they were dealing with had something to do with "women." Some expressed frustration that their reports, emails, and other requests went unheeded and that they often found themselves on the outside looking in. One adviser matter-of-factly stated, "Most of the time, you're just out of the loop!" (Personal interview, October 12, 2005), and others concurred that the gender units were a much underutilized resource within the missions.

These gender advisers also stated that the lack of appreciation for their contributions to the mission translates into a subsequent lack of staff, resources, and support from both the mission and UN headquarters. Most of the units are quite small, considering the workload they are expected to carry, and some are grossly understaffed. Among the nine gender units whom I contacted, the largest consists of nine people, which is in one of the larger missions (with nearly 15,000 troops), and the smallest consists of just one person: the senior gender adviser herself. At least three of the gender units are currently requesting additional staff—requests that, up until now, have gone unanswered.

Furthermore, the gender units operate without an official budget; much of their funding coming from external donor organizations or countries, making it difficult for gender advisers to plan for projects or initiatives. Several complained that it impeded them from assisting those underserved communities outside of a capital as a result of insufficient travel funds. One explained that in the country where she works it is traditional to offer a cocktail when conducting business, but that her lack of funding proved to be "a big handicap" in terms of her forging partnerships with local organizations because she was not able to secure a room for a cocktail party (Personal interview,

January 18, 2006). This may seem an insignificant worry in the context of a peacekeeping operation, but when one considers the importance of the UN's attempts to respect and follow the local culture of the host country, a social event may go a long way toward offering the UN badly needed credibility.

Gender Advisers' Strategies

In light of this reality, what strategies do gender advisers use to overcome challenges to assist in mainstreaming gender in their respective peacekeeping missions? In many cases, they are quite creative in terms of approaches they take to fulfilling their job duties; in others, their success is a result of pure hard work and determination. This section outlines and discusses four strategies that emerged from my conversations with the gender advisers: (1) Working "from the outside-in," (2) Using human rights as an "entree," (3) Using male staff in gender units, and (4) Engaging in independent prioritization. It also examines how they were able to use them to their advantage in efforts to implement gender mainstreaming policy.

Strategy #1: Working "From the Outside-in"

Several gender advisers felt that it was effective to highlight the gender mainstreaming successes they had in local communities to capture interest and make gender issues more relevant to members of the UN mission. They called this strategy working "from the outside-in." In this way, they used their two-pronged mandate (to work both internal and external to the mission) to their advantage by using concrete examples from the community to show UN mission staff not only what it means to mainstream gender but, more importantly, the cost of *ignoring* gender. This strategy proved useful for one gender adviser in particular who told me that her work training female political candidates within the population had a very real, positive impact on the different units within the mission because they could appreciate the concrete, tangible results she was showing them (Personal interview, August 18, 2005). It was an approach to which she had clearly given some thought:

> Nobody understands gender mainstreaming within the peacekeeping missions, you know, nobody understands. Once they see concrete results, something they can understand on a daily basis, it makes a big difference, so maybe we should revise our own strategy and, and

put a lot of, uh, emphasis on the work we are doing outside—the capacity-building—and trying to use that work to implement our strategy within the mission. (Personal interview, August 18, 2005)

Another gender adviser emphasized the importance of including the cultural context in the trainings she does with UN mission staff, explaining how it impacts men's and women's postconflict roles, responsibilities, and experiences. In this way, she advocated making the "outside," or local context, visible and pertinent to mission employees as they carried out their specific jobs.

Strategy #2: Human Rights as an "Entree"

Another strategy was the idea of using human rights as an "entree" to talking about gender issues, especially working within a host population. Several gender advisers explained that this approach proved useful in mitigating the threats that gender issues typically pose. For instance, one explained that, when she helps facilitate human rights workshops for community members, she leads the group through a set of questions to get them thinking about different levels at which men and women access their rights, and why that discrepancy might exist.

Interestingly, another gender adviser disagreed with this strategy, fearing it might be moving too far away from what gender mainstreaming is all about. She believes in the importance of making distinctions between gender mainstreaming inside and outside the mission and dealing with human rights violations, for which there is usually a separate office within the mission—worrying that, "Gender issues will be watered down to some kind of human rights" (Personal interview, July 27, 2005) if gender advisers blur the distinction and align themselves with the human rights unit or sector. This issue resonated with another gender adviser, who felt she should be reporting to the Deputy Special Representative of the Secretary General (DSRSG) for Political Affairs, as opposed to the DSRSG for Humanitarian Affairs; she said, "[M]y work is basically political work...and I just think I'm a misfit there [within the Office of Humanitarian Affairs]" (Personal interview, July 22, 2005).

So, whether approaching gender issues through a human rights perspective proves to be a successful strategy seems to depend upon the gender adviser's own level of comfort with merging certain aspects of the Gender Unit's mandate with that of the Office of Humanitarian Affairs. Yet, it seems clear that even those gender advisers who do use human rights as an entree to discussing gender issues with certain populations also recognize that this strategy is limited in terms of implementing other parts of the gender-mainstreaming mandate.

Strategy #3: Male Staff in Gender Units

Many of the gender advisers told me that their use of male staff in the Gender Units was strategic in terms of offering them more credibility with certain members of a mission or local population. In fact, this was a very popular strategy: Six out of the nine advisers told me outright how valuable they thought it was to have male staff members—explaining that, when offering training for the mission personnel, male trainers added a different dimension and perspective and were able to offer different experiences for trainees to consider. The gender advisers said male members of the mission's military contingent are more receptive to trainings facilitated by male staff from the Gender Unit than by female staff. One adviser told me that one of her male staff members received a comment from a soldier after a training that it was good to hear "a real man" talk about gender issues instead of a woman (Personal interview, August 18, 2005). While it is unclear how difficult it is to recruit men to work in the Gender Units—although the gender advisers did not cite this as a problem—it seems evident that this strategy has many potential benefits to offer in terms of engaging men and offering a fresh perspective to the task of gender mainstreaming.

Strategy #4: Independent Prioritization

A fourth, and somewhat controversial, strategy emerged consisting of gender advisers engaging in what I term *independent prioritization*. The idea is that the gender advisers themselves use their own judgment to determine what projects and initiatives they will work on, despite what is being dictated by DPKO or the mission mandate. For example, one explained that she had decided to focus more of her efforts on addressing instances of GBV within the population as a result of conflict rather than on enforcing the UN's recent policies on sexual exploitation and abuse (SEA) by members of the mission, which have been generated from the scandal that has rocked the UN over the past several years. She said she certainly does not ignore issues of SEA if they come up, but that, through her conversations with the local population, she came to realize that they were more concerned about the sexual violence they were experiencing at the hands of the armed militias and rebel factions in the country than the risk of SEA from members of the peacekeeping mission. Expressing frustration at the amount of resources and attention being directed toward SEA, she suggested this situation was more a result of the UN's trying to save its image than trying to respond to the most urgent needs of the population (Personal interview, July 22, 2005).

> *Gender Adviser*: We pay so much attention on investigations, on sending people away, on... I don't see how it has impacted the population, really. It may have, I might not have had time to focus on it, really (unintelligible). Our office thinks that we have other priorities...
> *Interviewer*: Right.
> *Gender Adviser*: For example, sexual violence as a result of the conflict in the communities. To find out how these people are doing and what resources they are having to address it and how their capacities are being built to be integrated into, into their communities, you know, when this, when the trauma is all over, etc. For us, that is more of a priority than the strategy of making a big noise in *The New York Times* and all these things and, you know, sending people away and that I don't, I don't see, I don't get it yet. I have yet to get it.

Initially, I found her comments quite surprising, not only for their candor, but for the apparent discrepancy between what she perceived to be of the utmost importance in her work. She was one of the first gender advisers whom I interviewed, and I had expected them to "toe the UN line" in terms of mandates and activities of the Gender Units. As I began speaking to more gender advisers from other missions, though, I found they agreed with her comments, and also felt frustrated at the amount of resources dedicated to addressing SEA within the missions.

> *Gender Adviser*: I think there's a lot of emphasis now on SEA. I mean, there's compulsory training for everybody; there has been a directive that there must be a roll-out for training for everybody, so that's obvious, but it is really the "flavor-of-the-month" (laughs). It is so obvious because we are now dreaming, we are eating, we are sleeping, we are talking...
> *Interviewer*: (Laughs).
> *Gender Adviser*: (Laughs) I hope it works and it won't cloud the general gender problem.
> *Interviewer*: Do you think that it has? Do you think that it's kind of overshadowed the GBV [gender-based violence] work that you've been doing?

Gender Adviser: I think so, I think so. It' just my opinion, but I think so. The money, the positions, I mean, do you know how much we have (unintelligible), I am telling you I am one, but look at the number of personnel conduct officers that are coming up there [to the mission's Personnel Conduct Unit, dedicated to SEA issues], D1s, D5s, what have you, it's (laughs) something that, we have been struggling!
Interviewer: Yeah.
Gender Adviser: But there seems to be so much resources directing towards it—not that it's bad, but I think a balance needs to be, you know, maintained.

The gender advisers expressed frustration that politically controversial issues for the UN, such as incidents of SEA within peacekeeping missions, are privileged at the expense of the equally important work of the gender advisers in dealing with issues of sexual and gender-based violence within the population as a result of the conflict.

As previously mentioned, these gender advisers sense a lack of support for gender mainstreaming in their missions; as a result, they feel isolated and separated. It appears that this relative, or perhaps involuntary, independence creates, in some cases, the sense that gender advisers are able to—or are, in fact, expected to—determine their own agendas. However, this is not always perceived to be a positive strategy, but one that calls into question what the Gender Unit is trying to accomplish. With the confusion already surrounding the role of gender advisers, this is a risky strategy. One NGO worker I interviewed (Personal interview, August 4, 2005), who had worked alongside one of the UN peacekeeping missions, told me how she struggled to understand the actions of the Gender Unit:

> Um, you know, the other issues that, again, that we raised consistently and were incredibly frustrated about was sexual exploitation particularly regarding DPKO and other UN staff sexually abusing, exploiting girls and women, and they [the Gender Unit] just, you know, time and time again, failed to address it. There were these kind of big, glaring issues that they could have jumped on and done something very concrete with, but they just failed to see that as a priority or it wasn't their task.

This calls attention, again, to the fundamental questions plaguing peacekeeping missions: What does it mean to mainstream gender in a peacekeeping operation? What tasks and responsibilities fall under the mandate of the Gender Unit? What tasks and responsibilities *should* fall under the mandate of the Gender Unit? How is this information best communicated to the mission personnel and members of the local population? Certainly, these are questions that DPKO and the gender advisers themselves are still trying to answer, but it seems that the distance from UN headquarters in New York to the forgotten Gender Units in the field is tangling vital lines of communication, risking even greater confusion around gender mainstreaming in peacekeeping operations.

A Promising Strategy?

Clearly, the role of the gender advisers in peacekeeping missions demands a certain level of patience and creativity in order to achieve success—evident through the various strategies they use to overcome numerous obstacles in their respective missions. Yet, it appears that some of these strategies may be more promising than others. I would argue that the strategy of working "from the outside-in" offers the potential for the most success, as it combines the ability to address the need to apply a gender perspective within both the mission and the host community and the need for the UN to address adequately the needs of that same community.

Interestingly, the idea that the strategy of working "from the outside-in" might hold the most promise is counterintuitive to what I had originally anticipated. Since the gender mainstreaming policy is mandated by UN headquarters, not generated from within the local population in-country, I expected the UN mission personnel to have a better understanding of the policy and its value, but that does not always seem to be the case; in fact, one gender adviser told me she actually sees results more quickly in the work she does with the population and that the same progress seems to happen over the long term within the mission, if at all (Personal interview, August 18, 2005). In the course of my conversations, gender advisers offered several examples of some of the positive work they were able to do with the local population. For example, one told of how her efforts at conveying the importance of a gender perspective in a postconflict situation to the local population were so successful that she had observed that "gender" was now a buzzword among the locals (Personal interview, July 22, 2005). She discovered that it is often more useful to begin the arduous process of mainstreaming gender with the local population, who are often open to new solutions, and then to attempt to engage the mission personnel in the process after they have seen the effects that have been achieved locally.

It would seem that members of local populations may have more to gain from innovative solutions than do members of UN missions. It seems plausible that gender as a concept may be more salient to a society that is very likely experiencing social upheaval in the aftermath of conflict than to the UN staff who, by comparison, have relatively stable experiences. The development and implementation of more inventive, original solutions—such as gender mainstreaming, need to be approached cautiously. In fact, gender advisers and NGO workers alike told me that, "They [mission staff] think we [Gender Units] are too troublesome and, you know, they do not want us to disturb the status quo" (Personal interview, July 22, 2005), and that "There's not a lot of 'boat-rocking' in the UN" (Personal interview, August 16, 2005)—both comments pointing toward the conclusion that, with more at stake in adopting a gender perspective, the local population seems a reasonable place for the gender advisers to start that process.

Furthermore, mission staff may be less receptive than locals to mainstreaming gender because they perceive it to be adding more work to their already stacked workloads. One gender adviser tried to combat this attitude by reasoning that it is just the same work from a different perspective and that, in fact, it is part of their overall responsibilities (Personal interview, January 18, 2006). In other cases, UN staff could not be bothered with adopting a gender perspective no matter what kind of workload they were carrying. Another gender adviser used this example in a personal interview of July 22, 2005 to illustrate the staff resistance:

> It [gender mainstreaming] is still a separate issue to be dealt with by this section [the Gender Unit], and they think that you should be doing little, little activities. When I say, for example, that the DDR [disarmament, demobilization, and reintegration] policy should be gender-sensitive or I say to them, "We must make sure that the electoral process is engendered" and I actually give ways in which it should be done, it comes back to me that I have to do the action and, um, still today, apart from DDR, you know, not one of them has come back with a plan of just two activities and what's the intent to do to integrate gender.

This is not to say that there are not hardworking, dedicated individuals working within UN peacekeeping missions; there are many. Having said that, in my conversations with gender advisers, NGO workers, and other UN peacekeeping mission staff, their arrogance, insularity, and passivity were emphasized time and again. One disillusioned

NGO worker reflected on her time working alongside a UN mission, saying, "You know, I used to think that everyone working for the UN appreciated what they were doing and had a good heart. That's not true. It's the money" (Personal interview, September 23, 2005). Again, there are certainly exceptions, but it appears that in many cases particular units and sectors within the UN peacekeeping missions are functioning reactively, as opposed to proactively, especially in cases involving implementing the gender mainstreaming mandate.

By way of contrast, some gender advisers were able to offer numerous examples of gender mainstreaming successes from their work; in fact, most of my conversations started out with their relating stories or anecdotes about such efforts with local individuals, groups, or governments. One explained how her office was successfully able to use radio in public outreach efforts regarding violence against women, and how she witnessed real attitude changes as a result (Personal interview, October 12, 2005). The chaotic changes often present within a postconflict environment may provide opportunities for positive social change by opening up spaces where previously taboo or taken-for-granted cultural assumptions—especially those relating to women's social roles and identities, can be challenged and potentially transformed.

Certainly, a strategy such as working "from the outside-in," requiring extensive partnership and collaboration with local communities and government, depends upon how well-received a UN peacekeeping mission and its efforts have been within the host country. Under these adverse circumstances, gender advisers obviously find it very difficult. For example, I interviewed one gender adviser on January 18, 2006, during a period of rioting by the host population against the UN's presence, and she told me how trying it had been to collaborate with local organizations and institutions on issues of violence against women in the hostile environment:

> We decided to do a training-of-trainers, actually at the university level to, uh, well, to try to help and we spoke with the head of the professors union and he invited us in his office and we went there and we sat down and then he started to criticize the UN, but in a way you cannot imagine. He said he will never sit in any training organized by the UN; he said that it's true violence is a problem at the university, but he will never do anything which is supported by the UN and he said, "When I see a UN car, I feel like taking a Kalashnikov and firing over."

In another example, a gender adviser discovered that the locals had a nickname for the UN peacekeeping mission there: "The [mission acronym] Occupation Forces" (Personal interview, August 18, 2005). So, while working "from the outside-in" does seem to hold tremendous potential for the gender mainstreaming policy in general, there are certain factors that may determine the level of success gender advisers and other UN mission staff are able to achieve—such as receptiveness of both locals and UN employees toward addressing gender issues, the initiative of the UN employees to step out of their comfort zones and become involved in activities external to the mission, and the positive acceptance of the UN mission on the part of the host community.

Integrative versus Transformative Gender Mainstreaming Strategies

Next, it seems important to situate the efforts of gender advisers and other UN staff within some of the more relevant academic literature on gender mainstreaming strategies. Examining pertinent theoretical work on gender mainstreaming can offer insights into some of the more pressing questions regarding the UN's potential for success in this area, such as (1) Are the UN's current polices aligned with what scholars widely acknowledge as the most successful approach to mainstreaming? (2) Are there improvements to be made in the UN's efforts?, and (3) Is success possible and through what means?

Rounaq Jahan (1995) has identified two different types of mainstreaming strategies: The first is an integrative strategy—meaning that a previously invisible issue is brought in from the margins and made visible within an existing framework. For example, in the case of the UN, the concept of "gender" and its importance in a postconflict situation has only recently been recognized at headquarters, in DPKO, and in the field missions. Second, Jahan has identified agenda-setting, or transformative strategies, where the goal is not only to center the issue, but also to alter the entire system that had previously masked it. In terms of gender mainstreaming, this means application not only within the UN system, but also in the male-dominated culture of the UN. However, based on my evidence, it seems that the UN is stalled in the very early stages of an integrative approach—highlighting gender equality issues, but doing little to change its systemic approach to them.

A transformative approach would require major changes to the culture of the UN itself and to the ways in which gender equality is framed within the organization. Currently, gender equality in the UN means increasing women's representation, achieving gender balance—whereas a transformative strategy would require a broader understanding of what gender equality entails. It might include acknowledgement and resolution of unequal power relations existing between men and women, along with the adoption of radical new goals, strategies, and evaluative benchmarks to assure the systemic acceptance of equality issues. These changes are not optional if the UN is to achieve success in its gender mainstreaming efforts; merely pursuing an integrative strategy is not enough to effect real change where gender inequality is concerned. In an overview article, Beveridge and Nott (2002: 300) reach a similar conclusion, "It seems to be generally accepted that mainstreaming can only adequately address the pathology of inequality where it pursues a transformative agenda."

However, there are other elements that make up a genuinely transformative agenda beyond gender. A feminist perspective reveals that gender inequality is not the only form of inequality restricting and limiting women's possibilities for action and identity in the postconflict environments specific to this analysis. Multicultural and global feminists have rejected the idea that all women experience gender inequality identically and have called attention to the need to recognize the intersecting axes of oppression that women of color, poor women, disabled women, lesbians, and other underrepresented groups of women experience (hooks, 1984; Collins, 1990; Mohanty, Russo, and Torres, 1991; Brown, 1992). So, this begs the question: Does part of the transformative agenda for the UN include an attempt to mainstream race, class, religion, nationality, ethnicity, and (dis)ability along with gender in its peacekeeping missions? As part of their assessment of the appropriateness of mainstreaming as an instrument in achieving feminist goals, Beveridge and Nott (2002) make the distinction between *gender mainstreaming* and *equality mainstreaming*, the latter taking the aforementioned other social locations and identities into consideration. They argue that a sole focus on gender is somewhat myopic—and ultimately ineffective in efforts to address social inequalities.

The UN's policy of gender mainstreaming lacks real transformative potential because it has this same one-dimensional focus on gender. The diverse populations that the UN peacekeeping missions serve demand the establishment of security and the provision of humanitarian aid and assistance that take into account the multiplicity of identities that shape the postconflict experiences of war-affected populations. Again, the gender advisers' strategy of working "from the outside-in" seems to offer the UN peacekeeping missions the best chance of moving toward this transformative mainstreaming agenda.

Beginning with concerns of the local population and focusing on their daily realities, gender advisers and other UN staff, working "from the outside-in," must acknowledge the intersecting identities of those whom they assist, wrestling with social complexities operating in and governing postconflict environments.

Conclusions

This chapter has offered a discussion of strategies used by UN gender advisers to mainstream gender in peacekeeping missions, providing an analysis of strategies in terms of their potential to help the UN achieve its gender mainstreaming goals. It has argued that the UN must pursue a transformative agenda in its efforts at mainstreaming gender and that, ultimately, this agenda cannot be transformative without acknowledging the influence of other social identities beyond gender on individual and group experiences in a postconflict setting. Further, it identifies the strategy of working "from the outside-in" as the most promising in offering the UN the ability to achieve its gender mainstreaming goals and to address the needs of the populations it serves.

Having said that, it is important to note that the integration of a truly transformative *equality mainstreaming* agenda into the UN's peacekeeping efforts seems a distant possibility. As noted, the UN is experiencing limited success in achieving its gender mainstreaming goals. At some level, this is to be expected. Mainstreaming a gender perspective in peacekeeping missions and postconflict environments involves the arduous process of changing long-held cultural beliefs and attitudes about men's and women's social roles on both the part of UN mission staff and local populations.

Fortunately, many of the gender advisers saw progress in this respect since the introduction of Security Council Resolution 1325, which calls for increased protection of women and girls during armed conflict and increased participation of women in peace and security processes, peacekeeping operations, and decision-making processes at all levels. However, despite how difficult it may be to promote these essential attitudinal changes, there are also ideological, administrative, and practical factors that impede the progress of the gender mainstreaming policy—factors over which UN and peacekeeping missions have control, but which they have addressed belatedly or refused to address at all. Over a decade after the concept of gender mainstreaming was introduced at the UN, ten years since its gradual introduction into peacekeeping, the UN, and the DPKO in particular, seems to have reached a crossroads in its attempt to address gender inequality in postconflict settings. It remains to be seen whether they will continue on the path of employing integrative strategies, giving the illusion of success in mainstreaming gender, but offering limited progress—or whether they will take the more difficult path of embracing transformative strategies, which present the possibility of overcoming gender inequality as well as addressing the roots of other social inequalities.

REFERENCES

Barkley Brown, E. 1992. What has happened here: The politics of difference in women's history and feminist politics. *Feminist Studies* 18 (2): 295–312.

Beveridge, F. and S. Nott. 2002. Mainstreaming: A case for optimism and cynicism. *Feminist Legal Studies* 10: 299–311.

Cockburn, C. 2001. The gendered dynamic of armed conflict and political violence. In *Victims, perpetrators, or actors? Gender, armed conflict, and political violence*, ed. C. Moser and F. Clark, F. (Eds), *Victims, perpetrators, or actors? Gender, armed conflict, and political violence*, pp. 13–29. London: Zed Books.

Cockburn, C. and D. Žarkov, eds. 2002. *The post-war moment: Militaries, masculinities, and international peacekeeping: Bosnia and the Netherlands*. London: Lawrence and Wishart.

Enloe, C. 2000. *Maneuvers: The international politics of militarizing women's lives*. Berkeley: University of California Press.

———. 2002. Demilitarization—or more of the same? Feminist questions to ask in the post-war moment. In *The post-war moment: Militaries, masculinities, and international peacekeeping*, ed. C. Cockburn and D. Žarkov, 22–32. Bosnia and The Netherlands; London: Lawrence and Wishart.

Hill Collins, P. 1990. *Black feminist thought: Knowledge, consciousness, and the politics of empowerment*. Boston, MA: Unwin Hyman.

hooks, b. 1984. *Feminist theory: From margin to center*. Cambridge, MA: South End Press.

Jahan, R. 1995. *The elusive agenda: Mainstreaming women in development*. Atlantic Highlands, NJ: Zed Books.

Mohanty, C., A. Russo, and L. Torres. 1991. *Third world women and the politics of feminism*. Bloomington: Indiana University Press.

Niarchos, C. 1995. Women, war, and rape: Challenges facing the international tribunal for the former Yugoslavia. *Human Rights Quarterly* 17: 649–669.

Nikolić-Ristanović, V. 2000. *Women, violence, and war: Wartime victimization of refugees in the Balkans*. Budapest: Central European University Press.

United Nations General Assembly. 2003, February 13. *Report of the Secretary-General* on gender mainstreaming in peacekeeping activities, A/57/731. New York.

7

Aftermath of U.S. Invasions: The Anguish of Women in Afghanistan and Iraq

Hayat Imam

War looks like a male enterprise: The majority of soldiers are men; decisions about launching war and its conduct are made by men; the wounds of the frontlines are experienced mostly by men; peace is called and settled by men. But war and violence impact women in very significant ways, both short and long term.

War imposes a double burden on women. Not only do they experience the violence of war just as their fellow citizens do, they also encounter gender-specific harm. Shared by men and women are blows to their sense of nationalism, to pride about history and culture, and to respect for religion. Women in Afghanistan feel the same rage and helplessness as Afghan men, seeing civilians and children bombed and killed. Women in Iraq felt the same sense of betrayal and anger as Iraqi men, watching the looting of their treasures from the Baghdad Museum while U.S. soldiers looked on.

But women also have to deal with particular traumas. When their husbands, sons, families, and community members are targeted, kidnapped, imprisoned, tortured, or killed, women are not only overcome by grief and fear, they must pick up the pieces, be strong for children and other dependents, and ensure the family's survival. And this is often required under conditions of extreme hardship, where basic infrastructure and services, food, water, and healthcare, become scarce to nil. Often, war forces communities to flee, adding the burden of loss of home, loss of memories, and loss of cherished items.

Two outcomes are inevitable in wars: Impoverishment and lack of security. In many societies, if the breadwinner loses employment or if the wife is widowed, it is next to impossible for her to find work or income. She and her children become dependents of other family members, the state, or the occupying power. Starvation is rampant. Under lawless conditions, women often become victims of rape and other sexual violence. According to a 2004 Amnesty International Report, *Lives Blown Apart*, sexual violence is often an intentional strategy to terrorize and defeat an entire population. An attack on women is an affront to her, but also to those who should have protected her. One outcome is greater restriction on women's movements and further emphasis on their seclusion. Young girls are married off earlier to ensure their safety and position in a husband's care.

This chapter focuses on the impacts on women resulting from U.S. invasions and occupations of Afghanistan and Iraq. No country, ethnic group, or culture has a monopoly on violence, as every group has proven itself to be quite capable of violence and war. My rationale is twofold: First, as an American, the actions of my country are my responsibility; second, the United States is the most powerful nation on earth, and there is currently no other country or body capable of curbing its actions. There is only "We the people," and we people must raise our voices.

Roots of the Invasion: Afghanistan

Beginning in the late 1970s, the United States positioned itself in Afghanistan. Strategically placed between the huge oil and gas reserves of the Caspian Basin, the Central Asian States of Turkmenistan, Uzbekistan, Kazakhstan in the North, and the Arabian Sea in the South, Afghanistan is an ideal location for a pipeline to transport oil to tankers in the Arabian Sea (Meacher, 2003). In the 1980s, our government spent billions of dollars to arm and train local and imported militia to oust the Soviet presence in Afghanistan (Weaver, 2000). A key figure we nurtured and supported was Osama Bin Laden; once successful, the militias took turns ruling an Afghanistan devastated by the war—first, a set of warlords in the North (the Northern Alliance) and then the Taliban. Both groups were known to subjugate and suppress the rights of the Afghan people, especially women.

The United States funded the warlord Gulbuddin Hekmatyar, whose claim to fame is that he led fellow students in throwing acid in the faces of unveiled women (Mahajan, 2002). We also funded the Taliban, one of whose first acts in power was to close girls' schools. Despite systematic human rights violations by the Taliban, we tolerated many years of their rule while negotiations on the pipeline continued. Until July 2001, we saw the Taliban as a stable regime that would enable the construction of hydrocarbon pipelines from Central Asia, through Afghanistan and Pakistan to the Arabian Sea; yet, negotiations broke down as they refused to accept our conditions (Meacher, 2003).

After the September 11, 2001 attacks, the United States declared its intention to bomb Afghanistan in order to capture Osama Bin Laden—despite the fact that the Taliban government was reportedly willing, under certain conditions, to hand him over. We refused that offer and continued to bomb and invade (Mahajan, 2002: 30). We conclude, then, that the real agenda was to get rid of the Taliban and bring on a government that would be more amenable to our interests. Hamid Karzai, our preferred candidate for the country's 2005 presidential election, was once a consultant for the US oil company negotiating for the pipeline (Ibid., p. 124), and Zalmay Khalilzad, US Ambassador to both Afghanistan and Iraq during these invasions, had also been a consultant to this same oil company.

For some Americans, the invasions of Afghanistan and Iraq are explained and justified by 9/11, but we have to take into account that these plans were put in place long before. In 1997, some neoconservative Americans set up a think tank called the Project for a New American Century (PNAC) to promote U.S. global leadership, founded by people whose names are familiar, including key members of George W. Bush's administration: Secretary of Defense Donald Rumsfeld; Vice President Dick Cheney and his Chief of Staff, L. Scooter Libby; Deputy Secretary of Defense Paul Wolfowitz (later head of the World Bank); Governor Jeb Bush; Richard Perle; and Elliot Abrams. In 2000, the PNAC issued *Rebuilding America's Defenses: Strategies, Forces, and Resources for a New Century,* calling upon the United States to take steps to dominate global resources and boldly stating that the best way to realize this goal was to take advantage of "some catastrophic and catalyzing event—like a new Pearl Harbor." 9/11 provided just such an excuse to launch a worldwide war plan under the rubric of "the war on terror," and since then we have established bases at the gateways to all major sources of fossil fuels (Pilger, 2002). Prime among them is the pipeline across Afghanistan, the rationale for U.S. military bases in this key region.

There was a lot of press about the successful democratic experiment in Afghanistan and the miracle of the peaceful parliamentary elections held in 2005. This is far from the truth. Members of the Northern Alliance, some of whom committed crimes such as mass rape, ran as candidates for the parliamentary elections. Allegations of vote rigging and intimidation were rampant. In districts outside the center, many women did not dare go out to vote because of security concerns. According to Human Rights Watch, warlords dominate the new parliament, 60 percent of whom are directly or indirectly linked to human rights abuses. Their power can be seen in the fact that Hamid Karzai invited warlords into his cabinet to serve in critical positions. The result of these U.S. supported elections has been to legitimize many human rights abusers as lawmakers.

Since then, there has been a weakening and a breakdown of central authority in Afghanistan, accelerated by rampant corruption within Karzai's government. According to an August 30, 2005 Reuters interview with Dr. Ramazan Bashardost, Afghanistan's former Planning Minister, billions of dollars in aid has been squandered. The country's bombing has allowed vast areas to fall into the hands of warlords of the Northern Alliance, paving the way for the current resurgence of the Taliban. The warlords' power stems from growing poppies and trafficking in narcotics, a trade that has jumped dramatically with Afghanistan producing 90 percent of the world's supply of opium—traded openly, under the U.S. occupation. Chair of the U.S. Joint Chiefs of Staff said he has serious doubts about the ability of the Afghan government to stop the rise in the Taliban's influence, given that the heroin trade accounts for 50 percent of the Afghan economy, and pours $100 million a year into the Taliban coffers (Schmitt, 2008).

Essentially, Karzai's government controls Kabul and its environs; as it loses its grip, the Taliban steps in to fill the vacuum. In one village in Logar Province, just forty miles from Kabul, thieves were terrorizing the local populace. The government was unable to respond to pleas of the villagers so they turned to the Taliban, who stepped in and meted out justice, albeit a harsh one. Increasingly, the Taliban is forming a shadow government, with its own police chiefs, judges, and education systems, and winning support by bringing law and order back to these communities (Gopal, 2008).

Roots of the Invasion: Iraq

The Project for a New American Century (PNAC) also created a plan for Iraq. Its September 2000 report recommended increasing military spending by $48 billion so the United States could "fight and win multiple, simultaneous major theater wars" and that, should Bush take power, Iraq should be a target (Pilger, 2002). Early 2003, leading up to the invasion of Iraq, was a time of war fever among our leaders.

Suddenly, Iraq's president, Saddam Hussein, was our enemy—even though we had remained allies during his worst excesses, giving him diplomatic cover and selling him $1.5 billion of high-tech military goods (Goodman, 2004).

Although now it is increasingly clear that the invasion and occupation of Iraq was part of a long time plan for economic and political control of the region and its energy resources, in the run-up to the invasion in March 2003, all we heard was that Saddam Hussein posed an immediate threat with his "weapons of mass destruction"—the infamous WMDs that soon were brought into question. In fact, after the Gulf War of 1991 and subsequent years of bombardments, sanctions, and United Nations inspections, Iraq had been brought to its knees: Weapons scrapped, infrastructure destroyed, the health and well-being of the Iraqi people devastated. There was no legal mandate from the U. N. and no public support for an invasion. Millions of people around the world protested our preemptive invasion of a country that posed no threat to us.

When WMDs could not be found, the Bush administration's rationale for invasion took various twists and turns: A finger was pointed at Iraq's involvement with al Qaeda and 9/11 and, when that notion was discredited, we settled on being "the U.S. liberators who would bring democracy and freedom to Iraq." But, it turns out, what democracy and freedom really means is the freedom "to seize new markets for Western multinationals on the battlefields of preemptive wars" (Klein, 2007: 343). Naomi Klein shows that Iraq was a target for two reasons: First, it sits on the third largest proven oil reserves in the world; second, Iraq was one of the last remaining hold-outs against a free-market economic system. The plan was that by bombing, shocking, and terrorizing the entire population, deliberately destroying its infrastructure, and allowing its history and culture to be looted, a state of such disorientation would be induced that sweeping economic change could be implemented, practically overnight. President Bush's top envoy to Iraq, Paul Bremer, facilitated this investor friendly transformation with some 100 legal decrees, resolutions, and orders, privatizing Iraq's 200 state-owned companies producing staples, lowering corporate tax from 45 to 15 percent, decreeing that foreign companies could own all Iraqi assets, and ensuring they could take all the profits made in Iraq out of the country.

Bremer was more cautious with the petroleum industry. There is a long history of suppression of Iraq by the West over oil, but Iraqi resistance has been equally long and fierce. I have seen this resistance first-hand. As a young girl, I lived with my family in Iraq. On the one hand, it was magical to experience the fabled bazaars of Baghdad, boat rides on the Tigris River on full moon nights, the hospitality of the Iraqi people. But I also witnessed the bloody 1958 coup, when Iraqi nationalists demolished a monarchy they thought had sold their patrimony to Western oil monopolies. Six years later, the CIA organized a countercoup, paving the way for the Baathists and Saddam Hussein to come to power. However, even Saddam Hussein ensured Iraqi control of its own oil by nationalizing the oil sector for three decades.

The Coalition Provisional Authority (CPA), the initial governing body for the occupation, lacked local or international support to privatize the oil industry; instead, the U.S. government has pressured Iraq's government to amend its constitution to pass a new petroleum law creating a fiscal and legal framework beneficial to foreign investors. The original draft, vetted by the U.S. government, U.S. oil companies, and the International Monetary Fund, was not seen by the majority of Iraqi members of parliament or the Iraqi public. This pro-Western petroleum law would have locked Iraq into 30-year production sharing agreements (PSA) with U.S. and U.K. oil companies to extract Iraq's oil, claiming some 70 percent of its profits. When the draft became public, there was an outcry and tremendous resistance among Iraq's parliamentarians, the public, and members of the oil workers unions, who saw this as an economic disaster that would strip away Iraq's profits and control of its oil reserves. A letter signed by Nobel Laureates pointed out that a nation under occupation should not be forced to make such sweeping decisions when it has no power to negotiate.

From spring, 2008 until autumn, the Bush administration and the Iraq executive branch of the government tried to hammer out a Status of Forces Agreement to allow the United States to stay on in Iraq after the U N mandate expired. The United States lobbied for an agreement with no end date to occupation, provided sweeping rights and immunities to occupation forces, and legalized long-term bases and indefinite numbers of troops. In October 2008, tens of thousands of Iraqis, both Shias and Sunnis, took to the streets to protest the terms of the agreement and demand the withdrawal of U.S. troops. Responding to the furor, the Iraqi cabinet negotiated a bilateral agreement containing key concessions, including a final end-date of 2011 for our occupation, no arrests of Iraqis by U.S. forces without warrants from Iraqi courts, and no long-term U.S. military bases (Sheridan, 2008).

Impact of the Invasion on Women in Afghanistan

The military occupation of Afghanistan has left the country in chaos, with high unemployment, homelessness, and a total lack of law enforcement. The administrative infrastructure has been destroyed by war, making it impossible to implement laws. With the central authority eroded, armed militias belonging to local warlords, the Taliban, and influential landlords act with impunity. Seven years after the invasion of Afghanistan, according to a September 9, 2008 report in *Middle East Online,* the level of violence there was higher than in Iraq. The situation for women is particularly desperate, as they have become increasingly vulnerable and unprotected.

Afghanistan is in its worst shape since 2001, mainly due to the growing number of civilian deaths (Smale, 2008). According to a United Nations Assistance Mission in Afghanistan (UNAMA) Human Rights Report, from January 1, 2008 through August 31, there have been 1445 civilian casualties, which are up 39 percent since 2007. Civilians are directly targeted, or caught in the crossfire of numerous attacking parties. There has been an increase in bombing and house raids by United States and International Military Forces (IMF), assisted by Afghan government forces. The Taliban has responded to bombings with untargeted blasts, executions of civilians whom they see as collaborators, and suicide bombers. In a riveting account, Anand Gopal (2008) moved among the people and recorded their anguished responses to the killings and deaths, pointing out that, when civilians see their loved ones mutilated, beheaded, and killed in U.S. raids and bombings, they willingly turn to the Taliban to fight back.

In August 2008, a U.S. missile attack in the village of Nawabad killed ninety civilians as they slept, including sixty women and children. There are many other stories of brutality, such as the forty-five women and children killed at a wedding party, among them the bride, or members of a family killed in a midnight raid. According to an Afghan Human Rights Organization (AHRO) report of September 3, 2008, 98 percent of the casualties caused by United States and coalition forces are intentional. Philip Alston, U. N. Special Rapporteur on Extra-Judicial, Summary or Arbitrary Killings, says the worst of it is that relatives of those killed are unable to get any information or accountability; no one tracks the outcome of investigations and prosecutions, or makes information public. Women in Afghanistan have particular difficulties in mobility and pursuing public information, so the chilling outcome is that loved ones disappear and women are simply left in the dark.

Murder, robbery, kidnapping, and the rape of women and children are routine, and there is no centralized, effective system of justice to protect them. In March 2008, the Afghan Independent Human Rights Commission (AIHRC) said deteriorating security had contributed to increasing violence against women. There have been some high profile stories about brutal rapes of women in the news, but too many other such incidents have not been reported or recorded. One woman, who complained to a local commander about his abducting her son, was dragged off in broad daylight, raped, and had her private parts cut with a bayonet. President Karzai later pardoned the perpetrators, releasing the rapists back into the community (Clark, 2008). Very young girls are being kidnapped and raped. The son of a powerful official was accused of raping twenty-two girls in the northern province of Sar-I-Pul; Syed Nurallah, the father of one of the victims, says his daughter, "Wakes up in the middle of the night screaming. Her arms, legs, her body is always tense and frightened. I have one question for Mr. Karzai: if this was your little girl, what would you do?" (cited in Abawi, 2008). Radhika Coomaraswamy, the UN Special Representative for Children in Armed Conflict, found that sexual violence against young boys is also a problem. In what is known as "bacha-bazi", or "child's play," little boys are forced to dress in female attire, dance, and perform sexual acts.

Amnesty International has stated that the United States has not fulfilled its promises of safety, freedom, education, and healthcare for Afghan women. Veiling and restrictions are still being imposed on them in places outside of Kabul, and women are being trafficked into prostitution and forced into marriages—sometimes to settle family debts. Women have no power, no mobility, and no resources of their own. Beatings, kidnappings, and other forms of intimidation are preventing them from holding public office or other jobs, or even from registering to vote and going about their daily business.On September 28, 2008, in Kandahar Province, Malalai Kakar, a female police officer was shot in the head outside her home, and in June of 2008, another police woman was shot in Herat.

Although the Karzai government has signed the UN Convention on Ending Discrimination Against Women (CEDAW), no government report has been submitted for CEDAW as required under the agreement. Women of Afghanistan wrote a 'Shadow Report' and submitted it to the UN in 2007. This report documents that violence against women: forced marriages, sexual harassment, domestic violence are all on the rise. 60 to 80 percent of marriages are forced and 57 percent of brides are under 16 (Gopal, 2009). Many women see suicide or running away as their only options.

Women's rights have deteriorated in the last eight years as a direct result of policies by Karzai's government. The first was empowering anti-women warlords, many with private armies of their own. Sonali Kolhathar, founder of Afghan Women's Mission, writes on www.commondreams.org that Taliban-style edicts are still in place in many parts of the country. The warlord of Herat arrested women for driving cars, appearing unveiled and speaking to journalists. He even conducted chastity tests on unescorted women.

The second was to appoint a conservative, fundamentalist judiciary. In April 2009, misogynistic elements in the judiciary proposed a shocking Afghan law that legalizes marital rape, further confines women to their homes, denies them inheritance rights, sets minimum age for marriage at 16 and requires women to obey their husbands in all things. As a result of an international outcry, this law has been shelved for now.

Girls are still deprived of education in most provinces. School attendance has dropped overall and, in a 2006 speech, Karzai said 200,000 children have been driven out of schools by disruption and violence in the country. In addition, the Taliban directly targets girls' schools, going against centuries of Islamic tradition supporting women's literacy. In Islam, every man and woman is encouraged to read the Quran, automatically upholding the principle of literacy.

Essential services are disrupted. Safe water reaches only 12 percent of the people, and a 2005 UN Environmental Program (UNEP) Report found medical waste going into the water supply. Maternal and child health is in tremendous jeopardy, mortality risk for pregnancy-related causes are one in fifteen (versus one in 3,500 in the United States), one in nine woman are dying during or after pregnancy (Sahil, 2007). For children under age five, the mortality rate is 257 per 1000—at least double that of other Asian developing countries; so, one child in four will not live to see his or her fifth birthday (Oot, 2002).

In stark contrast to the situation before the invasion, when the Taliban had banned all poppy growing, about half a million Afghan households are now involved in poppy cultivation, on 30 percent of the arable land. This is driving the world's opium production and a flourishing drug trade. Inevitably, drug use is on the rise in Afghanistan, where there are about 920,000 drug users, 120,000 of them, according to a 2008 report of the Afghanistan Independent Human Rights

Commission (AIHRC), women. Also, the AIHRC has reported a rise in self-immolation, forty-seven women having doused themselves with gasoline and burned to death.

Given these conditions, it is not surprising that people are fleeing their homes by the thousands. According to the UN High Commission for Refugees, as of 2006, 200,000 Afghans were refugees, leaving behind everything they own. With the prevalence of high unemployment and lack of NGO assistance or humanitarian aid, there is little chance these refugees can return home in the near future—or maybe ever, given the climate of violence and danger. For many Afghan women, the loss is permanent.

IMPACT OF THE INVASION ON WOMEN IN IRAQ

To understand the full extent of what we have destroyed and what Iraqi women have lost, consider what Iraq was like before the first Gulf War, in 1991—a prosperous, modern, secular state with universal education and one of the best healthcare systems in the region. Most women were well educated, many working in professional fields as doctors, lawyers, and engineers. There were progressive civil laws governing women's rights. Basic necessities and infrastructure such as electricity, clean water, transportation, and hospitals were fully functional. During the Gulf War, our government specifically targeted this infrastructure, and daily bombings throughout the subsequent ten years of sanctions on Iraq devastated the rest.

By 2006, there were in excess of 650,000 deaths in Iraq due to the invasion, according to the *Lancet Medical Journal*. Still, this enormous figure does not begin to capture the suffering attached to every death by those left behind to grieve and cope. By 2007, there were 2.3 million widows in Iraq, including those who lost husbands during the Iran-Iraq War (Ali and Jamail, 2008). When men were wounded and disabled, women typically bore responsibility for caring and tending to their needs, often under impossible circumstances. Many hardly had time to recover from the terror, deaths, and rubble left after the "Shock and Awe" bombings before nearly 500,000 soldiers, civil servants, teachers, and doctors were fired from their jobs by the Coalition Provisional Authority (CPA). Not only was this a frightening prospect, jeopardizing sustenance, women also had to deal with the anger and rage of men feeling impotent and humiliated. This is often the hidden subtext of war: Men are punished, tortured, and made powerless and then women, in turn, are targets of that transferred anger and violence.

Human rights violations by the U.S. military have been frequent, further entrenching the spiral of violence. Soldiers forcibly break and enter houses, even with women and children present, which is a grave insult to Muslims for whom modesty is an added concern. They search and arrest people, without warrants, charges, access to lawyers, or limits on how long they are held in prison. From 2003 to 2006, almost 60,000 men were imprisoned, and the 2007 estimate was 19,000 men in jail (Klein, 2007), family members waiting anxiously to hear their fate. Fears are high that loved ones will be humiliated and tortured, as many were in the Abu Ghraib prison, with electric shock, sexual abuse, water-boarding, and attacks by dogs.

The safety of the civilian population is the responsibility of occupying forces under international law, but the U.S. authorities have failed in this duty. According to Amnesty International, violence against women has increased. Iraqi women face arrest, torture, rape, and execution simply because their male relatives are sought by occupation forces. Our military held dozens of women as bargaining chips to put pressure on their relatives to surrender. In the first year of the occupation, nearly 1,500 women were in prison and, according to General Taguba's report on Abu Ghraib, Iraqi women have been abused, raped, and forced to strip naked at gunpoint.

With this kind of repression, it was only a matter of time before Iraqi men began to react and resist. Thus, the war began—after President Bush declared victory. Thousands of soldiers fired by the CPA still had their weapons and were fully trained, and armed militias formed to resist U.S. forces in a lawless environment. With no other source of income, many turned to extortion and crime. Kidnappings for ransom have become so common that children, girls, and women are afraid to leave their homes. These militias are often associated with Muslim extremists with controlling and rigid views about women's roles and societal behaviors. By these strict dictates, women must wear *hijab* (head-covering) and stay at home. Female unemployment is now twice as high as that for males (UN Humanitarian Information Unit, 2006). Another direct consequence of the violence and instability has been a huge drop in school attendance, especially by girls. The tragedy is that, before the Gulf War 1991 and the subsequent decade of sanctions, Iraq had the best education system in the region, with the highest literacy rates in the Arab world (Klein, 2007). This drop in education will have long-term negative consequences for prosperity and health well into the next generation.

Sixty percent of Iraqis are unemployed, putting one-third of the population below the poverty line. Malnutrition is increasing, and thousands of children can be seen picking through garbage dumps, begging, and stealing (al Samaraie, 2007). Inevitably, thousands of Iraqis have fled, becoming refugees in neighboring countries. Millions have also been internally displaced. This exile and displacement covers untold stories of human misery and deprivation: Separations from loved ones, disintegration of families, loss of homes and belongings, and, for women, the danger of sexual abuse and harassment.

While the American-occupied part of Baghdad, the Green Zone, is lit up like the United States, the rest of Iraq is dark, with just a few hours of electricity per day. This has serious, reverberating consequences as, amid soaring temperatures in the desert climate, old and young suffer from the heat, and families who can ill afford to waste food have no refrigeration. Traffic lights and streetlights don't work, causing chaos and insecurity on roads. Telephone and Internet services are all affected, not to mention the dire effects on businesses and industries. Water sewage plants don't function, so there is no clean water or even water delivery. The run-down water and sanitation infrastructure has been linked to the outbreak of cholera in 2008.

As might be expected, reduced electricity supply has had a disproportionate effect on healthcare facilities. At Baghdad Medical City, once the center of some of the best medical care in the region, there are only two hours of electricity a day, no air conditioning, no antibiotics, or no basic material for I.V. treatment. Medicines can only be bought on the black market, if they are available (Hamed and Jamail, 2008). Sanctions during the 1990s flattened Iraq's primary healthcare system, with estimates that 1.6 million "excess" deaths of children under age five occurred, and since 1990, infant mortality rates increased by 150 percent. The only way to fully grasp the tragedy embedded in these numbers is to remember that thousands of parents looked on helplessly as their babies died because a simple antibiotic, banned by the sanctions, was not available.

The deteriorating health situation of Iraqis can also be attributed to a traumatic brain-drain of some 2.5 million professionals (Susman, 2008). Along with others, thousands of physicians have left Iraq to escape the hopelessness, insecurity, and violence. In 2003, there were 30,000 physicians in the country; in 2007, there were 8,000 (al Samaraie, 2007). Since the Gulf War and the invasion of Iraq, poor health conditions for women have reached crisis proportions. Throughout the 1990s, health centers and hospitals were bombed, and an embargo was placed on medicines and vaccines, leading to high rates of maternal and infant mortality. This is also a form of violence against the population—the slow erosion of amenities that can make life unbearable. Here is an account from *Bulletin #3* (April 18, 2003) by Physicians for Human Rights, about conditions in a maternity and pediatric hospital in Southern Iraq:

> The maternity hospital in An-Nasiriyah has no prenatal vitamins, iron tablets, birth control pills...and medications to address the complications of pregnancy and childbirth. Scalpels to make incisions are re-used and tubing for IV's and catheters have been used for an entire month.
>
> Electricity in this hospital is provided by two generators. Due to short fuel supply, however, generator power is now reserved for emergency cases for nighttime use when needed. There is currently no source of water at the hospital. Not only can the floors and walls not be cleaned, but obstetricians and midwives have no water to wash before a delivery.
>
> Labor and delivery take place in the dark. Slivers of light reach the ward from the hallway windows...There are no towels, sheets or supplies...If an episiotomy is needed, this is done with a non-sterile, re-used scalpel or with old surgical scissors and without anesthesia. The use of non-sterile medical supplies not only invites life-threatening infection, it is also a source of infectious disease transmission, including hepatitis and HIV/AIDS.
>
> On the maternity wing of the hospital, the windows are without glass, floor tiles are not intact, and trash litters the hallway. Family members have been collecting water from swamps and rivers for the patients and this water has been used without being treated.... Swarms of flies are fanned away from newborns by new mothers and grandmothers.

There are two health issues that should be flagged for future study and investigation. The first is the use of depleted uranium (DU), a euphemism for Uranium 238 (U-238), a by-product of the uranium enrichment process. The U.S. military has dropped 1,700 tons of bombs with DU on population centers of Iraq (as compared to 300 tons in the Gulf War, which resulted in an epidemic of Gulf War Syndrome among returning U.S. troops). Its radioactive properties show their effects as strange and excessive cancers among Iraqi people (Koehler, 2006). It is known that children and pregnant women are especially vulnerable to radiation. Secondly, during the siege of the city of Fallujah in 2004, the U.S. military used White Phosphorus (WP) during the attack (Spinner, Vick, and Fekeiki, 2004); much the same as napalm, WP burns and melts the skin, and using it is illegal and against the Chemical Weapons Convention that the United States signed in 1993.

The ultimate catastrophe would be the partition of Iraq. Today, there is the prospect of civil war in Iraq, a previously unthinkable notion. Having lived among Iraqi people and having personally seen how Iraqis, particularly women, build bonds of community and relate to each other, I have observed a society where Shias and Sunnis live side by side, go to the same schools, intermarry, do business together, and think of themselves as Muslims first, rather than as Shias and Sunnis. In a recent survey, Iraqi women overwhelmingly (72 percent) demanded a unified Iraq (Kazakoff, 2008). The Iraqi women who were invited to a speaking tour by Code Pink made it clear that the sectarian ill-feeling and divisions between Shia and Sunni were introduced into Iraqi politics by Paul Bremer, the head of the Coalition Provisional Authority. The Iraqi people's analysis is that a civil war is being provoked in order to fracture the country and make it easier to control (al-Fadhily, 2007).

"Sting-back" Effects in the United States

There is an uncomfortable disconnect between what we believe is moral conduct and what we allow the state to tell us to do. Each of us believes we should not lie or kill or oppress others, that kindness and caring is what makes us fully human. Yet, no war can be conducted unless the state recruits and trains young people to kill, turning away from their natural inclinations for compassion and fairness and seeing another group of people as less than human. We are encouraged to believe that our own national interest is paramount and matters more than any other peoples' dignity and desires. These contradictory messages are bound to fracture the wholeness of our young people, resulting in startling levels of psychological distress and coping problems among returning war veterans.

A long-term United States presence in Afghanistan and Iraq will require enormous sacrifices by U.S. civil society in terms of a permanent war footing, both economic and social. For continuing wars to be palatable, the culture will need to become discordantly attuned to power, aggression, and racism. Creating a dehumanized enemy will require rewards for being tough and unsentimental. Machismo and masculinity will rule, pressuring men toward violence that so easily turns against women.

Are we there already? Maybe not quite, but the signs are there. Waging war tends to produce what I call a "sting-back" effect. Assault and rape of U.S. women soldiers by fellow soldiers are at an all-time high; in fact, female soldiers are more likely to be raped than killed by enemy fire. Some 41 percent of women seen at the Los Angeles Veterans Administration Healthcare Center say they were victims of sexual assault while in the military, 29 percent reporting rape (Herman, 2008). Under pressure from Congress, the Department of Defense announced a new policy on sexual assault in January 2005, but plans for addressing the problem are limited.

Other sting-back effects are low morale, suicides, or attempted suicides. Soldiers expect to be heroes, but they are often rejected and abandoned upon their return; forced into situations where they end up killing civilians, they experience trauma. If they leave angry at being disliked by the population they were supposedly liberating, perhaps they will be more xenophobic/Arab-hating or Muslim-hating. Then there are the wounded, physically and mentally, who may or may not receive proper care. There are many costs to society from war efforts. Clare Bayard (2008) has written, "Every bomb explodes twice: once shattering lives in Fallujah, Karbala, Basra; then burning up our schools and universities, healthcare, levees, social system." Our disregard for international laws and world opinion in the areas of preemptive action, collective punishment, and use of torture is bound to also have sting-back effects, and we have lost the right to protest if other countries take similar action.

Conclusions: Losses and Wins

Leading up to the 2008 U.S. presidential elections, the rhetoric was disturbing on the war issues. One party said, "We should divide Iraq up into three countries, then we'll win," the other, "The American public doesn't care how we got into the war, just as long as we win." One said, "We'll stay and fight for 100 years if need be, in order to win," the other, "Let's ramp up the war in Afghanistan, so we can win." There is only a narrow spectrum of difference. Poll after poll consistently shows that the U.S. public is overwhelmingly against these invasions, but our leaders don't seem to be representing us. The loser here is democracy. What is also lost is the suffering of people in Afghanistan and Iraq—men, women, and children whose lands have been devastated, whose people have been killed and tortured, whose thousand-year histories have been disrespected and betrayed. And at home, there are the incalculable losses from the civil liberties that have been taken away from us.

President Obama now has an opportunity to show what it means to really win. If we are to heal our society and regain our standing in the world, we have to firmly grasp that we cannot trample on the aspirations of citizens of other countries or plunder their resources. This small globe requires our attention, our restraint, and our need to share and be partners with the rest of humankind.

We can ally ourselves with peace movements, heeding the voices of women who have been loud and strong in United for Peace with Justice and its affiliates, such as the Dorchester People for Peace; in Code Pink; in the writings of insightful political analysts Arundhati Roy (2004), Naomi Klein, Amy Goodman (2004), and Antonia Juhasz (2006); in the courageous actions of Cindy Sheehan, mother of a slain soldier, who set aside her grief to fight for peace so others will not experience the same pain; in the honorable example of Barbara Lee, the lone voice in Congress in September 1, 2001, who voted against the use of force in Afghanistan, saying, "If we rush to launch a counter-attack, we run too great a risk that women, children, and other non-combatants will be caught in the cross-fire. We must be careful not to embark on an open-ended war with neither an exit strategy nor a focused target. We cannot repeat past mistakes." We can learn from the women of the Revolutionary Afghan Women's Association (RAWA) who continue to work for women's empowerment even when their lives are targeted for doing just that; also, we can listen to the courageous and outspoken voices of Iraqi women reaching out to the U.S. public.

The people of Afghanistan are facing a humanitarian crisis today, with high food prices, and a drought that will jeopardize the lives of millions of men, women, and children. We can win by realizing that there are no military solutions, no answers from bombs and escalation; instead we can move immediately to send aid and help. Let us jump feet-first into building a stable society in Afghanistan by working hand in hand with grassroots, democratic forces there, by giving support to the economy and local employment. Let us follow the lead of BRAC, a nongovernment organization (NGO) from Bangladesh with extensive experience in poverty alleviation that, among other actions, offers a Microfinance Program for loans to poor women for income generating programs such as carpet weaving, tailoring, and as vendors for fruits, vegetables, and groceries.

We can win by curbing our greed and by regulating the greed of multinational corporations. The best access to oil will be by having allies in oil-rich countries, not enemies. Instead of destabilizing Iraq, fomenting hatreds and sectarian strife, let us give the Iraqi people a chance to put their country back together. They have spoken loud and clear in every poll, blaming U.S. occupation forces for their violent resistance; they want our troops out of Iraq—today. Instead of insulting the Iraqis by criticizing them for the mess they are in, let us take responsibility for that mess and make amends by providing reconstruction money to rebuild the infrastructure that we destroyed.

Finally, in a burst of inspiration, we may realize we win if we all win.

REFERENCES

Abawi, A. 2008. Afghan children raped with "impunity", U. N. official says. *CNN* (August 7).
al-Fadhily, A. 2007. Fallujah fears a "genocidal strategy." *Inter Press Service* (March 30).
Ali, A. and D. Jamail. 2008. Home to too many widows. *Inter Press Service* (June 18).
al Samaraie, N. A. 2007. Humanitarian implications of the war in Iraq. *International Review of the Red Cross* (December 31).
Bayard, C. 2008. Not one more war. *Catalyst Project of War Resisters League* (March 25).
Clark, K. 2008. Afghan president pardons men convicted of bayonet gang rape. *The Independent* (August 24).
Goodman, A. 2004. *The exception to the rulers*. New York: Hyperion Books.
Gopal, A. 2008. Some Afghans live under Taliban rule—and prefer it. *Christian Science Monitor* (October 15).
Hamed, A. and D. Jamail. 2008. The biggest hospitals become sick. Posted on www.dahrjamailiraq.com (September 26).
Herman, J. 2008. Rapists in the ranks. *Los Angeles Times* (April 2).
Juhasz, A. 2006. *The Bush agenda: Invading the world, one economy at a time*. New York: HarperCollins.
Kazakoff, L. 2008. One barometer of Iraq's future. *San Francisco Chronicle* (March 19).
Klein, N. 2007. *The shock coctrine*. New York: Metropolitan Books.
Koehler, B. 2006. Spreading cancer. *Tribune Media Services* (June 29).
Mahajan, R. 2002. *The new crusade*. Monthly Review Press.
Meacher, M. 2003. This war on terror is bogus. *The Guardian* (September 6).
Oot, D. 2002. Save the Children testimony to Congress (March 28).
Pilger, J. 2002. John Pilger reveals the American plan. *New Statesman* (December 16).
Roy, A. 2004. *An ordinary person's guide to empire*. Cambridge: South End Press.
Sahil, F. 2007. UNICEF and partners come together to help reduce maternal mortality in Afghanistan. UNICEF Web site (April 2).
Schmitt, E. 2008. Taliban influence rising in Afghanistan. *New York Times* (October 9).

Sheridan, M. 2008. Iraqi Cabinet approves U.S. pact. *Boston Globe* (November 17).

Smale, A. 2008. Afghanistan is in its worst shape since 2001, European diplomat says. *New York Times* (September 15).

Spinner, J., K. Vick, and O. Fekeiki. 2004. U.S. forces battle into the heart of Fallujah. *Washington Post* (November 10).

Susman, T. 2008. Professionals see no future in Iraq. *Los Angeles Times* (October 8).

UN Humanitarian Information Unit. 2006. Iraq: Women were more respected under Saddam, say women's groups. *IRIN* (April 14).

Weaver, M. A. 2000. The real Bin Laden. *New Yorker* (January 24).

Part III

Reframing Twenty-First Century Feminism with Global Ethnic Struggles

8

WOMEN AND PEACE IN A DIVIDED SOCIETY: PEACE-BUILDING POTENTIALS OF FEMINIST STRUGGLES AND REFORM PROCESSES IN BOSNIA AND HERZEGOVINA

Anne Jenichen

Despite an improving international rhetoric highlighting the necessity of women's participation in postwar settings, women still tend to be disadvantaged in peace-building processes (Chinkin and Charlesworth, 2006; United Nations, 2002). This chapter argues that women's struggles for rights entail important potentials for peace-building in divided postwar societies. Women frequently are among the first who cooperate across ethnic divisions established and hardened during ethno-political wars. Feminist policy reforms often strengthen common state structures and their legitimacy, contributing to the overcoming of ethnic divisions. Women's participation and contributions should, therefore, be much more recognized and promoted in peace-building processes. However, it is *feminist* advocacy that is key, not women's participation per se. Women have often promoted nationalistic and violent agendas; yet, only if they champion the rights of women independent of their ethnic and political differences can peace-building potentials come into effect.

This chapter illustrates and discusses peace-building potentials of feminist advocacy and reform processes via the case of postwar Bosnia and Herzegovina (BiH). BiH is considered to be a prime example of ethno-political wars after the cold war, of ethnically divided postwar societies and of ambitious international postwar interventions (Bose, 2002). It was also the first war where massive sexualized violence against women received considerable international attention, eventually leading to its international recognition as a war crime and crime against humanity (Oosterveld, 2005).

Besides pursuing peace strategies such as the promotion of dialogue, reconciliation, and return (Kvinna till Kvinna, 2006), women in BiH have been very active in fighting for and achieving several women's rights norms and policies after the war. Three campaigns are presented in this chapter: (1) the promotion of women's political representation and participation, resulting in the introduction of an electoral gender quota; (2) the foundation of state machineries for the advancement of gender equality, including the adoption of a gender equality law, and (3) the support and recognition of victims of sexual war-violence as war victims entitled to state compensation. These campaigns and reforms sought to promote women's rights and status in society, which is why I call them *feminist*. However, my analysis does not deal with the question of whether they have achieved their goals. Discrimination and violence on grounds of gender continue in BiH, despite the adoption of relatively progressive norms and policies (Global Rights, 2004). This chapter is about peace-building potentials of advocacy and reform processes— unintended side effects rather than well-planned goals. Whether they really contribute to sustaining peace is hard to assess due to the multiplicity of variables shaping outcomes, but these processes counter divisions that are remnants of the war and impediments of peace in the country.

My argument is based on the distinction between "equity" and "efficiency" borrowed from studies on women in development (Razavi and Miller, 1995). Beyond the question of "What women need from peace-building," it asks, "What peace-building needs from women." There is a broad literature on the gender-blindness of peace-building processes and the negative consequences for women and their rights in postwar states (e.g., Pankhurst, 2008; Sørensen, 1998; Strickland and Duvvury, 2003). Given the enduring reluctance of national and international policy makers to systematically integrate women and their rights into postwar reconstruction efforts by reason of gender equity alone, efficiency-based arguments might be useful to mobilize support of decision makers and donors.

My reconstruction of feminist advocacy and reform processes in BiH is mainly based on interviews with representatives of women's organizations, the state, and international organizations, as well as the analysis of documents and publications such as parliamentary protocols, written reports, and Web sites. This chapter, first, lists some of the efficiency-based arguments about integrating women and their rights into peace-building processes. A brief overview of the causes, dynamics, and consequences of the war in BiH follows to illustrate some of the main impediments for peace there, succeeded by the analysis of feminist campaigns and reforms in BiH. The conclusions discuss the potentials and limits of feminist advocacy and reform processes for peace-building.

What Women Can Add to Peace-Building in Divided States

Women's contributions to peace-building have long been neglected in both theory and practice, yet feminists have much to highlight women's roles in postwar reconstruction, their arguments based on two rationales: Gender equity and peace-building efficiency. To begin with, women have the human right to equally participate in the reconstruction of their countries; yet, as women experience wars differently than men, their inclusion into peace-building efforts also introduces new perspectives to the process (Handrahan, 2004; Pankhurst, 2008; Rehn and Sirleaf, 2002; Sørensen, 1998; Strickland and Duvvury, 2003; United Nations, 2002). Some feminists have furthermore argued that women's activism can contribute to the building of sustainable peace and reconciliation—my primary concern here.

While women represent a population severely and distinctly victimized by war and its aftermath, the tendency to disproportionately portray them as victims perpetuates inaccurate assumptions about their contributions to war and peace. Women are not solely passive victims; they are often powerful agents, active participants both in peace initiatives and in the support of war. Focusing on the victimization of women while neglecting the significant roles they have played during and after wars can undermine their future potential as key participants in formal peace processes. Women's contributions to peace have often been overlooked because they mostly take unconventional forms, and occur outside formal peace processes. While their involvement in informal activities has been documented, women's more rare participation in formal activities remains a subject not often studied.

Women, often considered to be the best humanitarian workers and most committed peace-builders worldwide (Anderlini, 2007; Cockburn, 2007), can contribute much to peace and reconstruction processes. Frequently the first to attempt reconciliation, return, and interethnic cooperation, they occupy spaces to develop initiatives for peace across ethnic and national identities on the community level and in political arenas (Anderlini, 2007; Mladjenovic, 2002).

Cynthia Cockburn (1998) points out that feminism, antiessentialist and inclusive of women differently situated in ethnic, class and other structures, tends to "immunize" women against regressive constructions of ethnic and national identity. It helps some women reveal the contradicting nature of the seemingly innocent notion of "home" concealing confinement, divisions, oppression, and violence. Therefore, feminists may be more skeptical of "homeland" as well. "If you see home as a 'golden cage' you may suspect that homeland too has its contradictions," she has written (p. 45). Women who choose not to solve their problems through reifying male ethnicity and violence often choose to reject male control and form multiethnic and multinational groups with other women. The shared experiences that women have as women subjected to violence and discrimination may reduce the significance of ethnicity and strengthen gender identity. By cooperating across ethnic divides, these women reject ethnic violence directed against them and their position as "ethnic boundary-markers" (Handrahan, 2004).

This is not to say that women are "naturally" more peaceful merely because they are women and they share certain experiences, such as bearing children, but they are more often involved in peace activities than men. It is no consequence of "natural" inclination but is, rather, a result of their social experiences as women, such as gender-based discrimination and political marginalization, increasing their empathic capacities and decreasing their vested interests in fighting for a political system (Strickland and Duvvury, 2003). Maja Korac (2006) argues that, as women have not been exposed to masculine socialization, they may be better positioned not to accept the values of male-dominated societies and to formulate a transformative, nonviolent vision of conflict resolution. Women's ethnicity is often instrumentalized by male ethnic leaders. Women may therefore be less attached to an identity that locates them at the nexus of male violence. If women favor gender instead of ethnicity as a primary identity, they may be asserting their rights as women, independent of the dominant male ethnic community and identity. However, rejecting group identity and male control has repercussions. According to Lori Handrahan (2004) it is only logical that women in search of greater autonomy then seek out others, including women from other ethnic groups, also attempting to break from patriarchal-imposed ethnicity.

As elsewhere, feminists in BiH, albeit a quite marginal group, fought successfully for women's rights after the war, thereby pushing interethnic cooperation and contributing to the strengthening of common state institutions—important features of the peace process in the ethnically divided country.

THE WAR IN BOSNIA AND HERZEGOVINA AND ITS AFTERMATH

The war in BiH began in April 1992 after the country's declaration of independence from the Yugoslav Federation, and ended with the signing of the "General Framework Agreement for Peace in Bosnia and Herzegovina," also known as Dayton Peace Agreement, in Paris on December 14, 1995 (Burg and Shoup, 1999).

The considerable amount of interethnic violence during the war entailed its depiction as an ethnic war fought by three ethnic groups against each other: Bosnian Serbs, Croats, and Muslims (Bosniaks), even if these ethnic differences were not the cause of the war. Serious economic and power-political conflicts within Yugoslavia culminated at the end of the 1980s and were reinterpreted in ethnic categories. Rising political leaders mobilized ethnic differences and violence to legitimize their own leadership roles in the newly emerging states, succeeding in manipulating ethnicity by spreading fear, insecurity, and hatred, which advanced their political agenda of separate national states (Andjelic, 2003; Oberschall, 2000). In BiH, two secessionist movements sought to dissolve the country and join neighboring states. While the Serb secession triggered the conflict in 1992, the Croat project of secession soon followed (1993–1994). Both movements sought to expel and kill members of other ethnic groups to bring "ethnically cleansed" territories under their control.

Besides being ethnicized, the war violence was also highly gendered. Nationalist discourses regard women mainly as caretakers and guardians of the family and the community, so they become central to producing and maintaining cultural and group identity. The increase in violence, justified as the "defense" of the "engendered" ethnic collective, transformed women into symbolically important targets of sexualized war violence (Korac, 2006; Seifert, 1996).

Estimates range from 10,000 to more than 40,000 war-related rapes in BiH (Djurić-Kuzmanović, Drezgić, and Žarkov, 2008; Ward and Marsh, 2006), and reports indicate that most of the violence occurred during detention. While rapes and forced pregnancies in detention were also practiced in camps run by Croats and Bosniaks, in the case of Bosnian Serbs they were part of a policy of systematic "ethnic cleansing." Feminists have interpreted the sexualized war violence as a gendered war strategy by which women's bodies were ethnicized, turned into national territories (Djurić-Kuzmanović, Drezgić, and Žarkov, 2008). The war, as well as the subsequent peace agreement, prioritized ethnicity as identity, suppressing other identities such as gender.

The war left BiH a deeply divided society. After its three and a half years, with 200,000 Bosnians dead or missing and roughly half the population displaced, the country was territorially, politically, and socially segregated. The Dayton Peace Agreement recognized the division of the state into two entities: the Republika Srpska (RS) and the Federation of BiH (FBiH), plus the small multinational district of Brčko. The FBiH in turn is divided into ten cantons. Most of the Serb population today lives in the RS, while in the FBiH, Bosniaks dominate five of the ten cantons, Croats three, and two cantons have mixed Bosniak and Croat populations.

Governance structures in BiH recognize this territorialization of ethnicity by devolving much of the power to the ethnically relatively homogeneous entities and cantons. At the beginning of the peace process, the state was largely an empty shell, with the RS governing itself autonomously as a quasi-state and the cantons in the FBiH having a comparable degree of self-government. Only gradually have wartime elites transferred their powers to the newly established institutions, if often maintaining parallel power structures. Despite this weakness of the common state level, the degree of centralization nonetheless has gradually been strengthened—attributed to the influence of the international community, which has continuously pushed for the establishment of additional common state institutions and agencies and the transfer of competencies from the entities to the state.

BiH is a unique case of multinational governance (Bieber, 2006). Substantial involvement of the international community and extensive rules determining group representation and governance made it highly complex, with seven different types and levels of governance, fourteen constitutions, well over 100 ministries, and 600 deputies, as well as veto rights at most levels of governance. This complex and asymmetrical political system makes BiH a highly unstable and dysfunctional state; moreover, the risk of secession is still not totally banned. Nationalist Serbs of the RS have repeatedly called for independence or accession to Serbia (Alić, 2008). Serb as well as Croat nationalist parties still favor the restoration of considerable powers to the entities (UNDP BiH, 2007). Overall, the segregation and minimal contact between the three constituent peoples of BiH reduces their political and emotional investment in the state, precluding a reconstruction of trust through interaction on a daily basis (Bieber, 2006). One important feature of the Bosnian peace process has therefore been the continuous strengthening of state-level institutions as well as of interethnic and state-entity cooperation, last but not least also central conditions in BiH's accession process to the European Union (Commission of the European Communities, 2007).

Feminist Advocacy and Reform Processes in Bosnia and Herzegovina

Integrating effects of feminist activism and reform processes, which contribute to interethnic cooperation at the levels of society and state, strengthen the common state-level in BiH and increase trust in the ethnically divided FBiH, are discussed next. Three campaigns and reform processes illustrate these peace-building potentials of feminist activism in BiH: (1) the promotion of women's political participation and representation; (2) the foundation of state institutions for the advancement of gender equality; and (3) the support of victims of sexual war violence.

Feminists Advocating Women's Political Participation and Representation

Women were the first in war-torn successor states of the former Yugoslavia who cooperated across the ethnic divide both during and after the war. Although their groups were small and politically marginalized, they were among the first to voice publicly their opposition to nationalist policies, the tactics of spreading fear and hatred, and the process of militarization. Recognizing early on the centrality of maintaining old and developing new connections across ethnic lines, local feminists established antiwar groups and, later, centers for victims of war violence, and cooperated against sexual violence and in support of—mainly female—refugees (Cockburn, 1998; Djurić-Kuzmanović, Drezgić, and Žarkov, 2008; Korac, 2006). Once the war was over, another field of cooperation emerged: The feminist struggle for more political participation and representation of women.

Subsequent to the first postwar elections in 1996, women represented only two percent of members of the state-level parliament, but immediately began to work toward changing this untenable situation. Already in 1996 and 1997, women organized women's conferences in the cities of Zenica, Banja Luka, Tuzla, Sarajevo and Mostar, where they, among other things, discussed women's lacking political participation and representation. The more concrete work on the issue began in 1998 in the face of upcoming general elections. Women's organizations founded a "League of female voters" and started to campaign for women's participation in the elections. Women from political parties brought in the idea of an electoral gender quota of 30 percent on candidate lists (Borić, 2004; Nordlund, 2003). They organized public discussions, workshops, and radio and television programs, as well as a large women's conference in Sarajevo, to demand more participation of women in politics and to lobby for the proposed gender quota. Shortly after this conference, the Provisional Election Commission, an internationally chaired body in charge of the preparation and execution of elections in BiH at that time, eventually introduced the quota into the election legislation (Jenichen, 2009).

Given the chronic lack of resources predominating in war-torn societies, all these activities would have been impossible without the financial and logistical support of external actors. The women's activities became supported by transnationally active NGOs and foundations, such as "Kvinna till Kvinna" from Sweden, the "National Democratic Institute" (NDI), and the "Hunt Alternatives Fund" from the United States. The principal supporter of women's interethnic cooperation in those early postwar years was the Democratization Department of the Organization for Security and Co-operation in Europe (OSCE), which supported the organization of conferences and campaigns, and organized meetings with women from different ethnic communities. Most of the other international organizations and embassies were not responsive to women's issues at that time. Only later they began to tackle the issue of gender inequalities more seriously, even though not systematically (Kvinna till Kvinna, 2000).

The peculiarity of the described activities was that, right from the beginning, women cooperated across ethnic divides. In the first women's conference in Zenica in 1996, although it took place in the FBiH, a few women from the RS also participated. A few may not sound exciting, but crossing the "Inter-Entity Boundary Line" then was neither easy nor safe, due to checkpoints, harassment, and occasionally shootings. In the women's conference in Sarajevo in 1998, women from all over the country, from different ethnic backgrounds and from various civil society groups and political parties, including nationalist ones, participated, although nationalist parties tried to prevent their members from crossing the "Inter-Entity Boundary Line". These women acted in the sense of Nira Yuval-Davis' (1997) "transversal politics" by defining the boundaries between each other not in terms of who they were but in terms of what they wanted to achieve.

These women activists were among the first in BiH to cooperate across the ethnic divide. They laid the foundations for long-term reconciliation and trust. However, this observation must not lead to the essentialization of gender differences and according attitudes toward violence and peace. In BiH, many international donors and agencies deduced from the interethnic cooperation of some women that all women were basically more peaceful and antinationalistic, ignoring the great number who supported nationalistic and violent views and policies. Elissa Helms (2003) revealed that the international community often depicted women as "naturally" more interested in peace, more tolerant of ethnic and other differences, more willing to engage in dialogue and to compromise to diffuse conflicts. She argues that these donor representations of women in BiH charge women with achieving the very political goal of ethnic reconciliation while constructing them as apolitical—thus marginalizing them from formal political power. When women activists use these affirmative gender essentialisms, according to Helms, they risk closing off women's potential for influence in the formal (male) political sphere.

The OSCE, for instance, came to the rash conclusion that, if women were more willing to cooperate cross-ethnically, they would also support moderate rather than nationalistic political parties in elections. This was one of the major reasons why the OSCE supported women's political participation in BiH—it expected the breakup of the dominance of nationalist political parties. But the OSCE had to realize that this strategy did not meet Bosnian realities. Women in the 1998 elections predominantly voted for nationalist parties that won the elections by a clear margin (Manning and Miljenko, 2003; Nordlund, 2003).

The willingness of some Bosnian women to cooperate across the ethnic divide is not an innate characteristic, and therefore does not reveal anything about women's general political attitudes. It is rather, as Elissa Helms argues, a gendered construction of women's roles, determined by the nexus of discourses from foreign donors, international and regional feminists, local nationalists, and local, historically established understandings of gender allowing women different possibilities and incentives from men. Local gender constructions place men in the role of warrior and political actor, while women are seen as passive (war) victims, mothers, and nurturers. Women as a group, thus, fall outside the category of political decision making and, accordingly, of waging political violence and war, enabling them easier access to cross-ethnic cooperation. Facilitated by the support of international organizations, such as the OSCE, women were afforded more space than men to engage in these activities (Helms, 2003). It is therefore a significant qualification that it is not women per se but especially *feminist* women championing women's rights to equality that contribute to peace-building in the sense put forward here.

The Foundation of State Institutions for the Advancement of Gender Equality and the Adoption of a Gender Equality Law

Women's rights policies not only triggered interethnic cooperation between feminist groups and politicians, they also encouraged institutional cooperation between antagonistic entities at the government level. In 2000 and 2002, two government institutions for the advancement of gender equality were formed in the FBiH and the RS, and since their foundation they have cooperated in many instances, such as the formulation of a gender equality law.

The government of the FBiH approached the Finnish government in 1999 to request financial support for the formation of state structures for the promotion of the status of women in Bosnian society—an idea initiated by the then president of the FBiH, Ejup Ganić, who had developed a genuine interest in the promotion of women's status in society during the war. He had developed an awareness of discrimination against women and had recognized their societal potential that he felt could be utilized for the collective good. The Finnish government approved and, jointly with the FBiH government, later with the BiH state government, launched the bilateral "Gender Equity and Equality Project" (GEEP). It started in 2000 and ended in 2005, mainly managed by Bosnian project partners. The core of the project was the creation of state institutions responsible for the promotion and monitoring of gender equality, developing a coherent gender equality policy and introducing a "gender mainstreaming" strategy (GEEP, 2006). Consequently, each entity, first the FBiH in 2000, then the RS in 2002, set up a "Gender Center," independent government institutions responsible for the initiation and monitoring of policies and laws pertaining to gender equality and for the observation of the situation of gender relations within their respective entities.

Originally, the GEEP was initiated between the governments of the FBiH and Finland. But Finland requested the FBiH to include the RS as well. This was a painful process, as the idea was born in the FBiH, and the RS government was at that time not interested in gender equality, but the money went to both entities. From that point, both had to cooperate. Since their foundation, both Gender Centers, despite a chronic lack of resources, have become two key agents in the development of gender equality and women's rights policies in BiH, and have also become one prime example of interentity cooperation in postwar BiH. Both cooperated on a number of projects, such as the development of a national action plan on gender equality, the formulation and submission of the first official state report on the implementation of the international Convention on the elimination of all forms of discrimination against women (CEDAW), and, jointly with women's organizations and politicians, the defense of the electoral gender quota (GEEP, 2006).

One of the main joint projects was the initiation and formulation of the Gender Equality Law, adopted in 2003, prohibiting any form of discrimination based on sex and criminalizing gender-based violence and sexual harassment. Part of the law was the creation of a state-level institution responsible for the advancement of gender equality in BiH, officially instituted in 2005. The "Gender Agency," part of the Ministry for Human Rights and Refugees, is the main coordinating body responsible for the monitoring and development of legislation and policies in the field of women's rights and gender equality. It closely cooperates with the still functioning Gender Centers, thus promoting continuous cooperation between the entities.

Cooperation between the entities and strengthening of the state-level through the formation of gender equality institutions contributes importantly to the building of an integrated state. In other policy fields, large differences and lack of coordination between the entities have been a key source of BiH's post-war inertia, with Serb and Croat parties repeatedly blocking cooperation (International Crisis Group, 2001a and b). The cooperation between the entities' Gender Centers, by contrast, are an example of good cooperation. Yet, the majority of political decisions in BiH are still taken at the level of the entities, while the state level remains weak (Bieber, 2006). According to Christophe Solioz (2002: 38), only 20 percent of political decisions were taken at the state-level in 2002; in the meantime, this amount has risen to almost 45 percent (my calculation for April 2007–March 2008, based on Web sites of state-level and entity parliaments).

With the establishment of the Gender Equality Law and the Gender Agency at the state-level emerged another policy field in BiH whose regulation is mainly located at the level of the common state. Even though it is only a small, rather marginalized policy field in the country, it has nevertheless strengthened the state-level as a whole. One of the main causes to establish it at the level of the state and not of the entities was, as in many other policy fields, the influence of the international community. Although it had not requested the formation of these norms and institutions, the initiators of the law, particularly the Bosnian coordinators of GEEP, decided to lift it to the state-level to secure support of the international community. Otherwise, according to the then Director of the FBiH Gender Center, Samra Filipović-Hadžiabdić, the international community would not have taken the initiative seriously.

"For the Dignity of the Survivors"—A Campaign for the Rights of Victims of Sexualized War Violence

The war in BiH was characterized by a high amount of sexualized war violence. The number of women who survived—often multiple—war rapes is still unclear but it is for sure that there are thousands. Equally unknown is the exact number of children born out of these crimes. The situation of the survivors is still precarious. Most rape victims lack adequate healthcare and access to psychosocial support. Many of these women lack sufficient financial support, are unemployed, and have significantly decreased labor capacities as a consequence of trauma. The issue of their accommodation is unresolved as the trauma prevents them from returning to their pre-war places of residence and from filing applications for the return of property. Further, they do not receive any support for the education of their children (Georgievski, 2006).

The legal framework to accommodate the needs of these women is still insufficient. While the Law on Protection of Civilian Victims of War in the RS covered women victims of war, the law in the FBiH until recently did not. There was no law regulating their status as war crime victims, providing them with sustenance, employment, and professional and vocational training; likewise, no such law exists at the state level.

When the Law on Social Protection, Protection of Civilian Victims of War and Families with Children was to be amended in the FBiH, women from different women's organizations and the Gender Center of the FBiH took the opportunity to campaign for the inclusion of women survivors of war rape as a category entitled to claim specific social and other rights following from this law (Georgievski, 2006). The campaign "For the Dignity of the Survivors" demanded the adoption of amendments to the current law to enable women survivors of war trauma to exercise rights set for civil victims of war; in addition, it requested the passing of a respective law at the state-level to integrate and unify entity legislation on the rights of survivors of war torture—including women subjected to sexualized war violence. The campaign began in 2005 and culminated in 2006 on the day of the premiere of Jasmila Zbanić's movie *Grbavica* after it received the Golden Bear award at the International Berlin Film Festival. The movie deals with the life of a single mother and her teenage daughter in contemporary Sarajevo in the aftermath of the systematic war rapes of women. In less than thirty days, women activists collected more than 50,000 signatures at theaters where the movie was broadcast. The campaigners handed them, together with their demands, to the Chairman of the House of Representatives of the FBiH. About three months later, the FBiH Parliament adopted a law on modifications and amendments, including women survivors of war rape as a category entitled to specific social and other legal rights into the law. Yet, the request of passing respective state-level legislation has yet to be met.

The law gave women in the FBiH the chance to apply for recognition as civil victims of the war, entitling them to at least some state support. This not only has significant consequences for these women but also for political and social integration in general. Building a functioning state in a postwar situation requires a population that trusts the new institutions. Already shortly after the war, feminist scholar Ustinia Dolgopol (1997) had warned that shifting the responsibility for dealing with these women from the new governments on to the international community could create a serious problem for integration, "[i]t also means that the emotional and physical consequences of past violations can be ignored by the new government. One wonders what impact that will have on the individuals concerned; their sense of belonging to one country will not be fostered in a situation where their needs are not being addressed by their own government. And if there is no collective sense of belonging, then the peace may not be an enduring one" (p. 61).

The FBiH, given its multinational design, has long struggled with lack of support by its key constituencies. Particularly the Croats have repeatedly criticized the asymmetry of the current system of decentralization, demanding the establishment of a Croat entity mirroring the RS. Similar to the state, the FBiH has never developed a strong institutional identity of its own, and its sustainability remains questionable (Bieber, 2006). The step to integrate women into the legal system of support for war victims may at least improve their trust into these institutions—albeit this trust will still depend on the degree of implementation of the newly adopted legislation.

Conclusions

Women clearly need to be included in peace-building efforts. They not only have the human right to participate equally in the reconstruction of their country, their activities can contribute to the integration of divided postwar states. As demonstrated with the case of postwar BiH, women were among the first who cooperated across the ethnic divide, such as in their struggle for more political participation and representation. Furthermore, feminist reform processes, such as the foundation of the Gender Centers and the Gender Equality Law, contributed to cooperation between the otherwise antagonistic entities and the strengthening of the relatively weak common state level. However, the creation of integrated state structures needs not only institutional engineering but also legitimacy. The trust of the population in their newly created state institutions depends on how much they accommodate the specific needs of population groups violated by the war—as in the case of the inclusion of war rape survivors into the FBiH Law on Social Protection, Protection of Civilian Victims of War and Families with Children.

These integrating effects are all important aspects of the peace process in BiH even if how much they really add to the building of a sustainable peace is hard to assess due to the multiplicity of variables that shape this outcome. So, there are two qualifications following from the above analysis: First, it is not women's activism in general that overcomes ethnic divisions—women all over the world have pursued nationalist, separatist political projects as well as integrative, reconciliatory ones; rather, feminist activism championing women's rights for all women, irrespective of their ethnic or other affiliations, contributes to the transcending of ethnic partition. Second, due to scarcities of resources in postwar states, activities mitigating ethnic divisions require external support. The scope and effect of feminist activism will remain limited until the institutions of formal political power in the country truly embrace the politics of cooperation and postwar reconciliation. Reform processes of women's rights and gender equality often depend on individuals taking up the issues, but without broader institutional support they will not reach very far (Djurić-Kuzmanović, Drezgić, and Žarkov, 2008). Elissa Helms (2003) has argued that women more frequently cooperate across ethnic divides due to specific incentives rather than female traits. Indeed, the integrating effects analyzed here had not been possible without external support by the OSCE and the Finnish government. However, the international community in BiH has long ignored the issue of women's rights and gender equality until after the war, with serious consequences such as increased levels of violence against women. It took a while until these issues became more prominent on its agenda, albeit not in a systematic and sustainable way (Kvinna till Kvinna, 2000; Rees, 2002). But feminists represent important alternative voices within a context of nationalistic politics—a potential that should be utilized.

But an important caution is in order: The demands from reconstruction efforts for gender equity must not become secondary and conditional upon showing positive effects for peace-building. Efficiency-based arguments can be effective as a political strategy for having women's issues taken up by external agencies (Razavi and Miller 1995), but it must not push equity-based arguments aside. Gender equity should always be the primary concern of the promotion of women and their rights in a postwar setting. However, external agencies should simultaneously consider possible peace-building effects of the endeavors for women's rights that they support.

The international community already once failed to recognize the feminist antiwar movement as an alternative force for change during the war in former Yugoslavia, despite its unique attempt in developing elements of a culture of interethnic cooperation and reconciliation in the region (Korac, 2006). It should not miss the chance again and, hence, should continue to increase its support of local initiatives in the field of women's rights and gender equality—in BiH, and beyond.

References

Alić, A. 2008. Bosnian Serbs protest over Kosovo. *ISN Security Watch* (February 22). Available at http://www.isn.ethz.ch/news/sw/details.cfm?id=18677.
Anderlini, S. N. 2007. *Women building peace: What they do, why it matters.* Boulder, CO: Lynne Rienner.
Andjelic, N. 2003. *Bosnia-Herzegovina: The end of a legacy.* London: Routledge.
Bieber, F. 2006. *Post-war Bosnia: Ethnicity, inequality and public sector governance.* Basingstoke, UK: Palgrave Macmillan.
Borić, B. 2004. *Application of quotas: Legal reforms and implementation in Bosnia and Herzegovina.* Paper presented at the International Institute for Democracy and Electoral Assistance (IDEA)/CEE Network for

Gender Issues Conference, The Implementation of Quotas: European Perspectives (October): Budapest.
Bose, S. 2002. *Bosnia after Dayton: Nationalist partition and international intervention.* London: C. Hurst.
Burg, S. L. and P. S. Shoup. 1999. *The war in Bosnia and Herzegovina: Ethnic conflict and international intervention.* Amronk, NY: M. E. Sharpe.
Chinkin, C. and H. Charlesworth. 2006. Building women into peace: The international legal framework. *Third World Quarterly* 27 (5): 937–957.
Cockburn, C. 1998. *The space between us: Negotiating gender and national identities in conflict.* London: Zed Books.
———. 2007. *From where we stand: War, women's activism and feminist analysis.* London: Zed Books.
Commission of the European Communities. 2007. *Communication from the Commission to the European Parliament and the Council: Enlargement Strategy and Main Challenges 2007–2008.* COM (2007) 663 final, Brussels.
Djurić-Kuzmanović, T., R. Drezgić, and D. Žarkov. 2008. Gendered war, Gendered Peace: Violent conflicts in the Balkans and their consequences. In *Gendered peace: Women's struggles for post-war justice and reconciliation,* ed. D. Pankhurst, 265–291. New York: Taylor & Francis.
Dolgopol, U. 1997. A feminist appraisal of the Dayton Peace accords. *Adelaide Law Review* 19: 59–71.
GEEP. 2006. *Gender equity and equality project completion report.* Sarajevo: unpublished.
Georgievski, D. 2006. For dignity of the survivors campaign launched. *OneWorld South East Europe* (March 8). Available at http://see.oneworld.net/article/view/128961/1/.
Global Rights. 2004. *Shadow report on the implementation of CEDAW and women's human rights in Bosnia and Herzegovina.* Sarajevo: Global Rights.
Handrahan, L. 2004. Conflict, gender, ethnicity and post-conflict reconstruction. *Security Dialogue* 35 (4): 429–445.
Helms, E. 2003. Women as agents of ethnic reconciliation? Women's NGOs and international intervention in postwar Bosnia-Herzegovina. *Women's Studies International Forum* 26 (1): 15–33.
International Crisis Group. 2001a. The wages of sin: Confronting Bosnia's Republika Srpska. *Europe Report* 118 (October), Sarajevo: ICG.
———. 2001b. Turning strife to advantage: A blueprint to integrate the Croats in Bosnia and Herzegovina. *Europe Report* 106 (March), Sarajevo: ICG.
Jenichen, A. 2009. Multi-level advocacy networks in post-war settings: The case of the gender quota in Bosnia and Herzegovina. In *Gender dynamics in violent conflicts,* ed. C. Eifler and R. Seifert, 93–113. Frankfurt: Peter Lang.
Korac, M. 2006. Gender, conflict and peace-building: Lessons from the conflict in the former Yugoslavia. *Women's Studies International Forum* 29 (5): 510–520.

Kvinna till Kvinna. 2000. *Engendering the peace process. A gender approach to Dayton—and beyond*. Stockholm, Sweden: Kvinna till Kvinna.

———. 2006. *To make room for changes—Peace strategies from women Organisations in Bosnia and Herzegovina*. Johanneshov, Sweden: Kvinna till Kvinna.

Manning, C., and A. Miljenko. 2003. Lessons from Bosnia: The limits of electoral engineering. *Journal of Democracy* 14 (3): 45–60.

Mladjenovic, L. 2002. Caring at the same time: On feminist politics during the NATO bombing of the Federal Republic of Yugoslavia and the ethnic cleansing of Albanians in Kosovo, 1999. In *The aftermath: Women in post-conflict transformation*, ed. S. Meintjes, A. Pillay, and M. Turshen, 172–188. London: Palgrave Macmillan.

Nordlund, A.T. 2003. International implementation of electoral gender quotas in the Balkans: A fact-finding report. *Working Paper Series of the Research Program on Gender Quotas* 1, Stockholm University.

Oberschall, A. 2000. The manipulation of ethnicity: From ethnic cooperation to violence and war in Yugoslavia. *Ethnic and Racial Studies* 23 (6): 982–1001.

Oosterveld, V. 2005. Prosecution of gender-based crimes in international law. In *Gender, conflict, and peacekeeping*, ed. D. E. Mazurana, A. Raven-Roberts, and J. L. Parpart, 67–82. Lanham, MD: Rowman and Littlefield.

Pankhurst, D. 2008. Introduction. In *Gendered peace: Women's struggles for post-war justice and reconciliation*, ed. D. Pankhurst, 1–30. New York: Taylor and Francis.

Razavi, S. and C. Miller. 1995. *From WID to GAD: Conceptual shifts in the women and development discourse*. Occasional Paper, 1 (February), Geneva: UNRISD.

Rees, M. 2002. International intervention in Bosnia-Herzegovina: The cost of ignoring Gender. In *The postwar moment: Militaries, masculinities and international peacekeeping*, ed. C. Cockburn and D. Zarkov, 51–67. London: Lawrence and Wishart.

Rehn, E. and E. J. Sirleaf. 2002. *Women, war and peace: The independent experts' assessment on the impact of armed conflict on women and women's role in peace-building*. New York: UNIFEM.

Seifert, R. 1996. The second front. The logic of sexual violence in wars. *Women's Studies International Forum* 19 (1–2): 35–43.

Solioz, C. 2002. Bosnien und Herzegowina zwischen Abhängigkeit und Selbstverantwortung (Bosnia and Herzegovina between dependence and self-determination). *Südosteuropa Mitteilungen* 42 (4): 36–44.

Sørensen, B. 1998. *Women and post-conflict reconstruction: Issues and sources*. Occasional Paper 3 (June), Geneva: UNRISD.

Strickland, R. and N. Duvvury. 2003. *Gender equity and peace-building: From rhetoric to reality: Finding the way. A discussion paper*. Washington, DC: International Center for Research on Women.

UNDP BiH. 2007. *Early warning system. Annual Report 2007*. Sarajevo: UNDP.

United Nations. 2002. *Women, peace and security. Study submitted by the Secretary-General pursuant to Security Council resolution 1325 (2000).* New York: U.N.

Ward, J. and Marsh, M. 2006. *Sexual violence against women and girls in war and its aftermath: Realities, responses, and required resources.* A briefing paper prepared for Symposium on Sexual Violence in Conflict and Beyond, 21–23. Brussels: UNFPA.

Yuval-Davis, N. 1997. *Gender and nation.* London: Sage.

9

PEACE IS THE NAME OF AN UNBORN CHILD IN TURKEY

Simten Coşar

In Turkey, as elsewhere, structural violence characterizes politics and everyday life. Institutional power structures, along with mainstream media, reproduce, reinforce, and normalize violence by emphasizing survival of the Turkish state. Because women from all walks of life are the major subjects of this violence, feminist antimilitarist activists and organizations stand as the main reference points in the search for an alternative understanding of politics that privileges not killing and war, but life and peaceful coexistence. This chapter analyzes feminist struggles against structural violence in Turkey, focusing on those aspects that emphasize structural peace. It is based on my in-depth, semistructured interviews with Turkish sociologist and activist Pınar Selek, taken as the modal example of feminist antimilitarist activism. Selek, the author of several books focusing on issues of peace and war in Turkey (Selek, 2001/2007; Selek, 2004, Selek, 2008), is the founding member of *Amargi Kadın Kooperatifi* (Amargi Women's Cooperative), a feminist collective, and she participates in the editorial board of the cooperative's journal, *Amargi*.

BETWEEN SULTANIC AND REPUBLICAN VERSIONS OF PATRIARCHY: TURKISH WOMEN'S MOVEMENT

Tracing the women's movement in Turkey, the underlying context between when the (Ottoman) Empire dissolved and the (Turkish) nation-state was constructed needs be considered. It is also essential that republican ideology is regarded, as the major frame of reference for understanding how the nation and *its* state were imagined, and the place accorded to women in this imagination since it functioned as the dominant mode of nation-state construction, with roots in the late nineteenth century. Briefly, modernization first emerged as a major topic in the Ottoman-Turkish political agenda in the *Tanzimat* era (1839–1876), characterized with continuous attempts on the part of the Ottoman ruling elite to come to terms with the "West" (mainly, Continental Europe) in the face of defeats on the battlefield. Then, the decline of the Empire led to the flowering of discussions on alternative routes to modernization.

In the course of these developments, three strands of coming to terms with the West gained prominence: First, the Islamist version, after futile attempts to search for compatibility between the "modern" and the "Islamic," represented the rejectionary attitude toward anything deemed modern—that is, the "Western." As its polar opposite, the Westernist version argued for all-out Westernization: modernizing first the state, then the society. Lastly, the Turkist version, which emerged relatively late, opted for a synthesizing formula between the West and the "Ottoman"; in this synthesizing formula, not the Ottoman but the "Turk" was preferred as the new code for identity construction (Berkes, 1964).

In all three approaches, women's bodies and social status were utilized as symbols that attested either how civilized the Ottoman-Turkish society was, or the chastity, honor, and the quintessence of Ottoman-Muslim-Turkish society, or both. Westernists and Turkists shared the contention that, under the influence of Islamic-Ottoman tradition, it was difficult to have an image of a civilized society. The forerunners and supporters of both strands were also convinced that women's physical appearance in public life would evince the civilized nature of Ottoman-Turkish society. Besides, civilization would ensure women's emancipation, or equality with men before the law (Kadıoğlu, 1998; Sirman; 1989; Kandiyoti, 1987).

The Turkist formula provided a frame around which the new Republic was founded. The leading cadres of the National Independence War (1919–1922), the founding *fathers* of the Republican regime, were well informed of Turkist ideology—inspired from the ideas of the forefather of Turkish nationalism, Ziya Gökalp (1876–1924) (Berkes, 1959), for whom pacifism (*sulhseverlik*) was one of the central tenets; Gökalp (1972: 147) emphasized the revelation of heroic capacities—mainly, inborn and physical—for men to prove their maturity in public, and noted that in Turkish society "women...were generally amazons." The formula on sociopolitical militarization throughout the Republican history manifests itself in the construction of soldiering as an "ahistorical...[and]...unquestionable fact" (Altınay, 2007: 114–115).

Although discussions of modernization and nationalization in Ottoman-Turkish polity were carried by male intellectuals, by the late nineteenth-century women began to engage in the discussions concerning their emancipation (Yaraman, 2001; Çakır, 1996). In intellectual circles, pious associations, organizations, demanding women's education and employment, women worked to reverse the imperial decline (Çakır, 1996), and by the end of the century, the bulk of these organizations were articulated into the rising tide of the nationalist movement (Kandiyoti, 1991). Defining feminism as one of the central tenets of Turkishness, Gökalp (1972: 153) argued that

> the ideal of feminism arose simultaneously with the rise of Turkist movement. The reason behind the populism and womanism of the Turkists is not the value given to these two ideals in contemporary age; the fact that democracy and feminism were the two essential principles [of Turkishness] has a significant role in this. [Author's translation]

Thus, women's voices for equality were absorbed into the discourse of national salvation and nation-state construction. In parallel, women's demands for public visibility soon met with the sine qua non of a war-torn context: During World War I, Ottoman women increasingly gained a hand in economic life due to labor shortage, participating in the National Independence War as support actors. This state of affairs opened the way for the transformation of gender dynamics in the coming decades (Y. Arat, 1994), while nationalizing women's demands and women's movement. Women's organized voice, asking for equality in the socioeconomic sphere, gradually evolved into a stance for political equality. Yet, Durakbaşa (1998: 140) argued that Republican reforms retained the "Patriarchal norms of morality and...maintained the basic cultural conservatism about male/female relations."

This state of affairs is not surprising, when one recalls the construction of gender typologies in nationalist movements in general, and in nationalist struggles in the "Third World" in particular (Jayawardena, 1986). And, while Turkish nationalist struggles involved a modernizing spirit, women's chastity was perceived to symbolize the preservation of national authenticity vis-á-vis the highly possible polluting effects of modernization. Thus, its nation-state construction involved dualities: While the aim was modernization, calling for the adoption of "Western style" in politics and, eventually, in daily life, nationalists have always been on guard to preserve genuinely national attributes against the threat of foreign infiltration. Women, perceived as objects of modernization and as symbols of the authenticity of Turkish national identity (Kadıoğlu, 1998) were eventually subjected to strict control over their bodies and, thus, to a strict code of conduct. First and foremost imagined as the mothers and wives, in both private and public spheres, women of the new Republic were occasionally referred to as potential heroines. The most significant political and legal measures, including the unification of education (1924), the 1926 Civil Code, the right to participate in local elections (1930), and in general elections (1934), "were seen as tools for national development...rather than as means that would enable [the women] to develop individual...or...collective consciousness" (Z. Arat, 1994: 59). In such a setting women's organizational capacities were articulated into the nationalist credo.

In her analysis of the primary school textbooks throughout the Republican history (1928–2000), Tuba Kancı (2007) documents the connection between nationalization, militarization, and modernization in Turkish polity and society, tracing the continuity of the militarist discourse through seven decades with different facets. Four factors seem to be constant: emphasis on the soldierly nature of the Turks, sanctity of the homeland and the necessity of protecting it, and the continuous construction of enemies of the Turks and, thus, the homeland—though under different names; and lastly, representation of the military as "a school" for civic consciousness, civilized manners, and manliness. In this reproduction process, violence has been naturalized while, at the same time, alienated to Turkishness. As a quotation from a fifth grade textbook illustrates, the Gökalpian formula of the coexistence of peacefulness with warriorship was retained:

> Turks...knew how to kill and die when they were fighting. Outside the war and in their country they were never murderers. The hand of Turk, which uses the sword with extensive skill, is also skillful in healing the wounds of the people it has defeated (cited in Kancı, 2007: 255).

Militarist sociopolitical structuring was not peculiar to the Turkish experience. Nor was its entwining with capitalism, nationalism, and patriarchy (Jayawardena, 1986). The organic connection between nationalism and militarism fit well into an alliance with capitalism as the central constituents of what Peterson (1992: 32) calls "interlocking systems of hierarchy and domination." Different modes of patriarchy crosscut this structure of alliance: In the Ottoman-Turkish context, it was transformed from a sultanic to a Republican setting (Berktay, 2001), and has evolved in accordance with nationalist priorities.

In addition to wifehood and motherhood, Altınay (2007: 119–120) adds a third category portrayed as a version of the ideal model of Republican womanhood: the warrior. Not necessarily in contradiction, it requires abstention from other roles in that it involves a masculinized state of being; while holding onto the image of the nation's motherhood, this third category asks for a self-sacrificing attitude from the women in their essential roles, for participation in the manly endeavor of war-making, and/or it asks for sacrifice of their primary roles if they have the will for taking part in war-making and/or defense business. Thus, it can be argued that the Republican woman was imagined in a bifurcated identity. Underlying this bifurcation was the aim to establish control over women sexually and, thus, politically.

Ayşegül Yaraman (2001) classifies the development of the women's movement in Turkey into two periods on the basis of women's demands: The first phase, characterized by demands for equality with men, ends by the 1980s; and the second phase is characterized by demands for "equality with differences." In the second phase, women activists started to form woman-only circles in which they took issue with patriarchy in private and public spheres, organizing around "nonhierarchical and independent... organizations, issue-oriented ad hoc committees" (Sirman, 1989: 15). Taking inspiration from Western feminism, the women's movement included issues of sexual freedom, sexual harassment, rape, battering, and discrimination at the workplace into its vocabulary (Bora and Günal, 2002). In the meantime, women's rights organizations multiplied in number, at times crosscutting each other with respect to their spheres of action.

The deepening of the feminist outlook and the extension of issues culminated in significant achievements in recent legal regulations. Most recent examples are the feminist touch on the amendments to the Turkish Civil Code (2001) and the Turkish Penal Code (2004). However, despite this step forward, the "good old" ideological cleavages continue to have their reflections—such as between Kemalist feminists and Islamic/Muslim feminists. Increasing in its intensity with controversies over the ban on the headscarf—wearing them in public institutions, including educational institutions, this cleavage symbolizes one of the most significant fault lines. Briefly, the controversy stems from and continues with the discussion over secularization. For Kemalist feminists, reforms of the early-Republican era, including the dress code that banned wearing religious clothes in public, is the sine qua non for women's liberation; thus, they view those Muslim women who wear headscarves in public as unenlightened women who have no sense of gender equality. For Islamic/Muslim feminists, the ban on wearing religious clothes in public is nothing but a violation of one basic human right, freedom of religion and conscience.

Likewise is the Kurdish issue, which has been one of the most controversial political problems in Turkish political history—another fault line in the movement. The problem has increasingly occupied the agenda since the mid-1980s, when it turned into systematic armed struggle between the *Türk Silahlı Kuvvetleri* (Turkish Armed Forces, TSK) and the Kurdistan Workers' Party (PKK). Similar to the headscarf issue, the Kurdish issue, too, is yet unresolved, causing divisions within the women's movement along ethnic/nationalist lines. The women's movement got its share in this cleavage, too, as nationalist feminists regard Kurdish women activists who ask for cultural rights as separatists aiming at destroying the "indivisible unity of the Turkish state with its nation." Kurdish women activists and feminists regard this approach containing oppression: Deprivation from cultural rights through denial and the accusation stated above as a vital human rights violation. What is especially telling is that neither in the headscarf nor in the Kurdish issue, peace is considered as a categorical principle in the discussions on the resolution of these problems.

In the case of the Kurdish issue, among the parties to the controversy in the women's movement, concern with justifying resort to violence dominated the agenda—either based on the cause of (Turkish) nation's (read: state) survival or survival of the "oppressed" (the Kurdish people). In other words, the issue of peace has proved to be the most delayed theme for which the women/feminist activists took their time to discuss and act upon. In some rare instances where women from within the movement organized around a concern for peace, the attempts have, so far, proved to be sporadic and short lasting.

Searching for Peace in a Militarist Setting

The official understanding of peace in Republican Turkey has fit well into the Gökalpian formula, symbolized in the words attributed to Mustafa Kemal Atatürk, the founding president of the Republic:

> We are a military-nation. From ages seven to seventy, women and men alike, we have been created as soldiers. However, our understanding

of soldiering has nothing to do with imperialism (Cited in Altınay, 2004: 40).

The place of a nation, soldiering for the sake of peace, is beside the peace flag (Cited in Altınay, 2007: 124.) [Author's translation]

This approach to peace, which does not consider militarization in contradiction with peace, and which flirts with war as a means for the maintenance of peace, not only marked the official discourse but also has established its hegemony in the political discourse of the pro-peace opposition throughout Republican history. This hegemony has been reflected not only in the late coming and short lifespans of organizations, which were formed in the name of peace, but also in the fact that there has not been a categorical rejection of war(s), until recently. In her 2004 book, Barışamadık (*We Could Not Make Peace*), dealing with the absence of the culture of peace in Turkey, Pınar Selek documents the history of peace movement in Turkey. Starting with Barışseverler Cemiyeti (Association of Pacifists, BC, 1950), and continuing with *Barış Derneği* (Peace Association, BD, 1965–1968), and then *Türkiye Barış Derneği* (Peace Association of Turkey, TBD, 1977–1980), she examines the development of the concern for peace, as well as the nature of this concern. All three attempts to organize in the name of peace could not survive for long.

All three organizations shared a leftist heritage, and a rather delimited understanding of peace. Selek has noted that, in their declarations and publications, peace is understood not as a categorical principle but as an aim that can be achieved by dissolution of the capitalist system. Likewise, war in general is not totally denied: The organizations legitimized war and violence in the name of peace. Additionally, it is possible to observe a leftist/anti-imperialist version of nationalism in the organizations which, among other drawbacks, led to the disregard of exclusion and oppression of ethnic and social differences in Turkey. Worse still, the associations at times internalized the official nationalist discourse in their approach to conflicts over Turkish identity. Thus, as Selek sees it, attempts for organizing around peace could not suffice to lay the foundations of a peace movement that would problematize violence at micro and macro levels. Unsurprisingly, this limited approach was directly related to the absence of a feminist concern.

The problematization of nationalism, militarism, and war entered the agenda of pro-peace initiatives as late as the 1990s. By the first instances of conscientious objection, initial steps for organizing around an antimilitarist stance began. While antimilitarist and antiwar organizational activities have, so far, been carried out mainly by anarchist groups, public recognition of antimilitarist and pro-peace organizations has been insufficient to manipulate the political agenda. On the contrary, they have been cast out of the political space either by means of dismissal of their demands and discourse or through the accusation of treason—especially, in the case of conscientious objection. What is more important is that the attempts to connect feminism with antimilitarism and antiwar initiatives have proven to be marginal in antimilitarist organizations, in the women's movement, and in the wider political sphere.

Recently, a new initiative in the name of peace, concentrating on the Kurdish issue, was launched. Calling themselves *Türkiye Barış Meclisi* (The Peace Assembly of Turkey, TBM, 2007), the members have organized meetings and issued declarations asking for an unconditional ceasefire, as well as touching upon various aspects of structural violence, extending from violence against women to economic deprivation of the lower classes under the neoliberal economic programs. Although feminist activists are included in the TBM, it is apt to consider the integration of the feminist voice into the discourse of the TBM with reference to the liberal add-and-stir formula. Selek, in our 2008 interview, argues that because the assembly is too young, and because it aims to combine different political stances within its body, "It has a complicated structure," which eventually necessitates a party-like structure; for her, this necessity involves the risk of endangering the feminist touch on peace because it asks for bureaucratic styles in political activity. At this stage, it might be argued that in Turkey there has been a historical disconnection between pro-peace activism and antimilitarist organizations on the one hand, feminism on the other.

Peace at Home, Peace in Politics

In the Turkish women's movement, the dominant struggle against violence has been restricted to the issue of domestic violence. In this respect, the women's rights activists proved to be effective in the legal amendments that improved the protective measures for women who are subject to gender based violence. For example, the pressure by the women's movement is one of the main factors that led the governing Justice and Development Party (JDP) to introduce amendments to Turkish Penal Code (2004), which increased the penalties for gender based violence. Likewise, the law that was enacted by the same government (2004) made it compulsory for the municipalities whose population exceeds 50,000 to open shelters for women who are subjected to violence. Women's rights organizations have also been active in media monitoring to combat the normalization of violence through mass media. Since 2006, a feminist group, called Media Monitoring Group (MED-İZ) has been regularly monitoring the media, and publicizing those programs, advertisements and the news, which promote violence. Still, the problematization of militarist culture has not had significant appeal. In general, attempts among feminists to organize around the claim for peace have proved to be short lived, marginal, which is related to two factors: First, as noted above, due to the dominant conception of peace and the fact that violence has been a constant part of the political system in Turkey; second, peace has long been understood in line with the official discourse within the women's movement—that is, part and parcel of what Cady (quoted in Ruddick, 1993: 113) calls "Warism...the belief that war is morally justified in principle and often justified in fact." In this respect, women activists and/or feminists who attempted to form pro-peace organizations and initiatives either internalized the official discourse or experienced a double marginalization in terms of their stance as both feminists and "pacifists."

One such instance was *Barış için Sürekli Kadın Platformu* (BSKP, Women's Permanent Platform for Peace), formed in 2001 by a number of women's rights organizations, a lesbian initiative, women activists from human rights organizations, and leftist political parties. In its foundational manifesto, the platform openly argued for the connection between feminism and antimilitarism, offering structural peace as its basis. The platform announced its raison d'être as working for "expressing women's perspective and women's demands in the maintenance of permanent peace, personally, in the organizations, in society and in the world" (BSKP, n.d.) It might be argued that, while human rights activism formed the grounds for the formation of the group, women's direct experience of violence was posited as the essence of why to work for peace. In this respect, connecting violence at home with violence in politics can be cited as a major progressive step that marked the platform within the women's and peace movements. It had a patchwork character, which may be one of the reasons behind its short lifespan of three years.

A significant development is Women's Center (KAMER). The Center was established in 1997 and rapidly expanded to twenty-three Eastern and Southeastern provinces of Turkey. The Center has struggled against gender based violence, linking domestic violence with political and socioeconomic violence. The starting point for the founding activists was the struggle against the violence that stemmed from the political tension in Southeastern Turkey due to the armed conflict between the TAF and the PKK. Through time the Center increasingly focused on domestic violence as the point of departure to eliminate structural violence. KAMER is also significant in that it provides avenue for the women discover the connections between different forms of violence to self-questioning (http://www.kamer.org.tr/content.asp?c_id=278, 2009; Altınay, 2007).

Just when BSKP started its activities, a new women's organization was founded in İstanbul connecting the concern for peace at home with peace in the streets and in politics. Among the mentors behind the formation of the cooperative were prominent Turkish feminists like Pınar Selek and Aksu Bora. Amargi Women's Cooperative was initiated by a number of feminists with the aim of deconstructing patriarchy by "Developing the possibilities for the entwined institutionalization of academic knowledge, life, and politics" for liberation from violence (Amargi, n.d.). The cooperative is still too young to arrive at a decisive conclusion regarding its performance in formulating and internalizing an alternative discourse that runs counter to the established masculine and militarist discourse, but it is encouraging.

Women's activism has long been perceived as a way out of the dominant masculinist, militarist discourse in feminist literature on politics. In this reading, women, due to their inborn traits or due to their socialization, are supposed to be endowed with a capacity conducive to a peaceful state and to the resolution of problems by nonviolent means. However, at the current stage of feminist literature, the conviction that womanhood is, in itself, a sufficient starting point for seeking structural peace is at best dubious (Segal, 2008). Jean Said Makdisi (2008: 106–107) points out:

> Indira Gandhi, Benazir Butto, Margaret Thatcher, Golda Meir, Madeleine Albright and Condoleeza Rice as...powerful women [who] have merely lent their faces to disguise a brutally oppressive world system, to symbolize the fictional progress of democratic human relations, and above all to put a friendly, maternal, feminine face on the dark and deadly reality of wars of aggression and their legitimization.

Amargi was founded, and has so far functioned on the basic need of going beyond women's natural and/or socially acquired traits. While taking their experience with violence as the starting point, the cooperative aims at alternative discourses to counter masculinist/militarist discursive practices that have dominated domestic and international politics. In so doing, it differentiates itself not only from mainstream tendencies in the women's movement but also from pacifist and/ or antiwar organizations. This search for an alternative discourse is reflected in the horizontal organization of the cooperative, which has no Executive Committee or Board but an egalitarian distribution of responsibility and decision-making powers among members. Emphasis is on open criticism and reflexivity in deeds and arguments of all members, and in the care taken to integrate differences that cut across Turkey. It not only aims at struggling against violence at the level of institutional politics but also functions as a platform of learning to deconstruct and transgress the reflections of hegemonic discourse on peace in the daily lives of its members.

However, it is hard to imagine and reflect on peace in the nation-state setting. For, as is clear by now, nation-states are built on wars and nationalism (Poggi, 2001; Tilly, 1985). As elaborated in the Turkish case, and other nation-states, nationalism involves militarism not only at the state level but also at the societal. The founding manifesto of Amargi is telling, rejecting basic structural level features through which nation-states are reproduced: Patriarchy, power, private property, masculine discipline, male dominance, rejection and/or exclusion of differences (Amargi, n.d.)

CAN ONE CONCLUDE WITHOUT PEACE?

There is no doubt that peace is an unborn child in Turkey. It is also certain that none of the conventional approaches to peace, war, and security is sufficient to propose ultimate formulas for the constitution of peace in structural terms. Also, in a country where military expenditures are significantly high (between 1988 and 2007, military expenditure per population in Turkey accelerated from the already high amount of, in U.S. dollars, $6,989 to $11,066 (SIPRI, 2007), one has to *dare* to speak up for peace. Although the increase in the total amount of military expenditure corresponds to a decrease in the ratio of military spending to GDP (SIPRI, 2007), the fact that nationalism and militarism are the overwhelming themes in educational policy, starting from the primary school (Kancı, 2007) makes the pacifist task more difficult.

Pınar Selek is one of those women who could dare, and who still dares, to speak up for peace, despite the risk of being accused of treason, imprisonment, and exclusion at the sociopolitical level. Her personal and political history documents both militarism, established deep down in the political structure, and her individual and collective endeavors are attempts to peaceful coexistence that transgresses the official discourse and its everyday reflections. In this respect, her involvement with the outcasts or marginals of the society—street children, transvestites and transsexuals who earn their lives from prostitution—is telling. Her concern with these groups was shaped both by her academic tendencies, as a sociologist, and out of her pro-peace stance, which culminated in what was called the "street workshop." Participants produced artistic work out of garbage, staged theatrical performance, and published a journal: *The Guest*. Street workshop can be considered as an extension of the search for finding an alternative discursive practice that can get different, at times mutually hostile people together on collective platforms of action. The idea behind this practice also fits into the style of functioning in Amargi, which prioritizes collective production and transcending one's state of being in the course of production. It might also be connected to the principle of acting, rather than protesting. What Selek and the other participants of the street workshop revealed was the capacity of people with different mediums of communication to achieve a common platform for action through collective production. This experiment in transforming daily life might also be considered in relation to one of the principles in the cooperative's manifesto: "Life is the most important academic occupation." Academic activity, in this instance, corresponds to reflecting on one's acts and learning through action.

Apart from meetings focusing on feminist perspectives for understanding the interlocking facets of violence in everyday life and institutional politics, the quarterly *Amargi* offers an outlet for developing connections between gendered violence and militarism. Issues are organized on a thematic basis, selected with a view to topics ingrained in women's lives—such as headscarf issue, militarism, project-oriented activism in the women's movement, the way violence has been perceived in women's movement in Turkey, poverty, citizenship, socio-economic policies of the government, ethics, women and interactions, and women and local politics. In this respect, the journal hosts pieces that analyze micro and macro reflections.

Selek's choices in her individual and collective engagements have not been different from the principles of the cooperative: Theorizing through practice, and practice through reflection on liberation. If her work with the outcasts in the street workshop led her to approach the issue of freedom as a process where one finds herself in cooperation with "others," her research on PKK members was pushed with a concern for understanding the other side of the coin to reveal how state violence is reproduced and how it reproduces counterviolence, by "deciphering the memory of rebellions" against the nation-state construction. As she was approaching the end of her research, Selek has been subjected to first physical and then continuously psychological violence for more than a decade on the grounds of collaboration with PKK. The torture that she was subjected to under interrogation led her to reflect on how to struggle "with the evil, and not with the wicked" (Selek interview, 2008) that, in turn, opened the way for a comprehensive documentary on peace movement in Turkey (Selek, 2004). (In Spring 2009 Court of Appeals overruled the verdict of acquittal and sued thirty six years long imprisonment for involvement in terrorist activities. In February 2010 it decided for life sentence. For protests against the recent developments and support for Selek see http://www.pinarselek.com)

In her letter responding to the question "how to prevent war," Virginia Woolf (1938/1991) pointed at sociopolitical inequality between women and men as the reason behind different conceptualizations of war and peace. Woolf admitted that—despite some exceptions—men are more war-prone than women. She called women "outsiders," hinting at the necessity and indispensability of rising voices against war from a different— that is, a women's—discourse. Certainly, compared to early twentieth century Britain, contemporary Turkish women's sociopolitical status has reached to a more balanced level, at least in legal terms. However, the discourse of "the Outsiders' Society" has yet to be established. Likewise, asking for structural peace is still outside the margins of the dominant political discourse. This state of affairs asks for cooperation among those subjected to different levels of systematic violence.

Selek's individual and collective engagements, as well as organizations like *Amargi*, offer reasons for both hope and pessimism. Hope lies in the working of the cooperative, in its activities ranging from workshops for awareness-raising to liberation from violence in everyday practices of women; further, the cooperative has value for academics on different facets of the practice of violence in "outsider's" lives, demonstrating against the exclusion of and oppression on "others" of the nation-state. In these cases, it is possible to observe attempts to form connections between different levels of structural violence with the contention that domestic violence against women, violence against those who stand against established gender norms, and violence in the form of armed struggle all feed and reproduce each other. Pessimism, on the other hand, lies in the fact that the (nation-)state still has the forceful means to silence attempts for the construction of peace. This pessimism becomes all the more prevalent when one recalls the fact that organizations and activists forming connections between antimilitarism and feminism stay on the margins of the women's movement in Turkey. Today, the movement has come to a crossroads. On the one hand, its effectiveness in public policy making and public recognition has increased in the past two decades; on the other hand, the traditional cleavages still persist within the movement. In this respect, transcending crossroads for undoing the pervasiveness of nationalism and militarism in the women's movement for a world in which peace prevails, requires the extension of feminist antimilitarist principles. And, so long as activists like Pınar Selek and organizations like *Amargi* persist in their endeavors to search for an alternative discourse of freedom, the possibility for what Selek (2008 interview) terms "the problematization of the current masculine civilization and the imagination of a counter civilization" seems to increase.

REFERENCES

Altınay, A. 2004. *The myth of the military-nation: Militarism, gender, and education in Turkey.* New York: Palgrave Macmillan.

———. 2007. Künye bellemeyen kezbanlar: Kadın vicdani redçiler neyi reddediyorlar? (The Kezbans: What do the women conscientious objectors reject?) In Çarklardaki kum: Vicdani red (Sand in the wheels: Conscientious objection), ed. O. H. Çınar and C. Üsterci, 113–133. İstanbul: İletişim.

———. (16 September 2007). Damlaydı, okyanus oluyor (Once it was a drop, now it is becoming an ocean). *Radikal2*

Arat, Y. 1994. Toward a democratic society: The women's movement in Turkey in the 1980s. *Women's Studies International Forum* 17 (2–3): 241–248.

Arat, Z. 1994. Turkish women and the republican construction of tradition. In *Reconstructing gender in the Middle East: Tradition, identity and power*, ed. F. M. Göçek and S. Balaghi, 56–78. New York: Columbia University Press.

Berkes, N. (ed. and trans.). (1959). *Turkish nationalism and Western civilization: Selected essays of Ziya Gökalp.* Westport, Connecticut: Greenwood Press, Publishers.

Berkes, N. 1964. *The development of secularism in Turkey.* Montreal: McGill University Press.

Berktay, F. (2001). Osmanlı'dan Cumhuriyet'e feminism (Feminism from Ottoman Empire to the Republic). In *Modern Türkiye'de siyasi düşünce: Tanzimat ve Meşrutiyet'in birikimi (Political thought in modern Turkey: The accumulation of Tanzimat and Constitutional Era)*, ed. M. Ö. Alkan, 348–361. İstanbul: İletişim.

Bora, A, and A. Günal. eds. 2002. *'90'larda Türkiye'de feminism* (Feminism in the '90s in Turkey). İstanbul: İletişim.
Çakır, S. 1996. *Osmanlı kadın hareketi* (Ottoman women's movement), 2nd ed. İstanbul: Metis.
Durakbaşa A. 1998. Kemalism as identity politics in Turkey. In *Deconstructing images of "The Turkish woman,"* ed. Z. F. Arat, 139–155. New York: St. Martin's Press.
Gökalp, Z. 1972. *Türkçülüğün esasları* (Principles of Turkism). 9th ed. İstanbul: Varlık.
Jayawardena, K. 1986. *Feminism and Nationalism in the Third World.* London: Zed Books.
Kadıoğlu, A. 1998. Cinselliğin ınkârı: Büyük toplumsal projelerın nesnesı olarak Türk kadınları (The denial of sexuality: Turkish women as the object of grand social projects). In *Bilanço '98, 75 yılda kadınlar ve erkekler* (Balance Sheet '98, Women and Men in 75 Years), ed. A. Berktay-Hacımirzaoğlu, 89–100. İstanbul: Tarih Vakfı Yayınları.
Kancı, T. 2007. *Imagining the Turkish men and women: Nationalism, modernism and militarism in primary school textbooks, 1928–2000.* Unpublished Ph.D. thesis. İstanbul: Sabancı University.
Kandiyoti, D. 1987. Emancipated but unliberated? Reflections on the Turkish case. *Feminist Studies* 13 (1): 317–338.
———. 1991. End of empire: Islam, nationalism and women in Turkey. *Woman, Islam and The State.* Philadelphia, PA: Temple University Press: 22–47.
———. 1995. Ataerkil orüntüler: Türk toplumunda erkek egemenliğinin cözümlenmesine yönelik notlar (Patriarchal patterns: Notes on the analysis of male dominance in Turkish society). In *1980'ler Türkiyesi'nde kadın bakış açısından kadınlar* (Women from the women's perspectives in 1980s Turkey), ed. S. Tekeli, 367–382. İstanbul: İletişim.
KAMER'n feminizmi (KAMER's feminism) (2009). KAMER Foundation Official Website: http://www.kamer.org.tr.
Makdisi, J. S. 2008. War and peace: Reflections of a feminist. *Feminist Review* (88): 99–110.
Peterson, S. V. 1992. Security and sovereign states: What is at stake in taking feminism seriously. In *Gendered states: Feminist (re)visions of international relations theory,* ed. S. V. Peterson, 32–64. Boulder, CO: Lynne Reiner.
Poggi, G. 2001. *Forms of power.* Cambridge, UK: Polity Press.
Ruddick, S. 1993. Notes toward a feminist peace politics. In *Gendering war talk,* ed. M. Cooke and A. Woollacott, 196–214. Princeton, NJ: Princeton University Press.
Segal, L. 2008. Gender, war and militarism: Making and questioning the Links. *Feminist Review* (88): 21–35.
Selek, P. 2001/2007. *Maskeler, süvariler, gacılar* (The masks, cavalriers and gacıs), 2nd ed. İstanbul: İstiklal.

Selek, P. 2004. *Barışamadık* (We could not make peace). İstanbul: İthaki.
———. 2008. *Sürüne sürüne erkek olmak* (Becoming man by creeping). İstanbul: İletişim.
The SIPRI military expenditure database (2007). Available at http://first.sipri.org/search?country=TUR&dataset=military-expenditure.
Sirman, N. 1989. Feminism in Turkey: A short history. *New Perspectives on Turkey* 3 (1): 34.
Tilly, C. 1985. War making and state making as organized crime. In *Bringing the state back in*, ed. P. B. Evans, D. Rueschemeyer, and T. Skocpol, 169–181. Cambridge: Cambridge University Press.
Woolf, V. 1938/1991. *Three guineas*. London: Hogarth Press.
Yaraman, A. 2001. *Resmî tarihten kadın tarihine* (From official history to women's history). İstanbul: Bağlam.

10

Reconstructing Women in Postconflict Rwanda

Laura Sjoberg

On April 6, 1994 a jet carrying Rwandan President Juvenal Habyarimana was shot down, and "decades of conflict between the Hutu majority and the Tutsi minority erupted into a full-scale genocide (Power, 2002: 331). Prior to this, "There were between 900,000 and one million Tutsis in the population. At the end of 1994, only 130,000 Tutsis survived; between 70 and 80 percent of the Tutsi population had been killed" (Sperling, 2006: 639). Fifteen years later, more than 100,000 Rwandans remained in prison for their role in the 1994 genocide where an estimated 900,000 people were killed in 100 days (Melvern, 2004; Powley, 2003).

At the same time, "Rwanda is the world's grand experiment in forgiveness," including an organization called Living Bricks, which "brings convicted killers together with survivors of victims of the violence...the killers build homes for the families as a way of asking for their forgiveness" (Lamb, 2008). The stark transformation in Rwanda is often talked about in terms of gender relations, where "Women bore the brunt of the genocide" (Powley, 2003: 12) but, now, "Rwanda has the highest percentage of women in national parliament in the world," with women having won 56 percent of the seats in the Chamber of Deputies in the September 2008 elections (freedomhouse.org 2008; UNIFEM 2008)—up from 48.8 percent in the 2003 parliamentary elections, making it the place with the highest representation of women in the world.

This chapter examines discursive representations of the (landmark) inclusion of women in the governance of Rwanda in the years since the 1994 genocide. The conventional story is that women's "victimization and endurance" during the genocide meant that they "deserve a significant and official role in the nation's recovery. Men and women...repeatedly cited this as a primary reason women must be included in governance" (Powley, 2003: 12). Arguing that the story is much more complicated, traceable not only to women's victimization but also to their participation and perpetration, it contends that there is an important degree to which women's increased representation in Rwandan governance *reconstructs*, rather than removes, gender-stereotypical understandings of women's roles in Rwandan society.

After reviewing women's different roles in Rwanda during the genocide, I provide a short history of their involvement in the postconflict reconstruction process and their representation in government and lay out some concerns about women's situation in Rwanda. Arguing that the only way to make sense of women's increased representation in the social context of postconflict Rwanda is to understand it as embedded in a discursive, gendered symbolic politics influenced not only by their roles as victims and perpetrators but also by traditional notions of gender, it presents a case that women's increased presence in the Rwandan political arena can be seen not only as women reconstructing Rwanda, but also as Rwanda's reconstructing its images of women and femininity.

Women's Roles in the Rwandan Genocide

In the genocide, women were targeted not only for their ethnicity but also their Gender...subjected to sexual assault and torture, including rape, forced incest, and breast oblation....Women who survived the genocide lost husbands, children, relatives, and communities. They endured systematic rape and torture, witnessed unspeakable cruelty, and lost livelihoods and property. In addition to this violence, women faced displacement, family separation, and food insecurity, all of which resulted in post-conflict trauma. Their social structures were destroyed, their relationships and traditional networks were destroyed. (Powley, 2003: 12)

In her official capacity, Pauline Nyiramasuhuko has been accused of helping to plan and perpetrate the fastest and most effective genocide in human history. She "had been open and frank at cabinet meetings that she personally was in favor of getting rid of all Tutsis".... Allegations of rape, sexual assault, and other crimes of a sexual nature are part of the factual bases of the charge against Nyiramasuhuko for genocide. (Sjoberg and Gentry, 2007: 162–163)

Many accounts of the Rwandan genocide characterize women as either its victims or its perpetrators, but seem oblivious to the possibility that they could be *both*. There is overwhelming evidence that there were a number of ways women were disproportionately affected by the genocide, and also disturbing evidence that some Rwandans suffered at the hands of women perpetrators. Ruth Jamieson (1999: 142) has noted: "It is absolutely and consistently the case that in war women are victims of all kinds of abuse, including sexual abuse, but the events in Rwanda suggest that this is not the whole story. What is apparent from the Rwandan example, however, is that we are unlikely to arrive at an adequate conception of the human capacity to violence if we insist on endowing it only in the masculine." Some scholars (e.g., Jones, 2004; Ehrenreich, 2004) have argued that women's perpetration of genocide makes it unnecessary to document how women uniquely suffered; in reality, the situation is quite complicated.

Women as Victims of Genocide

In the Rwandan genocide, one of the most obvious strategies for women's victimization was the widespread use of rape as a weapon. As Biniafer Nowrojee (1996: 1) explains, "The extremist propaganda which exhorted Hutu to commit the genocide specifically identified the sexuality of Tutsi women as a means through which the Tutsi community sought to infiltrate and control the Hutu community. The propaganda fueled sexual violence perpetrated against Tutsi women as a means of dehumanizing and subjugating all Tutsi." Elizabeth Powley (2003: 1) recounts some of the content of that propaganda, identifying the gendered nature of three "Hutu Ten Commandments":

- Each Hutu man must know that the Tutsi woman, no matter whom, works in solidarity with her Tutsi ethnicity. In consequence, every Hutu man is a traitor
  - Who marries a Tutsi woman
  - Who makes a Tutsi woman his concubine
  - Who makes a Tutsi woman his secretary or protégé
- Every Hutu man must know that our Hutu girls are more dignified and more conscientious in their roles as woman, wife, and mother. Aren't they pretty, good secretaries, and more honest?
- Hutu women, be vigilant, bring our husbands, brothers, and sons to reason.

Alison Desforges (1999: 163) has noted that, "During the genocide, tens of thousands of women and girls were raped, including one who was only two years old" (ibid.). Often, these rapes were particularly brutal....RPF soldiers massacred unarmed civilians, many of them women and children, who had assembled for a meeting on their orders." Desforges continues, "Assailants sometimes mutilated women in the course of a rape or before killing them. They cut off breasts, punctured the vagina with spears, arrows, or pointed sticks, or cut off or disfigured body parts that looked particularly "Tutsi," such as long fingers or thin noses" (ibid.: 164). She notes that, in mid-May 1994, "The decision to kill women had been made at the national level and was being implemented in local communities" (ibid.: 227). While many women who were raped were killed, an estimated 200,000 Rwandan women were raped and survived (Newbury and Baldwin, 2000: 4). By fall 1994, the genocidal killing died down, but women's suffering continued. In the immediate aftermath of the genocide, "The population was 70 percent female"; as a result:

> Women immediately assumed multiple roles as heads of household, community leaders, and financial providers, meeting the needs of devastated families and society more broadly. They were the ones who picked up the pieces of a literally decimated society and began to rebuild. They buried the dead, found homes for nearly 500,000 orphans, and built shelters. (Powley, 2003: 13)

As Newbury and Baldwin (2000: 5) describe, "Women have had to shoulder enormous burdens, particularly since, in addition to caring for surviving members of their own nuclear families, many women are providing food, clothing, and school fees for orphaned children." This is especially difficult because some 70 percent of the population in Rwanda was living below the poverty line in 2000 (ibid.: 7). The economic and structural problems pile on: in 2000, 300,000 people (out of about nine million) were still in need of housing, 14 percent of women were undernourished, and more than half of households received some sort of food aid (ibid., 8–9).

The illiteracy rate in Rwanda in 2000 was 60 percent, and the majority of illiterate persons were women (ibid). Many women, unable to find other means of supporting themselves and their families, turned to prostitution. As Newbury and Baldwin recounted (2000: 9), "Although prostitution was once rare and found primarily in the capital and in major towns, it has now become common in some rural areas as well....Although fully aware of the risks of HIV infection, those prostitutes could envisage no other way of earning enough to stay alive." The HIV infection from prostitution just compounds the problems that women suffered during the genocide, where:

> Among the weapons of choice calculated to destroy while inflicting maximum pain and suffering was HIV. Eyewitnesses recounted later that marauders carrying the virus described their intentions to their victims: they were going to rape and infect them as an ultimate punishment that would guarantee long-suffering and tormented deaths.... For countless women and girls who survived rape only to learn that they were HIV positive, the end of the massacre in July, 1994, was just the start of their slow torture. (Donovan, 2003)

Even women who managed to survive the sexual violence *without* contracting HIV/AIDS still struggle with the repercussions of the sexual violence they suffered. Newbury and Baldwin (2000: 3) describe that, in Rwanda, "The stigma of rape is enormous." Attacks against women during the 1994 genocide were not only terrible and tragic events in victims' lives, but remain a determining factor in their social status in the postconflict era. Because women were raped during the genocide, "Their chances for marriage may be destroyed, and some have given birth to children who themselves are scorned" (ibid.).

In sum, women suffered disproportionately during the genocide, and, as a result, have been burdened with a number of social, political, and personal problems that make daily life a struggle in the still-ongoing process of postconflict reconstruction. Women were, along with most sectors of Rwandan society, victims. Women *as a group* experienced both the genocide and the immediate postconflict aftermath in ways unique to women based on gender.

Women as Perpetrators of Genocide

There are many important ways in which women were victimized in the Rwandan genocide. Yet, some have also been accused of its perpetration at almost every level, from leadership to complicity. First, many suspect that President Juvenal Habyarimana's wife, Agathe, was responsible for his assassination, paving the way for the country to be led by more extremist Hutus, who started the genocide (Prunier, 1995; Gourevitch, 1999). Carrie Sperling (2006: 653) adds that other "powerful women in Rwanda also assisted in the planning and incitement of genocide," recounting the story of two nuns:

> Two women receiving international attention for their roles in the genocide are sister Gertrude Mukangango and Sister Maria Kisito.

The two Benedictine nuns stood trial in Belgium for their role in the murders of thousands of Tutsis who took refuge in their convent in Suvu, Rwanda. Over seven thousand Tutsis...were killed. (ibid.: 656)

Mukangango and Kisito allowed Tutsis to take refuge in their convent, then betrayed their refugees by alerting Hutu *Interahamwe* death squads to the their presence and helping perpetrate a surprise attack and providing gasoline to burn down the convent with many Tutsis alive and trapped inside. Perhaps the most well-known female perpetrator is Pauline Nyiramasuhuko, who started her career in government as "a social worker...offering lectures on female empowerment and instruction on child care and AIDS prevention" (Landesman, 2002). In 1992, she became the Minster of Family and the Advancement of Women, "Where she was to supervise government policy in the area of family and women's affairs" (Sjoberg and Gentry, 2007: 161). Allegations of her participation in the genocide accuse her of driving through Rwandan towns announcing that the Red Cross would give away food and other crisis aid to people who gathered in a certain central location; then, unfortunately for those who gathered, "Nyiramasuhuko's announcement...was a trap, and refugees were surrounded by...thuggish Hutu marauders under her supervision...she commanded her *Interahamwe*, 'before you kill the women, you need to rape them'" (Sjoberg and Gentry 2007: 162).

It was not only elite women who participated in the genocide. As Sperling (2006: 638) explains, "Women, girls, and mothers also willingly and enthusiastically played important roles in the Rwandan genocide. As a female perpetrator of mass violence, Pauline is not an anomaly." "Regular" women in Rwanda "beat up refugees," "took an active part in selecting men who were to die," "went into the hospital with a machete," and "worked directly with killers...to burn people alive" (Jones, 2004: 120–122). Melvern (2004: 251) recounts that, "There was one woman who pulled out another's uterus." During the genocide, Jamieson (1999: 141–142) outlines some grim facts:

- Some women acted as cheerleaders to the rounding up and killing of Tutsis
- Some encouraged men to rape
- Some women acted as enablers and participants in the killing
- Women along with children acted as "finishers off." Their task was to locate those who were still living and kill them
- Women and children (typically mothers and their daughters) looted the dead and dying

Still, women's participation in the Rwandan genocide has been portrayed differently than their status as victims in scholarly and media accounts. Peter Landesman (2002) explained that, relative to women's participation in genocide, "Society does not have a way to talk about it yet, because it violated our concepts of what women are." While some identified "Rwandan women rapists" as raising "the problem of misogyny with a feminine name" (El Basri, 2004), many others ignored women's violent participation altogether, or denied their agency in violence (Sjoberg and Gentry, 2007). Pauline Nyiramasuhuko, claiming her innocence from behind bars, used phrases like "Can't kill a chicken," describing Rwandan women as essentially nonviolent, both by nature and because they live in a patriarchal society where they cannot "make men do anything" (Sjoberg and Gentry, 2007: x). Others, conceding that women committed violence in the genocide, argue it can be blamed on their maternal instincts, psychological instability, sexuality, or susceptibility to control by men (ibid.). For example, Adam Jones (2004: 122–123), emphasizing women's violence in the genocide, argues that, "Women's sexual competition with each other can largely explain any energy they put into attacking other women."

In sum, women were not only "victims" of the genocide in Rwanda, but also, in a lesser-known role, among its perpetrators. While women were still a small minority of perpetrators (estimates vary between 2.5 and 12 percent), their violence was very real and very brutal. These observations do not deny that women *as women* were victims of the genocide; they only suggest that the picture is more complicated.

WOMEN AND POSTCONFLICT RECONSTRUCTION IN RWANDA

In the postconflict transitions period, Powley (2003: 15) reports that, "The GNU [Government of National Unity] has made women's leadership and the inclusion of gender issues in government a hallmark of democratization plans" and, as a result, "Women have come forward to lead in unprecedented numbers and have helped shape governance." Now, "Rwanda is ranked number one in the world on an important indicator of gender equality: It has the highest percentage of female parliamentarians of any country" (Kingstone, 2008). In September 2008, "Women contesting in Rwanda's second parliamentary elections since the 1994 genocide...secured 45 out of 80 seats, or 56.25 percent, making the incoming parliament the first in the world to have women in the majority" (UNIFEM, 2008). In these elections, women's presence in the Chamber of Deputies exceeded even the gender quota in Rwanda's 2003 constitution, which specifies that women hold at least 30 percent of posts in all decision-making bodies (Powley, 2005). The "class of 2008" is not only the first in the world where women have been a majority of parliamentarians, but also the first in the world where women have been represented at a greater proportion than their representation in the general population.

In addition to posts held by women in the national government, Rwanda has cell (town), sector, district, and province women's councils, "Involved in skills training at the local level and in awareness-raising about women's rights...ensuring official representation of women's concerns" (ibid.: 156). Women play a numerically larger role in Rwandan government than progressive countries such as Sweden, Denmark, the Netherlands, and Norway, and, "There is a female chief justice of the Supreme Court, several female cabinet members, a female head of the influential National Unity and Reconciliation Commission and a female deputy police chief" (Lacey, 2005). Two explanations dominate the literature: Women's efforts to become involved as a result of their victimization, and explanations crediting elite Rwandans' belief that women are more suited to the task of forgiveness and reconstruction than men are.

Women Participate to Redress Victimhood

The first explanation is the initiative of individual women and of women's groups, proposing that women have organized politically to prevent a recurrence of the gender-unequal impacts of the genocide, while protecting and taking care of their families in the reconstruction process (Newbury and Baldwin 2000: 12). This argument emphasizes their self-interested entrepreneurship to improve their lives and those close to them. In response to women's needs for property, employment, and basic goods, women's groups have "sprung up across postconflict Rwanda to ensure legal entitlements" (Sorenson 1998: 20). They have focused on reconstruction, legal rights, and leadership. Newbury and Baldwin (2000: 6) explain that, "The activism of the Women's Ministry in the postgenocide government in promoting women's empowerment is a departure from the past"; as a result, "At the national level and in local communities, individual women, women's groups, and mixed groups in which women play an important role have demonstrated admirable initiative in addressing the challenges of rebuilding their communities." People focusing on women's activism credit their initiative with many of the successes of the postconflict reconstruction period, Sorenson (1998: 60) explaining that, "The strong co-operation between women from all social and ethnic backgrounds is an impressive example of a new Rwanda in the making."

Recruiting Women Peacemakers

The second argument about women's increased representation in government and civil society in Rwanda since the 1994 genocide focuses on the transitional government's recruitment—perceiving women more suited to the process of building peace and encouraging forgiveness. In Hunt and Posa's (2001: 38) words, this position contends that, "Allowing men who plan wars to plan peace is a bad habit," explaining that, "Exceptions aside...women are often the most powerful voices for moderation in times of conflict," stemming from women's "civil activism" and "family care." Powley (2003, 16) agrees, "Many Rwandans perceive women to be 'better' at forgiveness, reconciliation, and postconflict peace building than their male counterparts."

While, "In the past, Rwandan women normally remained silent in the presence of men and acted as if they knew little," in the immediate aftermath of the conflict, "the Rwandan government began a process of electing women's councils at the local level" and continued from there (Newbury and Baldwin, 2000: 112, 116). Women's participation was facilitated by "women's committees" in the cabinet structure, "women-only elections" at the national and local levels (Bouta and Frerks 2002: 41). Women's participation, both generally and in these specific issue areas, is emphasized because women have been framed as essential to the "reconstruction of the social and moral tissue of the nation" (Hamilton, 2000: 10). If women are more collaborative, they should be (and are) used strategically in times when governments are interested in building peace.

Are Women Equal in Rwanda?

It is important to note that women's record-setting representation in the Rwandan parliament is an important advance in a deeply patriarchal land. As Marc Lacey (2005) states, "The most remarkable thing about Rwanda's Parliament is not the war-damaged building that houses it...[it is that] mixed in with all the dark-suited male legislators are many, many women." Newbury and Baldwin (2000: 6) explain, "Patriarchy is alive and well in postconflict Rwanda. In some ways, the war and genocide have reinforced the subordination of women by the emphasis placed on militarism and military values."

These suppositions are backed by substantial evidence, Rwanda ranking 135 out of 146 on the Gender Development Index in the UNDP [United Nations Development Programme] 2002 report (Sweetman and Kerr, 2003: 84). This means, among other things, that its fertility rate (total births per woman) remains one of the highest in the world, averaging six births. Women's returns on labor are somewhere between 50 and 70 percent of men's (dependent on ethnic group). Because of a lack of collectible data about women's participation in the labor market, Rwanda is not ranked on the other UNDP, the Gender Empowerment measure, which measures political and economic participation in decision making along with control over economic resources.

Women in Rwanda also continue to deal with a substantial amount of gender-based violence. The WomanStats project has put together a composite scale of the physical security of women, ranging from zero (highest levels of physical security) to four (lowest); Rwanda ranks three, corresponding to a situation in which, "There are laws against domestic violence, rape, but not necessarily marital rape; these laws are rarely enforced; there are taboos and norms against reporting these crimes, which affect a majority of women. Honor killings may occur in certain segments of society" (WomanStats, 2007). The project notes the lack of legal framework against domestic violence in Rwanda, and a lack of enforcement of legal provisions about women's physical security.

News reports confirm that all is not well for women in Rwanda. Lindsey Hilsum (2004) reports that many women survivors still "Need housing, jobs, counseling, and medical assistance for life." Especially hard-hit are its HIV-positive genocide widows, who "Are largely overlooked in a country trying hard to rebuild and recover" (Itano, 2002). Domestic violence is still up from pre-1994 levels (Finch, 2008) and, "The crime of rape took, after the 1994 genocide, proportions never seen before," according to the Hirondelle News Agency (2007), which reported rape charges being more numerous, cases are often "resolved" in ways lacking stern denouncement, such as "marrying the victim with the rapist."

So, women in Rwanda may enjoy the highest representation in parliament in the world, but that does not mean that gender subordination has disappeared; instead, in a number of places, women are still second-class citizens lacking important rights and unable to rely on the law for physical or economic security. These limits can be seen all over Rwandan society: In struggles to translate government representation to government power, attempts to gain and hold economic power, rising rates of rape and domestic violence, and in efforts to pass and enforce laws to bring gender equality to Rwandan society.

Reconstructing Gender in Postconflict Rwanda

Women were victimized in the Rwandan genocide on the basis of gender, one of the most striking examples widespread rape, where "rape is a crime against its victim and women generally, and genocidal rape is those things *used* as a weapon against an ethnic or national group, attacking racial purity, national pride, or both" (Sjoberg, 2010: 2). They also experienced economic deprivation, social disruption, and political instability during the Rwandan genocide—their victimization difficult to reconcile with the traditional images of women as "beautiful souls" who are pure, innocent, and protected from war (Elshtain, 1987). Rwandan women's participation in the genocide also challenged traditional notions of women as peaceful, virtuous, and innocent.

As Rwanda was nearly destroyed by the 1994 genocide, so were traditional images of women and how they should be treated. In order to understand the gender implications of these stories about women's integration into Rwandan politics in the postgenocide era, some background on gender is necessary. *Genders* are socially assigned, expected roles on the basis of perceived membership in implicitly natural sex groups (Peterson, 1999: 38; Sjoberg, 2006). For our purposes, gender is "A set of discourses that represent, construct, change, and enforce meaning" (Sjoberg, 2007: 86). So, it is possible to see the women's situation in Rwanda and gender representations of Rwandan women as distinct (but interacting) forces. It is also possible to see that what is being reconstructed postconflict is not (only) the state but also the woman. If the pure, innocent, peaceful, and removed ideal of womanhood in Rwanda was destroyed by the combination of genocidal rape and women's perpetration of genocide, both revisionist narratives of women's roles in the conflict and stories about their inclusion in postconflict reconstruction use symbolic accounts of gender to preserve the subject of the "real" and "pure" woman in opposition both to violent women and to defiled women. Stories of women during and after the genocide do much to preserve the association of women with characteristics traditionally defined as feminine, such as peacefulness, passivity, emotion, empathy, and cooperation—downplaying their deviance.

Even as women in Rwanda are integrated into the state's governance structure in ways unprecedented there, and globally, inherited notions of what it means to be a woman remain prominent. The government characterizes women's participation as necessary because they are perceived as "better at" the sorts of things that Rwanda needs—including peace and forgiveness. In other words, gender stereotypes have been entrenched, rather than deconstructed, in the government's recruitment efforts. Women are not *less* marginalized into stereotypical characteristics, but the government has shifted its understanding of leadership qualifications from characteristics traditionally associated with masculinities to those associated with femininities. The symbolic association of women and femininity has not disappeared, but been reified. What it means to be a woman (in Rwanda, and generally) is complicated by accounts of the symbolic constitution of gender relations interacting with "women's place" in society.

Such accounts should be constructed first by noting that, discovering women commit violence in war and genocide, tells us the stereotype that women are necessarily more peaceful than men is not accurate—inviting a reconsideration of what it means to be a woman. If not bound by essential social characteristics, womanhood can be read as bound by living in a world defined by gender expectations and stereotypes. While feminist theory tries to complicate these ideas by highlighting differences between women (Mohanty 1988; 2003) and demonstrating that gendering is something that happens both to men and women (Zalewski and Parpart 1998; Hooper 2001), the reconstruction of woman in postconflict Rwanda can be used to begin to articulate a more sophisticated understanding of gender subordination.

The impact of perceived membership in and relationship with sex exists because gender subordination is fundamentally a symbolic power relationship—where those perceived as female/feminine are made less powerful than masculine/male. This power relationship extends through the perceived possession of gendered traits, and the gendering of perceived behaviors and actions. Gender subordination, then, is not something men *do to* women or women *do to* women, but the result of a systemic discursive framework of expectations and power relationships based on perceived membership in sex categories. As such, women can be (and are) perpetrators of a crime that disempowers and subjugates them individually and as a class. Women's participation in genocide and genocidal rape does not negate the gendered impacts of that genocide. In other words, women *as women* can be both the perpetrators and the victims in conflict situations. While some people have argued that women's status as perpetrators erases any unique status women may have as victims (e.g., Ehrenreich, 2004), it is obvious from the Rwandan conflict, filtering through gender-symbolic stylized accounts, that women as individuals can act as conflict perpetrators, victimizing on the basis of gender. Women *as women* can subjugate other women on the basis of gender.

Another complexity is that gender subordination is a complex problem that can be fixed and reified at the same time. Accounts of women's integration into Rwanda postconflict tend to fall into two categories: Those explaining their increased representation as a seachange (either through government recruitment or activism, or both) and those describing Rwanda as a backwards, barbarian place that continues to treat women as second-class citizens. The first class of narratives can be characterized as idealist (seeing the "good" and not the "bad"), the second as Orientalist (Said, 1978), sensationalizing certain practices on the basis of perceived cultural otherness and inferiority. Instead, an account of women's integration into political and social life that understands both tremendous successes (such as the government recognition of the need to integrate women into government, and the (global) first-ever woman-majority representative body) and real challenges (including doubts about how much a representational shift actually corresponds to power shifts) is essential to understanding gender relations in Rwanda.

Two observations can be made: First, women can succeed in some areas combating gender subordination (here, political representation) while simultaneously experiencing setbacks (here, domestic violence and rape). This makes sense because gender subordination is not one thing, one area, or one indicator, but a set of discourses and meanings that can interact in complicated ways. One of those complicated ways is specific to conflict and demonstrated in Rwanda. It has been extensively documented that war hurts women—they are, disproportionately, victims of war and conflict. The possibility that war could help women has been less explored. Women were the victims of the conflict in Rwanda in many, many ways—but that victimization was hybridized and complicated rather than clear and linear. The same can be said of women's *benefiting* from the conflict in Rwanda. For whatever reason, their inclusion in the formal structures of Rwandan politics increased exponentially after and as a result of the genocide; this is *a* benefit of the conflict situation, albeit not erasing or counterbalancing the tragedy and victimization women experienced, nor disappearing in the wake of the tragedy either. War is capable of both hurting and helping women, where women as women can be victims and beneficiaries, and where gender subordination can be corrected and entrenched in different areas at the same time.

Understand that in Rwanda, and likely elsewhere, women can subordinate women on the basis of gender; women can at once be victims and perpetrators; and women can make advances in some areas while experiencing setbacks in others shows "the status of women" is a much more complicated and multidirectional construct than it appears in either the idealist or Orientalist accounts. The "status of women" in Rwanda cannot be explained either by referencing women's increased participation in politics nor by ignoring it; instead, it is important to note that the story is not only *women reconstructing Rwanda* but also *Rwanda reconstructing women/femininity*. The reconstructed subject of the traditional woman needs to be deconstructed in order to understand, continue, and complete the project of the reconstruction of the Rwandan state.

References

Bouta, T. and G. Frerks. 2002. *Women's roles in conflict prevention, Conflict resolution, and post-conflict reconstruction*. Amsterdam: The Hague.

Desforges, A. 1999. *Leave none to tell the story: Genocide in Rwanda*. New York: Human Rights Watch.

Donovan, P. 2003. Rape and HIV/AIDS in Rwanda. *The Lancet* (December 1). Available at http://www.thelancet.com/journals/lancet/article/PIIS0140-6736(02)11804-6/fulltext. 12/1/08.

Ehrenreich, B. 2004. Prison abuse: Feminism's assumptions upended: A uterus is not a substitute for a conscience. *Los Angeles Times* (May 16). Available at http://articles.latimes.com/2004/may/16/opinion/op-ehrenreich16.

El Basri, A. 2004. Not so Innocent. *Liberation Daily* (January 19). Available at HTTP://www.voicesunabridged.org/article2.php?is_ss_article=196&id_rub=1&sous_rub=violence&numero=1.

Elshtain, J. B. 1987. *Women and war*. New York: New York University Press.

Fausto-Sterling, A. 2005. Bare bones of sex: Part I: Sex and gender. *Signs: A Journal of Women in Culture and Society* 20 (2): 1491–1528.

Finch, F. 2008. How Ambridge is helping Rwanda rebuild. *The Telegraph* (June 6). Available at http://www.telegraph.co.uk/arts/main.jhtml?xml=/arts/2008/06/12/nosplit/bvtvarchers12.xml.

Freedom House. 2008. Country Report: Rwanda. Available at http://www.freedomhouse.org/template.cfm?page=22&year=2008&country=7476.

Gourevitch, P. 1999. *We wish to inform you that tomorrow we will be killed with our families*. New York: Picador.

Hamilton, H. B. 2000. Rwanda's women: The key to reconstruction. *Journal of Humanitarian Assistance* (May 10). Available at http://www.popline.org/docs/1363/155391.html.

Hilsum, L. 2004. Don't abandon Rwandan women again. *New York Times* (April 10). Available: at http://query.nytimes.com/gst/fullpage.html?res=9A05E0DD1338F933A25757C0A9629C8B63.

Hirondelle News Agency. 2007. Rwanda: 1718 persons tried for rape in 2006, according to LIPRODHOR. *All-Africa.com* (December 12). Available at http://allafrica.com/stories/200712120625.html.
Hooper, C. 2001. *Manly states: Masculinities, international relations, and gender politics.* New York: Columbia University Press.
Hudson, V. M., M. Caprioli, C. Emmett, R. McDermott, S. M. Stearmer, and B. Ballif-Spanvill. 2007. WomanStats codebook. Available at http://www.womanstats.org/Codebook7.30.07.htm.
Hunt, S. and C. Posa. 2001. Women waging peace: Inclusive security. *Foreign Policy* (May/June) 200: 38–47.
Itano, N. 2002. How Rwanda's genocide lingers on for women. *Christian Science Monitor* (November 27, 2002). Available at http://www.csmonitor.com/2002/1127/p08s01-woaf.html.
Jamieson, R. 1999. Genocide and the social production of immorality. *Theoretical Criminology* 3 (2): 131–146.
Jones, A., ed. 2004. *Gender and genocide.* Nashville, TN: Vanderbilt University Press.
Kingstone, H. 2008. Rwanda buries the past, but can't forget it. *National Post* (October 23). Available at http://network.nationalpost.com/np/blogs/fullcomment/archive/2008/10/24/201916.aspx.
Lacey, M. 2005. Women's voices rise as Rwanda reinvents itself. *New York Times* (February 26). Available at http://www.huntalternatives.org/download/260_2_26_05_women_s_voices_rise_as_rwanda_reinvents_itself_.pdf.
Lamb, G. M. 2008. New ideas in fighting violence/finding forgiveness. *Christian Science Monitor* (October 26). Available at http://features.csmonitor.com/innovation/2008/10/26/new-ideas-in-fighting-violence-finding-foregiveness.
Landesman, P. 2002. A woman's work. *New York Times Magazine* (September 15). Available at http://query.nytimes.com/gst/fullpage.html?res=9505EEDA1F3EF936A2575AC0A9649C8B63.
Melvern, L. 2004. *Conspiracy to murder: Planning the Rwandan genocide.* London: Verso Books.
Mohanty, C. 1988. Under western eyes: Feminist scholarship and colonial discourses. *Feminist Review* 30: 334–358.
———. 2003. *Feminism without borders: Decolonizing theory, practicing solidarity.* Durham, NC: Duke University Press, 61–88.
Newbury, C. and H. Baldwin. 2000. Aftermath: Women in post-genocide Rwanda. U.S. Agency for International Development, Working Paper 303. Available at http://pdf.dec.org/pdf_docs/pnacj323.pdf.
Nowrojee, B. 1996. *Shattered lives: Sexual violence during the Rwandan genocide and its aftermath.* New York: Human Rights Watch.
Peterson, S. V. 1999. Sexing political identities/nationalism as heterosexism. *International Feminist Journal of Politics* 1 (1): 34–65.
Power, S. 2002. *A problem from Hell: America in an age of genocide,* New York: HarperPerrenial.

Powley, E. 2003. *Strengthening governance: The role of women in Rwanda's transition*. New York: Hunt Alternatives Fund.

———. 2005. Increasing women's political tepresentation: New trends in gender quotas, Rwanda. In *Women in Parliament: Beyond numbers*, ed. J. Ballington and A. Karam, 154–163. New York: International Institute for Democracy and Electoral Assistance.

Prunier, G. 1995. *The Rwanda crisis 1959–1994; History of a genocide*, London: Hurst.

Said, Edward. 1978. *Orientalism: Western Concepts of the Orient*. London: Pantheon.

Sjoberg, L. 2006. *Gender, justice, and the wars in Iraq*. New York: Lexington Books.

———. 2007. Agency, militarized femininity, and enemy others. *International Feminist Journal of Politics* 9 (1): 82–101.

———. 2010. Women and the genocidal rape of women: The gender dynamics of gendered war crimes. In *Confronting gender justice: Women's lives, human rights*, ed. Paula Gilbert, Debra Bergoffen, Tamara Harvey, Connie McNeely, and Suzanne Scott. New York: Routledge.

Sjoberg, L. and C. Gentry. 2007. *Mothers, monsters, whores: Women's violence in global politics*. London: Zed Books.

Sorenson, B. 1998. *Women and post-conflict reconstruction*. New York: DIANE.

Sperling, C. 2006. Mother of all atrocities: Pauline Nyiramusuhuko's role in the Rwandan genocide. 33 *Fordham Urban Law Journal* 637.

Sweetman, C. and J. Kerr, eds. 2003. *Women reinventing globalization*. London: OXFAM.

United Nations Development Fund for Women. (2008). Rwandan women security 56% of Parliamentary seats in historic election result. *UNIFEM News* (September 22). Available at http://www.unifem.org/news_events/story_detail.php?StoryID=736.

United Nations Development Programme. 2005. *Human development report 2005, International cooperation at a crossroads: Aid, trade, and security in an unequal world*. Geneva: UNDP. Available at http://hdr.undp.org/en/reports/global/hdr2005.

———. 2007. *Human development report 2007/2008. Fighting climate change: Human solidarity in a divided world*. Geneva: UNDP. Available at http://hdr.undp.org/en/reports/global/hdr2007-2008/.

WomanStats database. Available at http://www.womanstats.org.

Zalewski, M. and J. Parpart, eds. 1998. *The "man" question in international relations*. Boulder, CO: Westview Press.

Part IV

Confronting the Patriarchy of War as Women Combatants and Noncombatants

11

Relationships of War: Mothers, Soldiers, Knowledge

Steven L. Gardiner and Angie Reed Garner

Examining how knowledge of war is shaped by the gendered divisions of home front and front, and how people negotiate this divide, we focus on the relationship between a particular mother and her soldier-son to show how both military practice and well-established cultural forms shape the capacity to understand war-making. Drawing on interviews with soldiers, veterans, and family members, we demonstrate how knowledge requires the active integration of information into meaningful contexts, and how access to these contexts is not politically neutral. Mothers, as iconic representatives of familial interiority, are placed in an untenable position: They must learn about war-making in order to give support to their soldier-children, and yet they must not know too much about the caustic realities of wars to which their children are subject, lest they become less able or less willing to support soldiers fighting wars.

Contemporary women are part of war, and its ever-ready surrogate militarism, in various roles—as soldiers, aid workers, journalists, civilian casualties, sex workers, and family members. Women, and the civilian population generally, are systematically disempowered in their relationship to the military. Through close analysis of the attempts of a particular American mother's efforts to come to terms with her lack of knowledge regarding conditions of service of her soldier-son, we understand how, seeking information, mothers face three significant hurdles: First, the military's official regime of information control; second, the inculcation and adaptation of this regime by soldiers as a gendered schema; and, third, the systemic difficulties of communication and understanding between the gendered realms of front and home front.

A military mother's quest for knowledge not only runs afoul of military censorship, but an entire world of discourse and practice constructed to separate them asiconic representatives of the private sphere from realities of the front. Rhetorically constructed as "for the good of mothers," the firewall between front and home front actually tends to serve the state and its war-making capacity, the military as institution, the collectivity of soldiers and veterans, and the individual soldier. Only as an afterthought does it serve mothers and family, if any residual benefit can be derived at the end of such a long chain of extraction.

The relation of war and violence to gender is complex. As Michel Foucault (1978, 1980) has famously argued, where knowledge touches us, so does power; and, power itself is constituted in and through knowledge. Its internalized process incurs a cost, and information becomes meaningful only as it is placed in a context shaped by social forces; what we know is formed by the norms, categories, and expectations supplied by our cultures—circumscribing our potential. Foucault refers to this as "power-knowledge," with emphasis on the linking hyphen.

Power-knowledge can seem a distant and obscure abstraction, with little relationship to our daily realities, but this is illusory. The immediacy of power-knowledge to ordinary lives is starkly evident in the nexus of relationships between parents, deployed soldiers, the military-as-institution, and—in the case investigated here, veterans and their organizations.

Back Story: A Mother and Her Soldier-Son

Jane Callahan (not her real name, as herein we follow the ethnographic convention of protecting confidentiality) is the mother of soldier-son Ken, deployed to Iraq in the early stages of Operation Iraqi Freedom. Enlisted in the United States Army before the events of September 11, 2001 and the rush to war that followed, Ken was trained as a Russian translator at the Army's famed language school in Monterey, California. With little reason to suspect he would be deployed to the Middle East, he found himself in Iraq, his mother hungry for information about what was happening to him and what was likely to happen. "It came as a shock to me," Jane told us, "when the recruiters started showing up at our door. Growing up when I did, through the seventies and eighties, we were so antimilitary. But Ken said, 'Mom, I'm 18.'"

Jane lives in the same small, Midwest town where she grew up. She graduated from a private liberal arts college, and since the deployment of her son has become extremely active in the local veterans service organizations—the American Legion and VFW. We interviewed her at a pizza place next to the town library, where she works, and she described her feelings about Ken joining the army as a kind of resolved ambivalence, "Now I think it's one of the best things that he could have done. It was the best thing for him. Of course, when he went in there was no sign that we would be going to war. But he probably didn't tell you about my hitting him with a rolled up newspaper, asking him what he was trying to do?"

The ambivalence—*"best thing he could do"* and *"hitting him with a rolled up newspaper"*—indexes an affective accommodation to a difficult reality. Many veterans report regretting joining in the first place, intensely disliking much of what they did and experienced in the military, and yet are glad they served once their service is safely in the past. Military nostalgia tends to increase with age, leading some veterans to join organizations twenty years or more after completing their service obligations.

Jane's position vis-à-vis military service, however, was different from that of a soldier or veteran. Her father fought in Korea, her grandfather in World War I, several cousins served in Vietnam and more distant ancestors and collateral relatives fought in every American war since the Revolution. Like many Americans of her generation, however, Jane had been profoundly alienated from the military as an institution prior to her son's enlistment. The Vietnam War created a rift in a multigenerational narrative that equated patriotism, military service, and honorable sacrifice. With her son actually in a war zone, her critical position became enormously complicated. At the urging of a Marine Corps veteran and old college friend, Larry, Jane consented to her son's recruitment to the American Legion; indeed, she actively facilitated it:

> Ken had enlisted and Larry came to see me one day, and said, "We've got to get him signed up for the American Legion." Well, I thought about it and said, "Okay, we can do that." It was something my father was in and everything. Then one of the local members wanted to see his DD-214 [an official record of military service, issued at the end of service], but of course we couldn't show it, because Ken is still active duty. It was one of the member's wives who wanted to see it. So eventually we got a copy of his transfer orders, and that satisfied them. I had sent the paperwork off to Ken with a note that said, "Sign this—it's not optional."

That matter squared away, Jane joined the American Legion Auxiliary and forged a connection to her own son far away in Iraq via exhaustive service work with veterans. She took on a supportive and nurturing role, forbidding her friend Larry to watch post-World War II-era war movies—"old movies okay, but nothing with M-16s in it," having learned that the sight of that specific weapon was a trigger for his PTSD—speaking to the depth of her effort to glimpse what was becoming of her son. Her efforts can be appreciated across three versions of the same story about a photo of her son.

Version One—From Jane

Some time after arriving in Iraq, Ken sent his mother a grainy color photograph of himself and another soldier, standing in a dry swimming pool under the harsh Iraqi sun. They were dressed in the full uniform of a combat soldier: fatigues, boots, and body armor with weapons slung over their shoulders. Rather than speaking the proverbial thousand words to her, the photograph was fairly mute.

Partly from a mother's pride and partly in search of information, Jane showed the photo to two American Legion friends—the aforementioned Larry, and Colin, a highly decorated Vietnam vet. They glanced at the photo and suggested, "Ask Ken why he has a SAW [Squad Automatic Weapon]." Jane had no idea what a SAW is, or why it should matter, but it was clear from their comments that it did matter, very much.

Lacking even the dubious back-channel lines of communication available to spouses living on military bases (Harrell, 2003), parents and other civilian family members dwell in categorical isolation from the realities of war; in traditional wartime usage they live in the *home front*. But, in America's most recent wars, fought entirely by volunteers, the idea of a national civilian sphere dedicated to supporting troops in the field has become a notion mostly trotted out by campaigning politicians. Beyond the immediate environs of military bastions like Lawton, Oklahoma and Fayetteville, North Carolina, there is little in the way of an American home front, little sense that the *nation*—as opposed to its armed forces and military families, is engaged in a violent struggle. Most Americans go about their lives barely affected by the deployment of America's sons and daughters "in harm's way." Accordingly, in the wars that the United States has fought since 1945, the home front has come to be referred to by American military personnel simply as "*the World*."

To explain how power-knowledge touches people in real life, we see how it does so via a matrix of categorical expectations. Each type of family relationship indexes a densely woven set of narratives, both generalized cultural forms (stories held in common) and particularized knowledge that emerge when people integrate their own experiences into the existing forms. To the extent that individual experience and available narratives are poorly matched, friction is inevitable. How any individual copes with this friction varies as a function of his or her resources, which include previously integrated forms of knowledge, commitments, and expectations. Responses can range from paralysis to the repression of incoherence (usually via the application of ideological grease) to conscious resistance.

Resistance, at a minimum the questioning of available narratives, if not their outright rejection and replacement, requires an attempt to produce new knowledge which, in turn, requires someone to exercise a power that can only be deployed from a particular subject position. There are subject positions besides those related to kinship; a mother or father who also was, say, a senator or a general (or the friend thereof), who seeks knowledge about his or her military son or daughter, might well mobilize power in relation to other positions. Still, most Americans lack such options, and must rely on kinship.

The private sphere, where caring takes place, is gendered. In spite of generations of effort by American women to open the public sphere, the workplace, and the military to their fullest participation, the *home* is still considered a feminine space. By custom, and in many instances by law, mothers are not only presumptive primary caregivers for young children; they remain the nerve center of parental concern. Never mind that in many families the key nurturer may be a father, or an aunt, or a grandmother, or an older sibling, or a combination of persons—it is mothers who stand categorically for the interiority of American families (Goldstein, 2001).

This gendering of categories, the imputation of feminine and masculine qualities, is a prime example of how meaningful contexts emerge from the integration of information into categories—such as that women have traditionally been most responsible for domestic chores, child-tending, and other home-based tasks. Such contexts allow a person to extrapolate from *is* to *ought*—from "women tend to be caregivers," "to women ought to be caregivers." Rephrased, there are Gold Star Mothers but no Gold Star Fathers—those who have lost a child to war. It is mothers who are constructed as suffering the loss of children, especially sons, in war. Likewise, it is mothers who are understood to long for specific information from the front—and, indeed, they may actually do so.

We may say that *"ignorance is bliss,"* but we say it largely of children or those whom we wish to infantilize—or, worse, those we see as *setting themselves up* for a *rude awakening* to the *harsh realities of life*. In spite of this hackneyed and transparently hierarchical language that divides those in the know from those who know nothing, war remains a privileged realm of discourse. All other elisions and occlusions of knowledge present in the situation—from the military's official "need to know" policy to the individual soldier's often unstated position that there are some things "Mom doesn't need to know," follow from this gendered, categorical division of reality.

Version Two—From Ken

Ken Callahan joined the Army during peacetime, his enlistment shocking his mother and baffling his father, a college professor and nonveteran. He chose to train as an intelligence specialist, and studied Russian to work as an electronic interceptor translating radio communications. In spite of the fact that his training did not include Arabic and he was ill-equipped for intelligence work in Iraq, Ken (like so many other soldiers, reservists, and national guardsmen and women) was sent to the war.

We had the chance to speak with Ken after he returned from his first tour and, when asked if he was able to talk about his experiences in Iraq with friends at college, he replied, "I don't talk about it, and they don't ask." Like all soldiers, he had many stories to tell; like most soldiers, he found those stories difficult to share with people who had no way to understand them. A photograph depicting his platoon sleeping on the metal hoods of their trucks and a single laconic comment about "sand spiders" (scorpions) served as his effort to describe field conditions to friends and family. He sent pictures to his mother, so the burden of interpretation was borne entirely by her. Ken's version of this particular story ends here.

Ken's mother made an active effort to learn military jargon, which in some ways made him more willing to talk to her. Asked about the SAW, Jane reported his agitation: "You tell Larry, you tell Colin: the image of army intelligence sitting behind a desk shuffling papers is just wrong. *You tell them we go right in behind the tanks.*" His response was every bit as condensed and telegraphic as that of the two veterans. From this exchange we can begin to imagine something of the context for Jane's knowledge about military culture. It is not too difficult to imagine her next questions, even if unspoken. What is a SAW? *Right in behind the tanks:* what does that mean? Ken's reactions have been layered into American ideas of what it means to be a soldier and a man, especially into gendered presumptions about the separation of home and front.

As political scientist Joshua Goldstein (2001) argues, the relationship between masculinity and soldiering forms a key underpinning of the gender system itself: To be a *real man* is to be a *good soldier*. The ideal qualities of masculinity in war-fighting societies are virtually identical to those of the good soldier: physical and emotional toughness, loyalty to group and cause, strength, and skill. Trying to separate masculinity from soldiering is like trying to cut the front side from the back of a piece of paper. It is perhaps possible. The link between soldiering and masculinity of course does not mean that all men are soldiers, or that women cannot be. Nor does it mean that there are no alternative masculinities to the soldierly variety. It means that, in war-fighting societies, normative regimes of self-constitution lead relentlessly to the production of men as *potential soldiers*.

The logic of women's participation or nonparticipation in war as soldiers is not simple. In the first place, as Mariam Cooke (1993) has argued and Cynthia Enloe (1983) has documented, women have always been present at the front—as soldiers at times, as victims of violence, as nurses, as camp followers and prostitutes, as insurgents and innumerable other roles chosen or forced upon them by necessity. In the American armed forces, women are increasingly visible as soldiers and casualties, as the amoebalike character of the "war on terror" makes the front everywhere and nowhere. As of March 2008, the U.S. armed forces had sustained a total of 3,241 "hostile" deaths in Iraq and 289 in Afghanistan; of this total 96, or about three percent, were women (Fischer, 2008: 1–2).

The *categorical* gendering of the front, however, remains extremely resistant to alteration. The participation of women in war—whatever the realities—is widely understood as a choice afforded by the power of the United States and its supposed commitment to an ethos of equality. The idea of women in battle remains controversial. Their presence in increasing numbers at the front has not *yet* changed the way in which war is imagined in much of the American heartland. This is not to deny the increasing presence of women in the military, nor the sacrifices they are making, but to highlight the gendered relationship of soldiering to regimes of power-knowledge, as war-fighting remains categorically masculine. Even as the nonveteran *fathers, sons* and *husbands* of soldiers remain ineligible to join the American Legion Auxiliary, it is still its *sons* that middle America imagines it sends off to war.

While father-son relationships and their potential fractures in relation to war and military service have been explored in American popular culture (Boose, 2006), mother-son relationships remain highly conventionalized and sentimentalized. Sons write "letters home," or emails to mom; mothers send *care packages* to their serving sons. Mothers hope and pray for safe return. This pattern is a dense schema of cultural forms, shaping a range of loaded expectations: Sons must *distance themselves* from families, particularly mothers, or their masculinity becomes suspect; mothers must not *doubt* the worthiness of the cause their sons fight, which could render potential "sacrifices" meaningless; sons must *protect* mothers from the truth of the front, preserving a sense of "back home" to which they may return; and mothers must perform grief at news of the death of a son, or relief at his safe return.

Central in managing the complex set of expectations in the mother-son-war schema is the control of information. While good sons are expected to write or call home, the gender-specific context of relationships redundantly marked between son/mother or soldier/civilian demands that such communications be radically uninformative. The communications of soldier-sons are systematically disciplined by the armed forces in a number of ways, varying from official censorship as an application of *operational security* (OpSec) to gendered shaming in basic training, directed at soldiers who "cry to their mommies." An entire discursive history of war-appropriate modes of communication, in films, novels, and war stories told to young men as they enter military service, models that real communication across the soldier (masculine)/civilian (feminine) divide is, in effect, impossible. This overly convenient categorical division becomes almost a mutual taboo, approached with trepidation from either side. It is reinforced by the soldierly fear of being misunderstood, blamed for wartime violations of civilian norms of conduct and how knowledge of war is so profoundly linked to social contexts, specialized vocabularies, and exotic place names learned experientially, through trial and error. Without the use of these divisions, it becomes difficult to communicate their linked experiences.

Version Three—From the Veterans

Military veterans occupy an ambivalent, even awkward place in the flow of information and construction of knowledge between front and home. As those who have been "there" and "come back," they occupy a liminal or interstitial space between military and society. Their minds and bodies have been marked by their experiences, often in ways that they may not even acknowledge. In some cases, parents are themselves veterans with access to military knowledge, albeit seldom for mothers. For mothers like Jane Callahan, veterans are crucial informants about the likely experiences and needs of their soldier-sons.

Veteran family members may or may not be forthcoming with information and interpretative aid. Fathers and brothers who are veterans have been inculcated with the man-making ideology of the absolute separation of military and civilian worlds. Key to this is the paternalistic duty to protect women-folk and civilians from military knowledge. Many former soldiers *consciously* evoke OpSec in their interactions with "civilians." As one long-time American Legion member told us when we began this research, "You'll have to watch out for OpSec. The idea is that you don't talk about this stuff with civilians. It's on a need to know basis. It will take some time [for people to talk to you]."

The habitual reticence of former soldiers is present even among antiwar veterans. The expressive possibilities fostered by the Internet and support groups do not facilitate communication with family and friends. Vocabulary issues aside, difficulty speaking to family are symptomatic of just how high the stakes are in such communications. To share "what I did in the war" risks alienating the very people who form an irreplaceable support system for a veteran. Even when the desire to shield the military as an institution from a critical civilian gaze is absent, veterans often have strong personal motives for remaining silent—rationalized in terms of protecting loved ones from knowledge that might be too distressing.

Jane confessed that there were self-imposed limits on her efforts, "There are some things I don't want to know. I've learned that no news is good news. If I'm not getting a phone call at 3:00 am and there aren't two guys in uniform knocking on my door, then it's okay." She also added, "I don't watch the news." Thus, what at first was a photograph of her son in the surreal but unthreatening environment of an empty swimming pool became a question about a SAW and a statement about what was behind the tanks.

In a separate interview, Jane's veteran friend, Larry—a past-commander of the local American Legion post, told this version of the story about the photograph, "When he was in Iraq none of us really knew what was going on with Ken. And then he sent his mom a picture, and Jane showed it to us, and we could see right away he was carrying a SAW, and so we asked her to ask him about it. So she asked him and it pissed him off, he was like, 'You showed them the picture, didn't you? Fucking Larry! Fucking Colin.'"

In Jane's version of Ken's reaction to her questioning, he reacted as if the two vets were "flipping him shit"—invoking against him a stereotype of army intelligence as rear echelon duty far from harm's way. This is exactly where Jane had reason to expect and hope he was. Except, and this is what the two veterans instantly noted: Soldiers far from harm's way have no need, ever, to be so heavily armed. ASAW, an M-249 light machine gun, is much heavier than the standard issue M16E1 assault rifle. Weapons of this sort are distributed by quota to particular individuals to provide support fire for their entire unit. It possibly never occurred to Ken, living with this weapon, that anyone would take special note of it when he sent the photo home. Or perhaps he hoped someone would; the implication of its presence was unambiguous. Far from being safe in the rear, he was close to the front lines, in actual combat—confirmed by his statement that his unit went in right behind the tanks.

It was through the exchange focused on the photograph that Jane discovered that her son was riding in the back of a canvas-sided truck, providing supporting fire while the rest of his team worked to intercept and triangulate on insurgent electronic communications. In Larry's version of of the story, Ken was not asserting his masculine claim to soldierly risk and sacrificebut on Ken's paternalistic anger. "He was a little pissed at us, for letting his mom in on things that will only keep her up at night," reported Larry.

Taken together, these three stories frame the difficulty experienced not just by Jane as a mother, but also by the larger society, in understanding war-fighting from the point of view of the soldier. While only one component of a fully contextualized understanding, such understandings must include points of view of enemy combatants, civilian victims, and others. But, as long as an absolute divide between home and front—at least for a powerful country like the United States—remains in force, then war remains distant, foreign, and unthinkable. The very unimaginable qualities of war mean that those who are "home" do not easily gain the power-knowledge that might position them to oppose it. On military matters and on issues of foreign policy, ignorance and credibility are thus (en-) gendered.

Much of the bitter knowledge of combat soldiers remains inarticulate. Trapped between the Scylla of masculine discipline and the Charybdis of military censorship, there is often no one to whom they may share their experiences while fresh. Later, the context of recall is often not only agonizingly painful, but mnemonically linked to the telegraphic jargon that is "soldier-speak," littered with profanity and laced with cryptic acronyms and place names. The same language condenses a radical separation of "us" and "them" in ways that strip "them" of humanity and is replete with racist epithets, gay-baiting, and the sexual objectification of women, including fellow soldiers. This language is unspeakable for the veteran in civilian contexts when s/he ceases to be a soldier.

The soldierly experience is not easily set aside. A significant number of veterans sooner or later find themselves involved with veterans' organizations, either traditional, such as the American Legion and Veterans of Foreign Wars, or oppositional groups such as Veterans for Peace or Gulf War Veterans Against the War. In various ways, and whatever else they do or do not do, such organizations provide opportunities for veterans to speak with one another. They also condense a lot of practical knowledge. Each local American Legion post, VFW group, and VFP chapter constitutes not an archive of information, but a living collectivity capable of producing discourses, grounded in soldierly experiences, about what is going on "up at the front" in the most current war. Such discourses, grounded in experiences that may not be commensurable, may be factually incorrect but they can provide a powerful context for understanding. Jane's level of access to military culture and insider knowledge did not come cheaply. In addition to the personally nurturing role she adopted with veterans, she cooked for their monthly pancake breakfasts, helped organize the Memorial Day parade, stood outside grocery stores and sold flowers as part of Legion fundraising activities, did outreach to military families, and basically anything else that needed doing just short of marching in uniform.

Conclusions: Gender, Knowledge, Power

The military enters into an oddly triangular relationship with mothers and their soldier-sons, particularly if the latter are unmarried. This may not be obvious at first, as relationships would seem to be mediated, making for more of a flat line than a closed polygon. The connection between mothers and the military, however, is more complicated than may be obvious at first glance.

It is mothers most of all who are imagined to *give* their sons, like a transfer of vested property, to the military. Wives and children also participate in this transfer, but military spouses and children are understood as *dependents,* belonging to an order of reciprocity for which soldiers and their families are compensated. Parental giving, symbolically represented as maternal is, by contrast, sacrificial. It is the mother who produces the soldier, both biologically, giving birth to him, and socially, nurturing and rearing him. Reciprocation, if it comes, is never welcome, for such is always postmortem. Mothers of single soldiers are the stereotypical beneficiary of a single soldier's death benefit, and any residual unpaid salary. Along with a check mothers are also the presumptive recipient of the news that their son has died and the flag in which his coffin was draped, if he died as a result of hostilities.

Besides these direct flows between human subject and concrete institution, there is also a more subtle flow of indexical discourse that points from military-world to mother-world, and vice versa. This is not so much mediated by the soldier-son as it is focused on his experience. The army places pressure on the soldier-son to separate himself from the mother-world in and through the process of becoming and living life as a soldier, requiring the military to reference a store of common knowledge about what mothers mean: comfort, ease, softness, nurturance, forgiveness—ideological representations and idealizations of civilian life that often bear little resemblance to the actual experiences of many recruits. Mothers, in turn, have preconceived views of the military both prior to the recruitment of their soldier-sons and after their deployment. Regardless of whether sons grew up hearing romanticized war stories or were strenuously warned away from the military, American mothers generally understand the military (along with its shadow counterpart, the prison) as institutionally other, a masculine world of legitimized violence, discipline, and hardness. Nonetheless, and somewhat paradoxically, it is the productive work of mothers and other caregivers that create the persons who become America's soldiers—"our boys," even "our girls."

When soldiers become injured beyond a capacity to continue in service, they often "go home" to their mothers, who are charged with providing a stereotypical romanticized civilian life of comfort, ease, softness, nurturance, and forgiveness that the military so denigrates. That mothers can and will accept this charge, and sacrifice themselves to the extent that the injured or disabled veteran may require, is by no means a foregone conclusion; thus, any information flows that might serve to jeopardize the disposition to maternal sacrifice can be the most constrained and dangerous for particular soldiers and the system of production of future soldiers alike.

Armies have their own set of institutional goals and tendencies, encoded in rules and regulations such as the Uniform Code of Military Justice and an unending stream of operations, missions, and orders. Information control is a central aspect. The OpSec rubric claims an enormous power to censor the flow of information, particularly from soldiers to civilians. Emergent technologies such as email, cell phones, and digital cameras have recently made the practical policing of information more difficult, but a total blockage of informational flows has never been possible. In spite of the famous watchwords—"Loose Lips Sink Ships," need-to-know censorship has never been primarily directed at enemy forces nor the civilian world. It has been aimed at soldiers, as a form of power that shapes their relationship to the civilian world. Soldiers are enjoined to accept the principle of OpSec even when many believe that sectors of the civilian population will learn from the media key elements of their mission details before they do. They are threatened with harsh disciplinary action for violation, so they generally inculcate the principle, if not always the practice. Living with OpSec is a form of soldierly discipline that tends to shape subsequent relationships, forming a model on which the world is coherently divided between those with a need to know and those with no such need. This military discipline, however, is not simply inflicted on the minds and bodies of soldiers, but on the whole structure of society, most intimately on those closest to soldiers: spouses, children, and parents.

Jane Callahan's quest for knowledge required her to take on a role in her community that she would not have chosen and could not have imagined before her son's enlistment and deployment. From a default antimilitarism legacy of the sixties and seventies, she moved to a "support the troops" practical patriotism that she lived intensely during her son's deployment. She went from hitting her son with a rolled up newspaper when he told her he was enlisting in the army to organizing the town's annual Memorial Day parade and acting as a kind of surrogate mother for the large group of veterans in the community though her work with the American Legion Auxiliary. Jane's journey was not an ideological conversion, but a reflection of her lived reality. Support for "the troops," or veterans, is not the same thing as uncritical support for military adventures such as America's war in Iraq. The context provided by inclusion in the subculture of veterans' organizations, however, shapes a deep distrust for civilian criticism of American wars. Jane's work with the Legion inducted her into a different world, where the principle of OpSec indelibly separates those with knowledge and authority to speak on matters military, and those who do not and should not.

The relations of war, as we have called them, suggest that the OpSec division exists to support a power differential that is ever more extreme as war becomes less the concern of the mobilized nation (however dubious the pretext) and more that of the state operating with imperial hubris. But it is not just soldiers, senators, and presidents who are implicated in the total system of relationships and exchanges that comprise the war system as we know it, but wives and husbands, sons and daughters, fathers and mothers—and the communities in which they reside. The military as institution is not separate in its self-understanding and rhetorical construction from kinship, but is parasitic upon it.

The relationship of kinship and militarization in contemporary society form a Gordian knot, too tight and complex to be unbound. Cutting it means constructing alternative communities of discourse capable of providing a meaningful contexts for interpreting our wars. This community must exist not just for peace activists and academics, but for soldiers, veterans, and their families—for mothers like Jane. This community of discourse must be strongest, not weakest, where soldiers and their families and communities actually exist.

If our understanding of power-knowledge, the military, and kinship is correct, then two groups of people are essential to the construction of the alternative discourse capable of bridging the OpSec divide: mothers, and veterans. The emergent voices of groups like Iraq Veterans against the War and Veterans for Peace, and the story of bereaved mother and activist Cindy Sheehan, suggest the possibilities of such modes of activism, and the perils. We have attempted to demonstrate some of the ways in which existing forms of power-knowledge shape understanding for mothers, soldiers, and veterans. Activist impulses are shaped in the real world not only by ideological commitments, but also by institutional frameworks that shape and authorize knowledge. It is our hope that this closer look at the institutional frameworks available to mothers like Jane Callahan will suggest ways to work for peace.

References

Boose, L. 2006. Techno-muscularity and the "boy eternal": From the quagmire to the Gulf. In *Hollywood and war: The film reader*, ed. J. D. Slocum, 275–286. Princeton, NJ: Princeton University Press.

Cooke, M. 1993. Women, retelling the war myth. In *Gendering war talk*, ed. M. Cooke and A. Woollacott, 177–204. Princeton, NJ: Princeton University Press.

Enloe, C. 1983. *Does khaki become you? The militarization of women's lives.* Boston, MA: South End Press.

Fischer, H. 2008. *United States military casualty statistics: Operation Iraqi Freedom and Operation Enduring Freedom.* Washington, DC: Congressional Research Service, Library of Congress. Available at www.fas.org/sgp/crs/natsec/RS22452.pdf.

Foucault, M. (1978). *The history of sexuality: An introduction*, Vol. 1. New York: Vintage Books.

———. 1980. *Power/knowledge: Selected interviews and other writings, 1972–1977.* New York: Pantheon.

Goldstein, J. 2001. *War and gender: How gender shapes the war system and vice versa.* New York: Cambridge University Press.

Harrell, M. (2003). Gender- and class-based role expectations for army spouses. In *Anthropology and the United States military: Coming of age in the twenty-first century*, ed. P. R. Frese and M. C. Harrell, 69–94. New York: Palgrave Macmillan.

12

FEMALE PARTICIPATION IN THE IRAQI INSURGENCY: INSIGHTS INTO NATIONALIST AND RELIGIOUS WARFARE

Karla J. Cunningham

WOMEN AND POLITICAL VIOLENCE: HISTORICAL OVERVIEW

Women are not new participants within the nationalist and/or religious conflicts existing within their respective countries. Consider that women in countries as diverse as Vietnam, Algeria, Iran, Chechnya, El Salvador, Nicaragua, Sierra Leone, Palestine, Turkey, and Lebanon have all participated in one form or another in the violence that shook their respective societies.

Women's involvement in political violence continually tends to shock us, no matter the context, challenging cross-cultural gendered normative assumptions about human behavior and subsequent socioeconomic-political structures and processes. Yet, assumptions that women are biologically, and thereby "naturally," peaceful have been largely disproved (Björkqvist, Österman, and Kaukiainen, 1992; Campbell, 1995; Campbell, 1999). Societal socialization of women—and men—regarding aggression and violence remains important, especially in traditional societies. Aggressive violence is almost universally ascribed as male, with one notable exception: When the threat to society is deemed overwhelming and conflict shifts into "total war." Within this narrowly proscribed framework, women frequently emerge as visible combatants.

In most instances, women's involvement in political violence has occurred within nationalist and secular settings. While these conflicts often espouse traditionalist themes, in part to distinguish cultural authenticity and opposition to foreign powers, they are rarely religious in nature. In contrast, most conflicts in the Middle East and North Africa, at least since the 1979 Iranian Revolution, have been ascribed religious characteristics, whether warranted or not. Islam is often used for public relations, mobilization, and propaganda purposes in these conflicts, but it is arguably tantamount to the traditionalist theme noted previously.

The modern period of Muslim women's involvement in Islamic religious violence began with the Iranian revolution (Reeves, 1989). For most observers, women's involvement in Islamic religious violence has widened since 2000, first in the context of the Chechen movement and then in the Palestinian and *Salafi* global jihadi movement (GJM). Three Salafi factions—purists, politicos, and *jihadis*, who share a common creed but who differ over their understanding of the contemporary world and its problems, offer different solutions. *Jihadis* take a militant position, believing that only violence can produce change. The *Salafi* movement includes a diverse array of people including Osama bin Laden and the Mufti of Saudi Arabia (Wiktorowicz, 2006, 207).

Situated firmly within the GJM are the current wars in Iraq and Afghanistan. While on the one hand they are about practical political issues of control and sovereignty, they also encompass the broader *Salafi* discourse regarding violence and most especially the source of law (human or divine). "The jihadi Salafis are pursuing a system-collapse strategy that seeks to install an Islamic emirate based on Sunni dominance...This faction uses suicide terrorism" (Hafez, 2007, 70–71).

Since June 2000, when women first participated in a Chechen car bombing, Muslim women have become increasingly associated with suicide attacks. While originally confined to the Chechen setting, this association has widened to include Palestine and Iraq. However, despite the commonality of female suicide attackers, the conflicts diverge and converge over themes of nationalism, foreign occupation, and religiosity. In contrast, the ongoing war in Afghanistan, dating from 2001 to the present, has been notably devoid of female combatants despite sharing these same themes.

Attention toward Muslim women's involvement in various conflict zones has overwhelmingly centered on their participation in suicide attacks. Information regarding their roles in other types of combat and support, in contrast, are generally unavailable for Chechnya, Palestine, and Iraq. Of central interest to many observers is whether—and to what extent—women's participation in suicide attacks impacts religious conceptions of *jihad*. In Chechnya and Palestine, the suicide attacks had nationalist goals, despite efforts to apply religious symbolism and terminology. Iraq constitutes a decidedly different case in that the lines between religion and nationalism have increasingly blurred; it has become a central arena for *jihadi* contestation, mobilization, and proselytism that involves equal measures of violence and media publicity. The incorporation of female converts from Europe into this environment suggests that the conflict in Iraq, while highly nationalist, has a more supranationalist *jihadi* current than either the Chechen or Palestinian cases.

David Cook's (2005: 383) argument that, "[T]o date, women fighting in *jihad* have only been a factor in these nationalist-Islamic resistance movements (Palestinian and Chechen), but not in other globalist radical Muslim warfare" seems to be both right and wrong if considered today. While Iraq serves as an important new benchmark for women's roles in *jihadist* war, Afghanistan has not involved female militants. One of the key differences may be that the Iraq War remains nationalist in intent, despite the religious branding used by militants, while the war in Afghanistan remains tied to the GJM and has not evoked a popular nationalist response. My focus here will remain on the emerging and growing involvement of women in politically violent actions. Palestine and Chechnya will be examined to identify general themes of women's political violence, nationalism, and religion; then, the Iraqi case will be examined to determine how it converges and diverges from the other cases.

Comparable Cases of Muslim Women's Involvement in Suicide Attacks: Palestine and Chechnya

There is great utility in comparing the war in Iraq with two other conflicts involving Muslim women: Both the Palestinian uprisings and the Chechen wars have given rise to female suicide attackers. The context of each war differs, as does the level of female involvement; however, all the wars share themes of nationalism, resistance to foreign occupation, and religion.

Palestine

While the Palestinian case has both secular and religious features, it is not a part of the Salafi/Wahhabi movement; instead, it resembles traditional nationalist movements and their goals, which tend to be geographically limited (i.e., the Occupied Territories) and politically straightforward—gaining political independence from Israel and instituting a Palestinian state. The ideological base of that state could range from secular to Islamic depending on whether one is considering Fatah or Hamas.

Palestinian women have been involved with nationalist-based movements utilizing violence since the 1960s. Historically, secular Palestinian leaders have allowed them to participate in a variety of roles to gain strategic advantage, as well as for operational reasons. Women have filled personnel requirements for a number of reasons when their male counterparts were killed, arrested, incapacitated, and/or injured. The individual and collective impact of occupation had direct meaning for women, whose political activism was an organizational basis for wider societal activism. While Palestinian leaders have understood the strategic value of women's participation in the conflict, their ability to mobilize women has been undermined by Palestinian society, which has only allowed for women's mobilization and expanded roles such as combat under conditions of extreme stress and for limited periods.

The most notable periods for women's involvement with Palestinian political violence have been the Six Day's War (June 5–10, 1967), the first *intifada* (1987–1993), and the second *intifada* (2000 to the present). At each juncture, women's mobilization was in response to heightened Israeli occupation and/or aggression. The case of Leila Khaled, who was affiliated with the Popular Front for the Liberation of Palestine (PFLP), and who planted a bomb in a Jerusalem supermarket during 1969, was unusual. Throughout the end of the first *intifada*, which means literally "shaking off," most Palestinian women were nonviolent, and limited their activism to protests, strikes, and various types of support efforts. Thus, while these women are often referred to as "warrior women," the term has more to do with the public nature of their roles than their individual activities.

The second *intifada* has been entirely different. Since 2000, Palestinian women have been more heavily attracted to an activist "warrior" stance, in response to three factors: (1) The deeper features of the conflict following the failure of the Oslo Accords; (2) The scope of Israel's response, which touches most households; and (3) A reaction to the grassroots features and general nonviolence of the first *intifada*, which was blamed for the failure to secure Palestinian rights. Beginning in late 2000 and then escalating throughout 2001, women were increasingly visible participants in a range of violent activities that presaged their role as suicide attackers. They assisted their male counterparts in planting bombs and other types of logistical support for violent attacks against Israeli targets.

Despite their evolving roles, the prospect of a female suicide attacker was remote, even in early 2002. But that changed with the January 28, 2002 attack by Wafa Idris, aged 28, who detonated a 22-pound bomb in Jerusalem that killed her, an 81-year old Israeli man, and injured more than 100. The Fatah-linked Al-Aqsa Martyr's Brigade (a.k.a. Al Aqsa Brigades) claimed responsibility for the attack, and branded Idris a "martyr." Between her attack and the end of May, 2006, sixty-seven Palestinian women were involved in planning or committing suicide attacks; of these, eight were successful, five by Fatah, two by the Islamic Jihad in Palestine, and one by Hamas (Schweitzer, 2006).

The Palestinian case is an example of a traditional nationalist movement; religion in this instance is not of the GJM variant, and has more ostensibly political implications for mobilization and potential government structures that might emerge from the conflict. The goals and recruitment potential for the conflict, especially as they relate to women, are geographically limited to the Occupied Territories, although attacks occur in and around Israel. The goals of the combatants are politically straightforward, focused on gaining political independence from Israel and instituting a Palestinian state.

Women's mobilization into the conflict has been generally limited with respect to overall numbers and roles. Female suicide attackers have been selectively and judiciously operationalized. Societal support for them has been generally supportive, albeit that this support has been rescinded when female suicide bombers have not conformed to socially accepted norms of "acceptable" combatants. For example, Reem Rayishi, the mother of two young children, committed a suicide attack on behalf of Hamas in January, 2004, and this attack provoked a popular backlash as society rejected the use of mothers in this warrior capacity. Traditionally, though, it should be remembered that many Palestinian mothers have sacrificed their children—namely, their sons, to the war effort (Peteet, 1997).

Chechnya

The Chechen case, according to Speckhard and Ahkmedova (2006a: 440), "Is linked ideologically to the global Salafi jihad but fine-tuned to fit local circumstances." *Salafi* influence in Chechnya, and its prominent role in introducing terrorist violence, has created complex social dynamics, and Chechen society advocates a more traditional nationalism and Islamism akin to the Palestinian model. *Salafis* emerged during the second war with Russia (1999 to present), and have advocated a more fervent religiosity with links to the GJM, which represented an important shift in the Chechen confrontation with Russia. In the first war (1994–1996), the contest was highly nationalist in character with independence a central goal; however, since 1999, nationalist aspirations for freedom from Russian control and occupation have been coupled with the larger global battle of *jihad*. The Chechen conflict remains geographically contained to Russian targets, although many are in Russian territory. The secular nationalist aspects of the Chechen wars generated a pathway to women's violence that evolved slowly. This process increased during the second Chechen war, prompted by the protracted and costly ramifications of war with Russia on operations and personnel.

There is limited evidence that a small number of women were combatants in the first Chechen War, as well as that some of these women were Wahhabis (Nivat, 2005), most of the information journalistic. The combination of violent conflict, geographic and cultural constraints, and Russian media controls has significantly limited observer scrutiny of the Chechen wars. Indeed, it was the introduction of female suicide attackers in 2000 that prompted an increase in observer interest in the second Chechen war.

The first Chechen war (1994–1996) witnessed significant levels of violence and international condemnation of Russia for human rights violations. Russia withdrew in 1996, but the new Chechen government was unable to establish control over its territory, laying the groundwork for Russia's intervention in 1999. The second Chechen war, from 1999 to the present, continues to be punctuated by rising levels of violence. Two women, as it turns out, perpetuated the first Chechen suicide attack, on June 7, 2000: Khava Barayeva and Luisa Magomadova. Between that date and August, 2005, there were 112 suicide terrorists, of whom 48 were women (43 percent) and 64 were men (57 percent). The attacks involved 2,043 hostages, took 939 lives, and wounded 2913 people (Speckhard and Ahkmedova, 2006a). Operationally, women have participated in 81 percent of the total suicide attacks involving Chechen rebels (Speckhard and Akhmedova, 2006b), and men working alone have carried out only 18 percent of the attacks (Speckhard and Akhmedova, 2006a).

The role of *Salifism* in Chechnya's suicide terrorism is disputed. *Salafism* grew more influential throughout Chechnya during the 1990s just as war broke out with Russia. Significantly, all of the women in Speckhard and Akhmedova's study reported being motivated by violent *Salafi* Wahhabism (2006a). In contrast, Nivat (2005: 417) argues that, for young women, "The *jihad* is not especially a question of religion, it is just that they understand the revival of Islam in Chechnya as a critical element in the identity-building of the torn region" (emphasis in the original). These differing perspectives on the roots of female violence in the Chechen setting illustrates that the highly nationalist features of the Chechen conflict have become religiously infused. For both Palestinians and Chechens, the wars they face are viewed as total (or *fard 'ayn*), but the importance of religion in these contexts differs from the *fard 'ayn* conceptualized by the *Salafi* GJM.

For Palestinians and the Chechens, *fard 'ayn* permits and even necessitates female political violence but it remains conceptualized and rooted in nationalist discourse. Religious justifications for female political violence have been unimportant in the Chechen case because secular nationalism remains such a powerful driver in this conflict. However, Palestinian religious leaders have been willing to issue *fatwas* (nonbinding Islamic religious opinions) permitting female suicide attacks to lend a religious justification to political contingencies and operational constraints. In stark contrast, despite the significant religious symbolism and narrative of the *Salafi* GJM, religious justifications have been slow to emerge.

The Chechen conflict blends the secular nationalism espoused by society and *Salafism*, the driving force behind those who have perpetrated terrorist violence since 2000. The role of religion has remained contained because the overall conflict has not been subsumed within the GJM, due to societal resistance. As a result, goals differ between a broad cross-section of society, which possesses more limited aspirations for political independence from Russia, and the *Salafis* who have sought to link the Chechen conflict within the GJM. The goals and recruitment potential for the conflict, especially as they relate to women, have been geographically limited to Chechnya.

Women's mobilization into the conflict has been limited temporally, with respect to overall numbers, and their operational breadth. Women were almost wholly absent from combatant roles in the first Chechen war; insofar as they have emerged as combatants in the second Chechen war, it has been in relatively low numbers and with highly proscribed roles as suicide attackers. Operationally, women have been systematically and meaningfully used as suicide attackers. Societal support within Chechnya has been mixed, in part because their operationalization has occurred within the context of *Salafism*.

Women's Political Violence in Iraq Since 2003

The war in Iraq, dating to March 2003, represents the next step of Muslim women's involvement in combat. While possessing characteristics associated with both the Palestinian and Chechen cases, its story is unique. Present in Iraq is both nationalism and religiosity and, for the purposes of this discussion, the war in Iraq—and the insurgency—will mostly focus on Sunni insurgent responses, with one notable exception, that will be discussed shortly. Iraqis, especially Sunni insurgents, want the United States to withdraw and to diminish Shi'a ascendancy and control. The Iraq conflict is *not* geographically limited in several respects: While general battles remain contained within its international borders, for the purposes of this discussion insurgents have been successful at recruiting female foreigners and have carried out attacks in neighboring Jordan. As with Chechnya, reportage on female suicide attacks is extremely poor, with widely divergent coverage, accounts, and accuracy. The figures presented here regarding women's involvement in suicide attacks inside Iraq represent a best-case estimate derived from various reporting between March, 2003 and May, 2008, open intelligence sources found in major American and international news sources.

Women's combat roles have been limited since the beginning of the Iraq war to suicide attacks, much as in Chechnya. There is no meaningful reportage regarding other forms of women's militancy and political violence in the Iraqi setting aside from suicide attacks. Women have participated in suicide attacks since the beginning of the Iraq War, with important variations. Almost immediately after the U.S. invasion of Iraq, the country's second suicide attack, on April 3, 2003, was credited to two women who attacked U.S. military forces close to Haditha. Nour Qaddour al-Shammari and Wadad Jamil Jassem (aka Nucha Mjalli Al-Shmmari and Widad Jamil Al-Duleimi) were nationalists, said to have committed the attack on behalf of Saddam Hussein. Following it, there were no similar discernable cases until 2005, although there are unconfirmed reports of two other incidents in 2003. Women's roles in combat remained highly limited through 2006. There were seven reported attacks by women in 2005, of which four failed and only one documented attempt in 2006 that failed.

Clearly, until 2007 Iraqi women were infrequently tasked and were often unsuccessful. That soon changed. By 2007, the Sunni insurgency began a sustained increase in female suicide attacks, with seven that year, of which six were successful. As of June 22, 2008 there were an estimated 21 attacks carried out by women in Iraq. Women have struck an evolving array of targets, as the insurgency has altered its goals and faced operational constraints. Until 2008, most targets had some type of official connotation (military, law enforcement) but, beginning in 2008, more attacks targeted crowded civilian targets (i.e., markets), especially those patronized by Shi'a. This has led to an escalation in the number of casualties from one wounded and three killed in 2003, to 73 killed and 121 wounded in 2007, to 243 wounded and 209 killed through mid-May of 2008.

There are also two other noteworthy topics associated with female insurgency in Iraq. Early innovations were common under the leadership of the former leader of al Qaeda in Iraq (AQI), Abu Musab al-Zarqawi, which included the following: (1) The use of women as suicide attackers; (2) The use of foreign women as suicide attackers; and (3) The use of women against a foreign target. While al-Zarqawi was not the first to use women in the context of Iraq's war against the United States, he does have the distinction of being the first Sunni insurgent to do so. The failed car bombing attack on November 9, 2005 by Muriel Degaque, a Muslim convert from Belgium, was also a troubling new precedent. Her appearance showed the linkage of the conflict to Europe and the broader international mobilization capacity of the *jihadi* movement. Finally, al-Zarqawi sent Sajida Mubarak Atrous al-Risawi to carry out an attack on November 13, 2005 against a wedding party in Amman, Jordan; although she failed to detonate her vest, her inclusion in the attack was shocking for many observers.

While al-Zarqawi was the first to use female militants, women's overall mobilization has been limited and sporadic. Since 2007, the Sunni insurgency has employed women more systematically and clearly, with greater capacity to carry out more successful attacks. This change suggests that the insurgency has succumbed to organizational and operational necessity in the face of the U.S. surge that began in June 2007 and was scheduled to end in July 2008.

The war in Iraq possesses traditionally nationalist goals of ousting a perceived occupation force and gaining political leverage in the structures that emerge from war. The Sunni insurgency, which has carried out the lion's share of attacks against United States and coalition forces, as well as Shi'a targets, is an amalgamation of traditional secular nationalists and *Salafi jihadis*. Despite the March, 2003 *fatwa* by Sheikh Tantawi, rector of Al-Azhar University, that it was an "individual duty" for Muslims to kill American soldiers in Iraq, the conflict's religious overtones have been more about branding and publicity than real religiosity.

Women have participated in the Sunni insurgency almost exclusively as suicide attackers but they were not widely or systematically operationalized until 2007, and then with a notable increase throughout 2008. The war in Iraq is notable because of its history of recruiting foreign women not only as fighters, but also into the broader global *jihad*. European women, especially those who have converted to Islam, have also been mobilized by the Iraq war, both as combatants and as supporters of the insurgency, mainly assisting the GJM as organizers, fundraisers, and teachers. Up to 47 female Muslim converts from Belgium, Denmark, and Germany reportedly were targeted for recruitment to carry out attacks in Iraq and Pakistan (Rosenthal, 2006). Malika El Aroud (a.k.a. "Malika" in various Islamist online communities) of Belgium is reflective of another side of this process: A prominent writer in Islamist online forums advocating for the global jihad, she has stated, "Normally in Islam the men are stronger than the women, but I prove that it is important to fear God—and no one else" (cited in Sciolino and Mekhennet, 2008: 2).

Conclusions

Women's participation in the Iraqi insurgency both converges and diverges with women's violent roles in Palestine and Chechnya. Their roles in all three conflicts capture the interesting tension between nationalism and religiosity, although this is not really novel because most nationalist settings have grappled with the interplay between traditionalism and modernism.

In all three cases here, participants have viewed the conflicts as total war, or *fard 'ayn*; however, its conceptualization diverges significantly. While the Palestinians and Chechens pay lip service to the idea of *fard 'ayn*, and conceptualize their respective battles as total war, the religious overtones of the conflicts are largely symbolic. What is left unresolved is the extent to which the Sunni insurgency in Iraq understands and operationalizes *fard 'ayn*. The Iraqi case appears to have much in common with Chechnya, with some of the most violent contingents understanding the conflict in its fullest religious meaning, as does the GJM. However, much of the insurgency—and the larger society from which it is drawn—have a more limited and traditional understanding of the conflict as nationalist, in the same way Chechen society overall remains decidedly secularist and nationalist in its orientation.

For years, Islamic leaders have been eradicating the intellectual and religious obstacles to female participation in suicide attacks either overtly or through their silence, and this discourse has included even the most radically conservative Wahhabi movement (Cook, 2005). The implications of this intellectual step cannot be overstated or underestimated.

In an expansion of earlier secular trends in which women's inclusion in combat signaled the conflict's immediacy and legitimacy, it has signified religious authenticity and the totality of the threat being confronted. When women are required to participate in *jihad*, the entire community is perceived to face an existential threat. Women then become a critical component of demonstrating to society—using religious justifications— the totality of the war they are waging. The result is a deepened legitimization of *jihad* and a reinforcement of its need for violence for both men and women.

The religious obligation of *fard 'ayn* is well-developed in the *Salafi* GJM setting and, as a result, women can become full partners in combat. The religious necessity of the war gives women rights that are not, and most likely will never be, reflected in nationalist settings where women's participation remains optional. It is thus no accident that women's mobilization into combat roles—through suicide attacks—has occurred largely at the hands of the most religiously grounded combatants. Religion provides an additional—and powerful—normative trope for propaganda, recruitment, and mobilization, especially in mollifying societal unease with women's political violence.

While the war in Iraq has once again catapulted female suicide attackers into international consciousness, their emergence is part of a larger trend that is visible in comparable settings in both Palestine and Chechnya since 2000. Women's combat roles have been largely limited to that of suicide attacker, especially in Chechnya and Iraq, whereas women in the Palestinian conflict have participated more broadly in the war against Israel. Part of this has to do with the broader and deeper organizational capacity of Palestinian women through their women's committees that formed around the 1967 war. The durability of the conflict between the Palestinians and the Israelis has given women and male leaders a great deal of time to experiment with women's participation in that conflict.

Iraq represents a new iteration of women's involvement in war, especially in the Middle East, even if it does not appear to represent a meaningful example of women's involvement in a truly GJM setting. Instead, the war in Iraq is resoundingly nationalist, and women's participation shares many common features with earlier nationalist wars. In contrast, the war in Afghanistan is perhaps the closest current approximation of globalist GJM conflict, where women have not emerged as suicide attackers. However, sporadic reports of female militants affiliated with al Qaeda and other GJM elements throughout the general region suggests that women's roles in that conflict may be more significant than currently understood.

Research on Muslim women involved in war settings is emerging and deepening. While most of the attention is concentrated on the more sensationalist aspects of suicide attacks, there is growing evidence that women's roles run deeper. Even the *Salafi* GJM has been under growing pressure by women to include them, and European women have been at the vanguard of this effort.

Further work is warranted for exploring why, when, and how women are operationalized in their myriad roles in multiple war settings. This work will likely remain hampered by the difficulties of obtaining detailed information on combatants in active conflict zones. However, its necessity cannot be overemphasized. Women have demonstrated their operational utility in numerous conflict zones. Military planners and strategists have systematically underestimated women's involvement in combat areas, especially those with significant Muslim populations (Cunningham, 2007). This is due to both gender and cultural biases, and has led to poor planning and strategy, as well as significant loss of life in some settings. Developing a more comprehensive understanding of women's roles in conflict zones may help offset some of these strategic surprises and operational failures.

References

Björkqvist, K., K. Österman, and A. Kaukiainen. 1992. The development of direct and indirect aggressive strategies in males and females. In *Of mice and women*, ed. K. Bjorkqvist and P. Niemela, 51–64. San Diego, CA: Academic Press.

Campbell, A. 1995. A few good men: Evolutionary psychology and female adolescent aggression. *Ethology and Sociobiology* 16: 99–123.

Campbell, A. 1999. Staying alive: Evolution, culture, and women's intrasexual aggression. *Behavioral and Brain Sciences* 22: 203–252.

Cook, D. 2005. Women fighting in jihad? *Studies in Conflict & Terrorism* 28: 375–384.

Cunningham, K. 2007. Countering female terrorism. *Studies in Conflict & Terrorism* 30 (2) (February): 113–129.

Hafez, M. 2007. *Suicide bombers in Iraq: The strategy and ideology of martyrdom*. Washington, DC: United States Institute of Peace.

Netzer, M. 2004. One voice? the crisis of legal authority in Islam. *The Fletcher School Online Journal for issues related to Southwest Asia and Islamic Civilization* (Spring): 1–5.

Nivat, A. 2005. The black widows: Chechen women join the fight for independence—and Allah. *Studies in Conflict & Terrorism* 28: 413–419.

Peteet, J. 1997. Icons and militants: Mothering in the danger zone. *Signs* 23 (1) (Autumn): 103–129.

Reeves, M. 1989. *Female warriors of Allah: Women and the Islamic Revolution.* New York: Dutton.

Rosenthal, J. 2006. German women answer the call (to jihad). *Transatlantic Intelligencer.* Available at http://www.trans-int.com

Schweitzer, Y., ed. 2006. *Female suicide bombers: Dying for equality?* Tel Aviv: Jaffee Center for Strategic Studies.

Sciolino, E and S. Mekhennet. 2008. Belgian woman wages war for Al Qaeda on the web. (May 27: 1–4). Available at http://www.iht.com/bin/printfriendly.php?id=13257511.

Speckhard, A and K. Ahkmedova. 2006a. The making of a martyr: Chechen suicide terrorism. *Studies in Conflict & Terrorism* 29 (5): 429–492.

———. 2006b. Black widows: The Chechen female suicide terrorists. In *Female suicide bombers: Dying for equality?*, ed. Y. Schweitzer, 63–80. Tel Aviv: Jaffee Center for Strategic Studies.

Van Natta, Jr., D. 2003. Big bang theory: The terror industry fields its ultimate weapon. *New York Times* (August 24): Sec. 4, 1.

Wiktorowicz, Q. 2006. Anatomy of the Salafi movement. *Studies in Conflict & Terrorism* (29): 207–239.

13

Agency and Militarization in the Heartland: Noncombatant American Women

Michelle M. Gardner-Morkert

Feminist analyses of war, militarism, security, and international relations have expanded greatly since the escalation of the "war on terror." This case study builds on feminist scholarship about the gendering of war by investigating the militarization of noncombatant women living in a small Midwestern town in the United States that I call "Harvestville," where I spent over two years analyzing women's lives in a Midwestern nonwar zone, nonmilitary base, nondefense contractor town. Harvestville presented a rich study opportunity because, lacking the more conventional and overt forms of militarization one might notice in, for instance, the United States Army post in Fort Bragg, North Carolina, or in Hartford, Connecticut, with its major defense-contracting companies. Militarization throws into sharper relief the roles played by patriarchal traditions of this onetime pioneer town that has been, and continues to be a nucleus for mostly white, heterosexual, middle class, Christian, two-parent families. This is the same American demographic group that, since the September 11, 2001 attacks, our civilian policymakers have relied upon to accept and support the principles of the government's "war on terrorism."

Like many formerly rural and now newly suburban communities, Harvestville's population, while having grown rapidly since 1990, remains quite racially, economically, and religiously homogenous. According to a 2005 U.S. Census Bureau report, it is located in one of the fastest growing counties. In 2003, Harvestville's population of 8,480 was expected to grow to 28,000 by 2010, 40,200 by 2020. More than 95 percent of the Harvestville population self-identifies as Caucasian, replicating the "red state" electoral phenomenon—a category created by the U.S. news media for those where a clear majority endorsed the Republicans. Dubbed the "Silent Moral Majority," many red state voters are observant evangelical white Protestants opposing abortion rights, legalizing gay marriage, and funding stem cell research, yet supporting capital punishment and the post-9/11 "war against terrorism." Harvestville's demographics reflect the political compass of the "Religious Right" that flourished under the George W. Bush presidency.

The women represented here are rarely the subjects of journals and conference papers because they are not soldiers, and seldom are they even relatives of soldiers, employees of weapons contractors, or live on or near bases. Harvestville's women may appear inconsequential in the war-making process; yet, their experiences indicate that gendered militarization occurs outside direct war zones when one adopts patriarchal beliefs that become militarized. They may seem far removed from Afghani women but, as you will see, they are not. They may seem far removed from weapons contractors, but they are not. And they may seem far removed from military strategists, but another theory is dispelled here.

Militarization here exposes the brotherhood of militarism and patriarchy in a way that prompts us to recognize diverse contexts. It influences the local, global, personal lives of individuals, and macrolevel political systems. As a transformative process, it relies on and fuels the gendering of political, social, and cultural processes that are so personal in the lives of Americans. The reciprocity of patriarchy and militarization are at the heart of my research. To create a publication about women, war, and violence is to not only identify women as a class of people affected by conflict and violence; it also claims women are active participants, that war and violence are gendered, and that some common threads exist globally among women's experiences. Thus, the story of Harvestville women's militarization is compatible. Like other women represented in this volume, a preexisting patriarchy prepared Harvestville residents for the intensification of their militarization and its knot tugged on their lives, creating a rigid, gendered, militarized code of conduct.

The Militarized Knot of Harvestville Women's Lives

The militarization of Harvestville women's lives is referred to here as a "knot" because their acceptance, and often even active support of, patriarchal power structures, contributed significantly to the militarization of their lives. Together and separately, the following strands deepened that militarization: (1) Socialized gender roles; (2) Fundamental religious ideology; (3) Conservative Republican Party politics; and (4) Complex systems of "othering." Individually, many of these sociopolitical processes were not militarized, but they might naturalize beliefs that became militarized. Here, both patriarchy and militarization must be taught— and accepted. Harvestville women internalize the contemporary gendered militarization in their lives as moral imperatives for their community and their country.

Patriarchy is a gendered process of domination and submission, inclusion and exclusion, power and control—qualities that make it susceptible to militarization. Investigating militarization, explaining when and among whom and why it proceeds, requires an analysis of patriarchy. Most of Harvestville women accept patriarchy, making them susceptible to militarization (see De Beauvoir, 1989; Gilman, 1898; Wollstonecraft, 1992; Woolf, 1938). Patriarchy fuels militarized power.

Cynthia Enloe's (2000) pioneering research into the militarization of women's lives influenced International Relations (IR) scholars and Women's Studies scholars to look at the relationship between the processes of masculinization and feminization in the study of militarization (for more in IR, see Cockburn, 2007; D'Amico and Weinstein, 1999; Pettman, 1996; Tickner, 2001). Reducing a macro-level approach toward militarization from impersonal foreign policies, war theories, and weapons systems to a micro view of the effects of militarization on individual lives and understandings of gender roles that influence, and are influenced by militaristic ideology, she investigates militarization in the lives of individual women to identify gendered patterns and norms. Patriarchy is not only present in each strand of the militarized knot of women's lives, but also flourishes when the knot tightens. Similarly, Cynthia Cockburn's (2007) findings about women's antimilitarist organizing have provided a foundation for my understandings of militarized femininities and wartime manifestations of patriarchy.

Militarization is ideology in action, influencing lives in subtle and overt ways. My research has convinced me that militarism's potency lies in its very banality—the daily practices and decisions one rarely contemplates but that are underpinned by gendered, militarized ideology. One of the most startling examples stems from an interview conducted with "Lisa" in late 2003, a time when popular American media outlets and the George W. Bush administration manipulated the image of burka-clad Afghani women to bolster support for the invasion of Afghanistan and to create a contrast of the "savage other" oppressing women and the "civilized" United States military's rescuing those women from oppressive gendered practices. At the time of our interview, Lisa, a college-educated, 45-year-old white, middle class woman had lived in Harvestville for about twenty-five years and worked in the Public Relations office for a company in a neighboring town. Although her children are grown, Lisa maintained ties with the local school board and was active in the community. While giving her exact governmental post would make her identifiable, and thus violate our agreed-upon confidentiality, it is significant to note that Lisa ran for and won a seat in Harvestville's local government. She shared her struggles to be heard in meetings, and the sexist comments frequently hurled against her by some of the male elected officials; in fact, Lisa referred to the political system as an "old boys' network," where the male mayor and his "cronies" tried to sabotage anyone expressing a dissenting opinion.

Lisa told me that, shortly after her swearing-in, she received a letter from a male resident of Harvestville who threatened physical violence against her and one of the only other females holding a political office in Harvestville, saying he believed women should submit to men—that it was against "God's will" for women to take leadership positions over men. At first, she requested a police escort to her car after evening meetings, and filed a police report; however, this was of little comfort, since the police department's representative on her town government committee was one of the men making disparaging comments. By contrast, think about media representations of women's militarized political oppression in Afghanistan.

Studying the processes of daily militarization as it shapes the ideas and actions of civilian women by charting the reciprocal relationships of militarism and patriarchal gender roles reveals the fluidity and complexity of this sociopolitical process. My chief finding is that patriarchy was a cause of the militarization of Harvestville women's lives. It set the stage for their embracing of militarization in their lives and practices—a necessary condition, validating women who subscribed to traditional gender roles. Further, the reverberations of this research extend past the boundaries of Harvestville, suggesting a theory that can be applied to outside contexts.

Gendering/Mothering

One strand in the militarizing knot of Harvestville women's lives is the gendering mandated by local and national patriarchy, performed and promoted by women within their community. Thus in the mid-2000s, a time of U.S. military conflict, Bush and his Republican Party strategists employed fear and "othering" to mobilize American mothers into maternal militarized service to their country. Harvestville's patriarchy, meanwhile, dominated local politics and government, churches, civil organizations, women's groups, political organizations, businesses, economics and families.

Pro natalist policies idealize the feminized private sphere as the center for learning national values with the mother as the teacher—creating a need to defend the home in order to maintain purity. Enloe (2000: 248) uses the phrase "pro-natalist policy" to describe a militarized regime's attitude toward mothers as breeders of future nationalists or future soldiers. Throughout the world, women identify and mobilize as mothers to support nationalistic causes. Yet, not all militarized motherhood exists in a war zone: When patriarchy dictates the scope of motherhood, it can be militarized in times of conflict or calm.

The Harvestville mothers whom I interviewed agreed that motherhood can be a transformative position of power, believing they could change the world by bestowing their conservative faith upon their children, by bolstering militarized patriarchy, heterosexism and traditional gender roles, and by acquiring the skills to successfully defend their children from cultural and spiritual evils. For example, in a 2007 interview with Meg, a 43-year-old married mother of a six-year-old son, she talked about her role as the director of the Mothers of Preschoolers (MOPS) mothering class open to the Harvestville community. Some seventy women were registered. When I asked if she thought the mothers in the program, including herself, paid attention to political debates and cultural issues she replied, "Sure we can learn how to fondle someone or learn what it's like to be inappropriately fondled or groped by a president. Or worry that the world is going to end, but that doesn't really affect my mothering. The Bible says to help each other, serve each other and put others first. That's what influences my mothering." When asked which "political" issues most influenced her voting, Meg smiled as if she has been waiting for that question, then replied:

> I'm for government tax credits for Christian schools. It's your job to manage the country for your child. But I think the Republicans will be out of office now. I stopped watching the 10:00 news and reading the newspaper except for the Business Section because it's all about murder, killing, and rape. I have no idea of what's going on in the world. I

also passionately pray—I fervently pray for the reversal of Roe v. Wade to save all those unborn babies— those precious babies.

Meg believes it is her job to manage the world for her son's future, to alter it and to secure it, and, even though she decided to isolate herself from learning about current events, she still believed it was her duty to transform the world for future generations in a feminized way. In what seemed like a contradiction from her earlier sentiment that world events do not influence her mothering, Meg tried to change the world and protect her child because her gendered religious beliefs delegated that maternal responsibility to her. She supported George Bush and the wars in Afghanistan and Iraq, escalating her allegiance to those militarized and politicized beliefs by tuning out of the news cycle. Ironically, the more she isolated herself from the "outside" world, the more capable Meg felt of making change in that world from her spiritual perspective. She knew her place in the patriarchal structure of her faith and conservative Protestant denomination, claiming it as a revolutionary site. Like most Harvestville women, Meg did not talk about the war often, nor did she promote an overtly militarized position.

Harvestville mothers believe fervently that their power to transform the world lies in promoting a militarized patriarchy and in instilling that same ideology in their children. Intensive mothering and its accompanying maternal guilt were embedded into their lives. They are the protectors of the morality of their children, representing home and the homeland, "security moms," symbols of civilian patriotism, nationalistic pride, and idealized femininity.

Conservative Protestant Ideology

Another strand in what has become the militarized knot of Harvestville life is women's application of conservative Protestant Christian ideology with militarism. Many of the Harvestville women whom I interviewed interpreted the world through their conservative beliefs about biblical inerrancy, which in turn legitimated a moral absolutism and female submission. They often spoke about spiritual warfare, proselytizing to convert "others," and interpretating early twenty-first century sociopolitical conditions as spiritual and cultural war. The women see what the Bush administration called the "war on terrorism" as a principle battle in that larger war. This conservative Protestant ideology was historically saturated with militarism, wars, and war imagery, thereby desensitizing its adherents to the influences of militarization. In addition, male clergy, male and female lay leaders, and male and female parishioners regularly used war metaphors to characterize their earthly battle against sin and temptation to fuel their quest to win souls for Christ.

The notion of religious sacrifice and militarized sacrifice made sense in this conservative Christian ideological realm because the shift from spiritual dichotomous thinking about right and wrong, and about sacrificing one's life for the Christian cause, was transferred to cultural beliefs that already concerned Harvestville women. Therefore, when George W. Bush and his political strategists framed the rhetoric about the war on terrorism into ideological terms, Harvestville women followed suit. They were willing to sacrifice our soldiers to fight against the terrorists, and to defend their country, communities, and families against all sorts of enemies—spiritual, cultural, and military.

The conservative Protestant concepts of martyrdom and patriarchal self-sacrifice to which Harvestville women have subscribed for generations fueled the contemporary cultural battles against which they fought. For example, when I interviewed Elizabeth, a 35-year-old who was coordinator of the Altar Guild at her church—responsible for cleaning and maintaining the altar, preparing the communion wine and wafers, ironing the pastors' vestments, and coordinating the sanctuary flower orders, she told me she, "Wanted to serve the church in some behind the scenes way. My mom had been a member of the Altar Guild for a long time and she and one of her friends talked me into it. I think it's fascinating to learn about the traditions of the church."

Both men and women support the traditional gendered division of labor in Harvestville churches. When I talked informally with a 62-year-old Harvestville woman named Carol, who had been a member of a conservative Lutheran church for her entire life, she recounted when she took communion from the first female helper, "I looked up and saw her in front of me. I got up, turned around and walked back to my seat without taking communion." Carol's refusal to take communion occurred in the early 1990s, and since that time, a few women have served communion, ushered, or held seats on the executive committee, but none has served as pastors because the seminaries affiliated with this Lutheran church do not allow women to enter into the pastoral course of study.

Serving on the Altar Guild and perpetuating gendered church roles are not militarized acts in themselves; however, when those actions support militarized ideas about femininities and masculinities, they help foster it. They reinforce women's submissive role and men's leadership, replicating male dominance and male authority. Therefore, when the male commander-in-chief, the male politician, the male soldier, the male husband, or the male pastor asserts his gendered authority to interpret scripture, to wage war, and/or to set family rules, many women accept this patriarchy and even teach it to future generations. Militarization builds on—and depends on— these spiritualized, traditional gender roles, and many Harvestville women believe that this hierarchy is needed to defend submissive femininity in the battlefields of spirituality, war zones, and national culture.

Othering

Othering in Harvestville is a complex system of classification based on a code of expectation and position concerning gender, sexuality, race, class, religion, and political affiliation. Those who fit the model are insiders and those who do not are considered "others," or outsiders. This generational categorization not only separates the insiders from the outsiders, but qualifies insiders as allies and outsiders as political, religious, and cultural enemies. The elevated American militarization during the course of my fieldwork in 2003–2006 caused Harvestville women to cling more fiercely to their spiritual beliefs and to intensify their othering of "non-Christians." This discovery demonstrated to me that, while preexisting patriarchy had made the women of Harvestville susceptible to heightened militarization, it deepened their beliefs in spiritual warfare and othering.

An insular community prior to the September 11, 2001 terrorist attacks on the United States and our military invasions in Afghanistan and Iraq, most Harvestville residents—men and women—routinely engaged in the othering of those who did not mirror their white, middle-class, heterosexual, Republican, conservative Protestant profile. In the wake of political changes after 9/11, many female Harvestville residents' suspicion of "others" intensified, as did their sense of urgency to protect their American way of life. Terrorism was framed as assaults on American freedom, translated by Harvestville folks as attacks on morality.

This newly militarized, spiritual, and political urgency to identify "others" in order to protect themselves was also gendered, because in Harvestville's patriarchal society, men and women went about the business of "protecting" by distinct methods: Women were responsible for practicing feminized, spiritualized protection of their family's beliefs, for teaching their children, and for keeping their belief systems safe.

Harvestville women further tightened the militarized knot in their lives and their community by creating a religious outlook interpreting the "war on terrorism" as a necessary spiritual and moral battle.

The process of othering combines not only community profiling based on race and class, but also incorporates religious and political beliefs. Either/or binary spiritual interpretations about gender roles and good/evil, is compatible with rhetoric that garnered support for the war on terror in order to protect "our freedoms" against those who "hate us." In the lives of Harvestville women, othering began with religion and become cultural and political othering. Many females there, like followers of the larger Religious Right movement, view traditional heterosexual families as the foundation of a moral American society, the springboard for converting secular America to a Christian nation. By way of example, the political debate surrounding gay marriage struck a chord with them. When the Harvestville newspaper (which will remain unnamed here) ran an op-ed supporting the legalization of gay marriage, one woman's letter to the editor (April 12, 2006) declared:

> Marriage isn't just two people living together with a license; marriage is the union of one man and one woman to create together through their love for each other, and their intimate lifestyle. Human families and animal families are built on this relationship. It is families and not individuals that are the cornerstone of society. Homosexuals shouldn't marry because they can't procreate, because they can't have the love that is in marriage. Nor do they have the biological potential, because God didn't create marriage for just anybody, but for a man and a woman.

She went on to explain that, "They do not want to create life and love, because homosexuality cannot create life and love"; as such, this writer articulated the insider/outsider, othering rhetoric identifying what she perceived as a sin—running contrary to God's divine plan. Once "sin" is identified and classified as harmful to an individual or to society, those people who support that "sin" in any way could be categorized as enemies. The battle lines are drawn, and Harvestville women see themselves populating the frontlines of this spiritual, political, and cultural war zone.

Tying the Knot: One Woman's Story

One female resident of Harvestville whom I interviewed soon after the presidential election of 2004 is called Dawn. A married WASP (white, Anglo-Saxon Protestant) in her early 50s, with several grown children, she was a full-time stay-at-home mother now working as a school secretary. Also, she remained active in her local conservative church, serving on many different committees and in a Bible study group. Having once been chosen as secretary of the local Republican organization, she still encourages her neighbors and co-workers to vote, wears patriotic pins, posts political signs in her office, places candidates' placards in her yard during election time, and stuffs envelopes for Republican candidates. Still, Dawn does not consider herself to be "politically active." Although Harvestville is a site where militarization grows, even thrives, it is in the town's insularity that encourages its residents to feel separate, fearing that which is "other."

This exclusionary small town atmosphere helped Dawn feel safe. Now that the population is rapidly growing, some Harvestville residents have moved to even smaller communities, or have resisted the rezoning in their neighborhoods that would allow for newcomers. In Dawn's opinion, newcomers, strangers, and detractors of this cherished atmosphere were marked by their political stripes, "By looking at the election results, there are more Democrats in town. Someone's not watching the gate close enough." Sameness is necessary.

After the terrorist attacks in New York, Washington D.C. and Pennsylvania on September 11, 2001, militarized discourse escalated in the United States. Harvestville citizens recalled their feelings of shock and fear at what they repeatedly saw unfolding on their television screens and in their newspapers. Bush spoke of hunting down the enemies and bringing them to justice, "dead or alive." Many Harvestville residents believed that their plain-spoken, Christian president felt that the terrorism involved personal attacks on their own freedoms and religious beliefs.

To show the strength of the American spirit, patriotism escalated and Harvestville residents felt compelled to support the families of the victims, the President, and one another as U.S. citizens uniting against unseen enemies. Militaristic ideology, gendered ideology, and anti-Arab sentiment flourished here. As the United States deployed troops against the Taliban and al Qaeda, militarized notions of masculinity and femininity were reinforced in daily life.

Dawn and about a dozen female and male members of her church rented two vans and drove to New York City to make a Thanksgiving dinner for a predominately Muslim community in November 2001. Looking back on that experience, she recalled that, "We felt helpless after September 11 and we wanted to do something to help the victims of the attacks." Sensing the anti-Arab racism in Harvestville and assuming that Muslims living close to "ground zero" must have experienced discrimination, the group of churchgoers picked an area in Queens, New York where an affiliated church was located, and decided to embark on a mission trip their. Her church group saw this opportunity as a mission trip to show generosity and compassion to a community less than sixty miles from the World Trade Center ruins. They chose a Thanksgiving dinner as an expression of "midwestern hospitality," a meal shared by two different cultures in the spirit of fellowship. "It was a tangible way for us to show God's love to others," said Dawn. Participating in this mission trip was a political activity because it was a result of the group's beliefs.

In preparation for their dinner offering, Dawn recalled, the group did not educate itself about the cultural practices of that community. In fact, Dawn and her group were unaware that they were planning to cook and serve a Thanksgiving meal on a Sunday afternoon during what happened to be Ramadan, an Islamic period of fasting and meditation. Therefore, the group did not serve as much food as they anticipated; instead of bringing residents into the church for the meal, many residents took plates of food back to their homes for themselves and their families to eat in the evening. Perhaps not surprisingly, even upon her return Dawn did not educate herself about the practices of the people for whom she drove twenty-six hours in a forty-eight-hour period. When I asked if she thought that this mission trip was a political activity, Dawn responded that it was not because, "I was simply doing what I do everyday for my own family. I cook for them to show them that I love them. It's what I do and we thought that since it was Thanksgiving, we could cook a meal for this community to show them God's love."

The patriarchal, militarized knot is at times impossibly tight and difficult to unravel. This simple example illustrates the interconnectedness of militarization, gender, religion, and politics in the practices of Harvestville life. From Dawn's perspective, cooking this meal in Queens was intimately connected to her domestic role as a Christian wife and mother, but it was not political to her. In fact, she and her group saw themselves as ambassadors of acceptance and reconciliation because they took steps to actively counter anti-Arab, anti-Muslim racism.

Conclusion: Harvestville Women Stranded or Representative of a Militarized Knot?

Feminist IR scholars have successfully made the case that militarization is gendered and relies on both men's and women's complicity for its success. Militarization and patriarchy dovetail consistently; thus, even when militarization increases and decreases, it is always linked to the pressure of patriarchy. Similarly, wherever there is sexism, militarization is close by.

Militarization takes on many gendered forms, some blatant and others more subtle. It can, of course, take those gendered, violent forms, but to begin to understand the inner workings of militarization, we must recognize that its processes may be present in communities long before anyone perpetrates any heinous acts. It can require a sustained effort to recognize the subtleties of militarization, regularly embedded into our beliefs systems. As we have seen here, some Harvestville women accept spiritual warfare as a familiar and naturalized articulation of their gendered, patriarchal, militarized beliefs, and many dutifully embrace their role in the domestic sphere because, they believe, it serves the community, the state, and the nation.

Harvestville women's experiences, consequently, can teach us that militarization is not always exemplified in the familiar faces of military commanders, political leaders, or even rank and file soldiers. More often, it is personified in unrecognizable faces of nonelite civilians carrying out its work by replicating and weaving militaristic ideology into gendered beliefs that often seem separate from its influence. Likewise, militarization can be reflected in the lives of citizens living in nonwar zones, citizens who work hard to live their lives by the "golden rule" by protecting their loved ones and leading "moral" lives. The banal face of militarization is that of a person who maintains the militarized status quo, who chooses to militarize but also ignores one's complicity in militarization and its far-reaching effects. This means that, to chart the course of militarization, we need to sit in the kitchens of exurbia and talk to noncombatant women about the beliefs and practices that create a naturalized knot of militarization in their lives.

Note

The interview transcript analyses contained in this chapter are taken from my dissertation, *Securing the Heartland: A Feminist Analysis of the Militarization of Non-Combatant American Women's Lives Living in One Small Town during the Afghanistan and Iraq Wars, 2003–2006*, and my forthcoming manuscript of the same title.

References

Cockburn, C. 2007. *From where we stand: War, women's activism and feminist analysis*. London: Zed Books.

D'Amico, F. and L. Weinstein. eds. 1999. *Gender camouflage: Women and the U.S. Military*. New York: New York University Press.
de Beauvoir. S. 1989. *The second sex*. New York: Vintage Books.
Enloe, C. 2000. *Maneuvers: The international politics of militarizing women's lives*. Berkeley: University of California Press.
Gilman, C. P. 1898. *Women and economics: A study of the economic relations between men and women as a factor in social evolution*. January 2, 2007, from http:digital.library.upenn.edu/women/gilman/economics/economics.html.
Pettman, J. J. 1996. *Worlding women: A feminist international politics*. New York: Routledge.
Tickner, J. A. 2001. *Gendering world politics: Issues and approaches to the post-Cold War era*. New York: Columbia University Press.
Wollstonecraft, M. 1992. *A vindication of the rights of woman*. London: Penguin Books.
Woolf, V. 1938. *Three Guineas*. .London: Harcourt Brace and Co.

14

Horror to Hope, Tragedy to Triumph: The Women of Rwanda

Tadia Rice

In April 1994 I was in South Africa, celebrating its rebirth and democracy, as Nelson Mandela became president. But that joy was shattered as the world became a global voyeur of televised images of young and old bodies piled like trash on Rwanda's dusty roads. Dismembered arms, legs, and skulls of Tutsis, and sympathetic Hutus, lay in stacks on the ground. Bloated bodies floated in rivers and corpses filled pits. Pregnant women with children wrapped on their backs lay hacked to death. In houses of worship clergy murdered church members, leaving their bodies to rot on the floor. Children were persuaded to kill parents as well as schoolmates. Mothers killed their half-Tutsi children, husbands killed wives, and brothers murdered sisters. This carnage tore at my soul.

God Goes about the World Doing Good, But He Sleeps in Rwanda
(Proverb of Rwanda)

The French call Rwanda, "Pays des Mille Collines." Rwandans say, *Igihugu cy'Imisozi igihumbi*, the "land of a thousand hills." It is a beautiful green patchwork quilt of hills and valleys set against blue skies and peaceful lakes. It is an inspiring site, but its people inspire even more.

In November 2007, I visited the Republic of Rwanda for an extraordinary celebration, the centennial commemoration of its capital, Kigali. Spotlessly clean, Kigali was founded as a colonial outpost in 1907 with only 357 people. It is now home to almost a million environmentally conscious residents who are committed to a "No Litter" policy. Plastic bags are illegal. No garbage, cigarette butts, or waste of any kind is allowed to litter the ground. At 7:00 am on the last Saturday of every month everyone participates in *umuganda*, the mandatory community cleanup. Businesses close, public transport stops, and until noon all adults, school-age children, and even the president, stop to clean wherever they may be. Rwandans are highly disciplined people.

Dotted with highrise buildings and noisy new construction, fast moving cars and pedestrians maneuver through Kigali. It is a safe place where laws are respected. When a crime occurs everyone knows about it. Corruption is not tolerated.

The embrace of the Rwandan women reminded me of my brown-skinned, brown-eyed, strong-willed grandmother. She was a humble woman of integrity and vision, creativity and courage. The matriarch of the family, she was fearless, generous, empathetic, and kind. In every way, she was in charge of the family, but just as her Rwandan counterparts she was poor and lacked a formal education. Yet, she and the women are among the smartest people I know. Women, in any culture, learn to work with others and carry on in the face of hardships. There are no female loners in villages.

As a management consultant specializing in leadership and women's empowerment, it was confirming that my grandmother and the women of Rwanda demonstrated what a ten-year research program, led by Wharton University Professor of Management, Robert House, proved. Using qualitative and quantitative methodologies, the Global Leadership and Organizational Behavior Effectiveness Research Program (Sage Publications, 2004) empirically confirmed that universally endorsed leadership theories and values reflect: vision; inspiration; self-sacrifice; integrity; decisiveness; and performance.

The women of war-torn, impoverished, postgenocide Rwanda demonstrated six leadership values under the most difficult of circumstances. The complexity of theories, and their applications, are repeatedly analyzed by academicians and applied by highly paid consultants in western business modules. However, the Rwandan transformed and simplified leadership into a new form—distilled, condensed, and filtered for survival and expedience. Rwanda gives new meaning to the art and science of leadership.

Spirited women learn how to turn challenge into success, and adversity into opportunity. Taking risks, problem solving, team building, and decision making are only a few of the attributes these women displayed as they got things done. The results of what happened in Rwanda's 1994 genocide demonstrate this essential truth.

LET US BE AGAINST WICKEDNESS
WRITTEN ON THE WALL OF THE KIBUYE GENOCIDE MEMORIAL

Churches were the one place in Rwanda where people felt safe, but the sanctuaries of two rural churches southeast of Kigali now represent the unspeakable horror and living hell that once were havens.

At the Ntarama Church sanctuary hundreds of genocidaires locked 10,000 worshipers inside. Then the rebel soldiers, called *Interahamwe*, murdered 5,000 of them. Where they prayed they now lay—500 disintegrating skulls, some with teeth intact, some with hair, some arranged on shelves. Wall-to-wall children, some with cracked craniums, are lined up in this genocide museum—a testament to the Rwandan horror. The dead are ever-present among the crumbling bricks where faceless remains will forever rest, strung together like dead pearls too numerous to count.

WHEN ELEPHANTS FIGHT, THE GRASS GETS TRAMPLED

Genocide is defined as the mass killing of a group of people with intent to destroy, in whole or in part, a national, ethnical, racial, or religious group. Experts consider the war crimes perpetrated in Rwanda among the most massive, systematic, and concentrated acts of genocide in human history.

More than 800,000 innocent men, women, and children were mercilessly killed within 100 days. According to Human Rights Watch (Human Rights Watch, World Report: Rwanda. Human Rights Watch Press release February 1, 2001), "the worst massacres had finished...perhaps half of the Tutsi population of Rwanda" in the first month. The French historian Gerard Prunier estimates that "this includes about 750,000 Tutsis and approximately 50,000 politically moderate Hutus who did not support the genocide...Only about 130,000 Tutsis survived the massacres."

The Rwandan government called this the fastest and most vicious genocide yet recorded in human history. An integral part of this viciousness was the use of rape as a weapon of war. Throughout history, whether during pagan Rome or American slavery, rape has proven an effective tool of sexual politics that keeps women vulnerable and fearful. Rape is political terror where the vagina becomes the battlefield. It is meant to defile the body and degrade the mind. It is genital terrorism that has no boundaries, and its fallout has no limits. It is meant to destroy the soul of its victim.

Rape is about violent power. It intimidates, humiliates, and controls women and communities. A dissolute strategy for extracting information and implementing systematic sexual slavery, rape is a weapon that requires hateful preparation. Often, victims are threatened with a brutal death, spared only to be raped, infected, and mutilated.

During Rwanda's genocide, Tutsi women became the symbolic enemy and the procreation foe. Rape was a justified tactical military operation. A standard weapon of war and tyranny, it has been perpetrated with impunity across Africa and is still being used around the world. Rwanda will happen again and again, wherever and whenever tolerated by governments and societies. Countless tales of horror from Rwandan survivors emerged. Human Rights Watch (1996) reported more than 250,000 women were raped during the genocide. A UNICEF Report (1997) reported witness accounts in the hundreds of thousands.

One twelve-year-old son raped his forty-five-year-old mother while her five younger children were forced to hold open her thighs as her husband was forced to watch. The *Interahamwe* held a hatchet to the boy's throat. Such an insidious legacy demoralizes entire communities and leaves survivors with a degradation and terror that defies rational thought.

In a twist of fate that only wars can create were reports that *Interahamwe* soldiers forced some Tutsi men to have intercourse with women strangers. Threatened that their loved ones would be killed, and beaten before or after the sexual act, the Tutsi men were told after coitus that these women were infected with HIV/AIDS. Whether these women were Hutu or Tutsi will never be known, but clearly the objective was to assure a slow and painful death for both. A 1996 report of the UN Special Rapporteur on Rwanda estimated that between 250,000 and 500,000 women were raped by men who were HIV-positive and knew their status. Sadistically, these men intentionally transmitted the virus to Tutsi women and their families.

The rape victims of Rwanda who survived these horrifying masochistic rapes were deeply scarred by this brutal chauvinism. They suffered physical injuries combined with psychological forces that rendered them inadequate protectors of their girl children, sisters, mothers, grandmothers—even themselves. Forced pregnancy, infections from sexually transmitted diseases (syphilis, gonorrhea, serious chronic medical problems such as vaginal fistula, life-threatening HIV/AIDS) were widespread consequences facing these victims.

Rape victims were likely to know the men who raped them; they also might be exposed to the rapists or their families during the subsequent reconstruction effort. With a new population resulting from the genocide, this fear became another layer of suffering for the women.

The Rwandan genocide left women, who were once productive, overwhelmed by trauma, loss, disbelief, and grief. The experience unleashed fear of both the known and unknown. There was no way to retrieve the life they once knew. They became, and many still are, dependant on charitable interventions in every aspect of life.

Many women were left with confused emotions about their survival, even leading to survivor guilt. Damaged lives, lost trust, self-confidence adrift, fear of the future, and an inability to maintain intimate relationships are only a few realities for rape survivors.

Rape as a primary weapon of war has taken unexpected proportions in Democratic Republic of Congo (DRC). As Rwanda's neighbor approximately 7,000 *Interahamwe* rebels fled to DRC. Escaping prosecution for Rwanda's genocide crimes, these rebels began unleashing further crimes in DRC—raping Congolese women, enslaving them, slaughtering babies, murdering villagers, looting and burning down houses.

As in Rwanda, gender-based violence in DRC also utilized low-tech weapons—guns, machetes, knives, cut bottles, tree branches, sticks, rifles, and other items that could penetrate. Action by Churches Together (ACT) International, a global alliance of related agencies working to save lives and support communities in emergencies worldwide, estimates that since 1996 nearly 200,000 women have been raped in DRC.

The American Bar Association runs a sexual violence legal clinic based in Goma. They estimate 75 percent of the DRC's rape convictions have been committed by military men. Compounding these crimes is military retaliation by Congolese forces against both civilians and Rwandan refugees suspected of collaborating with the *Interahamwe* rebels.

Rwanda and DRC share more than magnificent Lake Kivu and colonization by Belgian invaders. In 1998 insurrection by Rwandan rebels triggered two DRC wars that ultimately involved and influenced six other nations, destabilizing the Central African region. DRC's rich natural resources were plundered, and the U.N. accused a host of dubious factions as culprits, including foreign governments and international corporations.

After more than a decade of broken relations, Rwanda's President Paul Kagame and DRC's President Joseph Kabila met in 2009 and created a pact that would usher in a new era of peace in the region. They declared they would develop both economies, share military intelligence, and utilize natural gas reserves located within shared waters.

Despite presidential promises of peace, a new bombshell of reported rapes of Pygmy men in villages continues to astound officials. The accused are members of the Congolese army, rebel groups like the Democratic Forces for the Liberation of Rwanda, the National Congress for People's Defence, or the Mayi-Mayi (community-based *militias*). Congolese lawyer Me Mutumba Janvier, who is located in Goma, recalls the rape of a Pygmy man, "One of them is head of his village. He claims to have been raped by several men in front of his wife and children. His entire family was also attacked and made to suffer the same torture."

Janvier explains that the rapists are intent on destroying their victims and psychologically destabilizing them into total submission. Why Pygmies? Superstitious belief in the region is that Pygmies possess magical powers. According to Janvier, the soldiers rape men to destroy their invincibility, *kilembe* as it is known locally. The men are ridiculed, rejected, and emasculated in a society that considers homosexuality forbidden. Janvier says, "The people in my village say: 'You're no longer a man. Those men in the bush made you their wife.'"

Raping men has become an effective method by which to control citizens in villages where valuable mineral mines are located. Consequently, the number of *bushwives* is escalating. Men are now beginning to share the rape experience that women have long had to endure.

Reaching the Depths of Despair Is Not Dying

The phrase, "rape of rape" sounds like a conundrum, an ambiguous double entendre. In the Rwandan genocide women and girls were systematically gang-raped and then unimaginably mutilated. Witnesses detailed stories of *Interahamwe* obsessed with mutilating women's bodies, using spears, gun barrels, bayonets, cut bottles, machetes, and even the stamens of banana trees to penetrate their victims. Afterward, witnesses remember the men would slit their throats.

Armed militants, rogue soldiers, rebel fighters, thugs, prisoners, strangers, neighbors and even relatives, gang raped women and children—young, old, pregnant, disabled, even babies. With or without penile penetration, men thrust sticks, gun barrels, bayonets, broken bottles, glass shards and even hot plastic, into the vaginas of these suffering females. Some men would stab, slice, cut, or pierce the labia. Some women had their pubic hair set on fire. Some of the women were shot in the vagina, rectum, or breasts. Sometimes boiling water and acid was also used. Sometimes women's breasts were cut off. Reports from survivors recount how their sexual organs were mutilated: cut, gored, gouged, pierced, ripped, stabbed, speared, slit, or slashed with machetes, knives, cut bottles, sticks, rifles, and any object their perpetrators chose to use that would cause immediate agony and prolonged anguish.

One survivor was a woman giving birth (A Woman's Work, Peter Landesman, 2002). The men watching her waited for her baby to emerge only to spear and kill it while still in the vaginal canal. If the woman were lucky she would die and be thrown into massive pits full of dead relatives. If the mutilation did not kill her she would be left with vaginal and rectal injuries, diseases, infections, AIDS, and infertility—assuring her a life of intolerable torment and unending sorrow. Some women committed suicide.

I WILL LIVE

Global humanitarian failure to respond to Rwanda's genocide created more problems for rape survivors. Missed medical opportunities caused many fatalities and left survivors with vaginal fistula, a life threatening condition caused by one or more rapes that tear the walls between the vagina, bladder, and anus. The result is debilitating incontinence and severe pain. There is no way to control or camouflage the horrific smell of streaming urine and dripping feces. These infections will never go away without immediate care and vital reconstructive surgery to rebuild women's vaginas and rectums. Women who suffer this agonizing mutilation of genitalia cannot sit down because it hurts too much; they stink from the smell of continuous infection; and they can never deny what caused the condition that leaves a trail of urine and feces behind them. Even with medical care the condition leaves the survivor with life-long urinary and rectal problems, and infertility. They are the women who long for children they can never bear.

In Africa the proverb, "Children are the reward of life" takes on significant meaning. It is an important aspect of family life. Without children women will not enjoy the same status as those who are mothers.

Wives who suffer vaginal fistula are often abandoned by husbands or driven out of their villages. Rape was just the beginning of never-ending grief. These women are lucky if they are able to get diapers or colostomy bags, and wear them for the rest of their lives.

PREGNANCY AND FIRE CANNOT BE KEPT SECRET

Rwanda's National Population Office estimates the number of children born to survivors of rape range in the thousands. Progeny conceived through rape often represents the perpetrator, and in Rwanda, the perpetrator may have been a neighbor or relative. They may also have executed the family of the rape survivor—in front of her. The act of sexually violent rape dishonors her to their community, and this stigma can be as powerful as the trauma itself. For many indigenous women, culture censures them. For Rwandan women impregnated through rape there was an additional burden to bear: "Who will care for my children when I die from AIDS contracted during the rape?"

Sometimes it is their infected children who die first.

Families often disowned women impregnated by rape; and many of these mothers disowned their own unwanted children. The *enfants de mauvais souvenir* (children of bad memories) are the children of hate, a generation of children left with an identity of the savagery that conceived them. Many were orphaned, growing up on the streets along with other children whose parents died in the genocide. The tragedy for these children is plentiful. Stigmatized and often resented, these children of hate will never know who their fathers are—and they shouldn't. Now in their teens, they likely lack a positive identity so important in African culture. No one really ever wins in genocide, least of all the children.

IF YOUR MOUTH TURNS INTO A KNIFE IT WILL CUT OFF YOUR LIPS

Disturbingly, not all women were innocent victims. Rethinking militarism in a feminine context shattered my view of gender archetypes. African Rights reported, "Women, and even girls, were involved in the slaughter in countless ways, inflicting extraordinary cruelty on other women, as well as children and men. Women of every social category took part in the killings. The extent to which women were involved in the killings is unprecedented anywhere in the world."

UNICEF determined that by 1997 more than 5,500 women were in prison, most accused of crimes of genocide, and many with dependant infants.

To understand why women in the Rwandan conflict were both victim and villain, one must examine their participation in ethnic cleansing that constructs and sustains activist movements. According to Professor Lisa Sharlach of University of Alabama, "the nationalist radio broadcasters stressed that all Hutu, whether female or male, capable of killing Tutsi had the civic obligation of doing so...Additionally, the broadcasters demanded that all Tutsi, regardless of sex or age, must die."

Astounding reports have been documented: women killing with their own hands; stripping the dying and already dead of jewelry, money, and clothes; mothers and grandmothers refusing to hide their own Tutsi children and grandchildren; nurses compiling killing lists of Tutsi patients, refugees, and colleagues; stoning people to death; looting and burning down houses; rallying other women to participate in the killings.

The *Interahamwe* killing machine recruited their militia from amongst poor, uneducated young men, and the marginally employed or unemployed homeless. Overnight, these citizens on the lower rung of the social ladder became powerful authorities in soldier uniforms, able to exert revenge against those of a different ethnicity. These new soldiers killed with impunity. Sharlach adds, "They could steal, they could kill with minimum justification, they could rape and they could get drunk for free. This was wonderful. The political aims pursued by the masters of this dark carnival were quite beyond their scope. They just went along, knowing it would not last."

LAWS ARE HEAVIER THAN STONES

As Rwanda began rebuilding from genocide, the new government was challenged to dispense justice amid an emotional landscape of deeply wounded hearts and souls. Justice was a necessity. It was a moral decision needed for the survivors to recover from trauma and grief; to mourn adequately; to heal from emotional and spiritual wounds; to forgive; and to find unity from long-established divisiveness. No constitutional provision existed that could judge the perpetrators on the type of atrocities committed. Within six years jails were packed with more than 120,000 alleged criminals. Clearly there was no way to efficiently or economically prosecute this many prisoners.

In March 2001 Rwanda instituted what many considered the world's boldest experiment in reconciliation—*gacaca* (pronounced GA-cha-cha). As a trained mediator, it was enlightening to learn about this restorative traditional method of community justice. The intent is to heal the victim and to accept the offender back into their community. In the earlier days victim and perpetrator, as well as family and community, could gather under a shade tree or open grassland. In this natural environment the elder adult males dispensed justice.

Gacaca, in postgenocide Rwanda, developed into a more expanded version, but the intent was to assist an overburdened and inadequate criminal court system, and deal with the mass slaughter and widespread rape that occurred. It would become the acid test of leadership for a nation in recovery. *Gacaca* courts achieved several dynamics:

- Reconstruct the facts that occurred during the genocide
- Speed up legal proceedings
- Foster reconciliation
- Build unity among Rwandans

Hundreds of women, both Hutu and Tutsi, were trained as community leaders in the process. The women who performed *gacaca* broke traditional roles as they dispensed justice in a postgenocide society. Whether perpetrator in the genocide, survivor of the destruction, or victor in the reconstruction, roles for Rwandan women were forever fundamentally and dramatically changed.

BLESSED ARE THOSE WHO FORGIVE

"The people of Rwanda are still traumatized, but despite all that happened, life must continue," says Aloisea Inyumba, a Senator in Rwanda's Parliament. Once governor of Kigali-Ngali Province, Inyumba became the new government's first Minister of Family, Gender, and Social Affairs, replacing the infamous Pauline Nyiramasuhuko, who incited troops to rape thousands of women and orchestrated the slaughter of thousands trapped in a stadium where almost everyone was killed, even old women and unborn babies. She is now part of history as the first woman ever to be charged by the International Criminal Tribunal for Rwanda for rape as a crime against humanity. Inyumba understood that Rwanda's emotional considerations and legal challenges would require the country to create a new judicial system. It became her priority to insure that both victim, and accused, benefited from true justice, even though everyone who participated in the genocide could not be treated equally. More than 3,000,000 Hutus, who fled to border countries, had returned home. The Rwandans had to learn to live with neighbors who killed their family members, and perpetrators had to live with their victims.

Under *gacaca* law the accused might return home to face their victims and accusers. *Gacaca* law includes a Confession and Guilty Plea clause that allows reduced sentences for those who confess and plead guilty. Killers had a voice in this process. One killer said, "I have admitted to my crimes and asked for forgiveness. That is why I was released from prison after seven years. Since I was freed last year, I have visited fourteen homes to apologize for killing members of their families. I took part in the genocide from April 8, when we murdered many people in a hospital. I threw hand grenades, and I used a rifle. It is not easy to talk to the survivors because they are very traumatized. I helped one widow build a kitchen as a kind of compensation. I noticed that working together makes it easier for both sides. I've changed in prison. I realize how wrong I was."

The process often became an agonizing testimony for the victim, as well as a test of faith in a system that was experimental in many ways. Those who pursued justice could be rejected, disowned, or humiliated by family and community. The rapist, who may have regained freedom after trial, was often luckier than the women victims left behind, drained by illness, family rejection, and then imprisoned in immense poverty and social isolation. Women had to deal with tremendous anger and grief, and support networks were few.

As reconciliation moved forward, Inyumba became responsible for public debates promoting reunion between Hutus and Tutsis. The only woman on the ten-member executive committee of the Rwandan Patriotic Front, it was Inyumba who planted the seeds that encouraged Tutsi and Hutu women to talk to each other.

Surviving the catharsis of *gacaca* justice allowed many Rwandan to move beyond the futility of the killings and resume some normalcy in their lives. Profound acts of contrition from genocide conspirators proved to restore human dignity to many victims. Inyumba and her countrywomen recognized that reconciliation was the only future for Rwanda. Although divided into groups of Hutu, Tutsi, and Twa, the people of Rwanda share only one language, *Kinyarwanda*. They also share one homogenous culture, one country, and one indigenous history. Inyumba wanted to make sure another generation did not suffer like hers, so she is raising the children of her two slain brothers. She acknowledges, even fifteen years later that the memories are still fresh, and they are not good ones.

Some Rwandans claim that the "genocide industry" is now holding the nation hostage. French journalist Jean Hatzfeld collected oral histories of both Tutsi survivors and confessed Hutu killers. In his book, *Machete Season: The Killers in Rwanda Speak* (2005), his examination reveals more than physical scars. It considers whether justice has been sacrificed for national recovery.

One Tutsi, Innocent Rwililiza, lost his wife and children in the Nymata Church Massacre. His response to the early release of thousands of perpetrators, "If you think about it, who is it talking about forgiveness? The Tutsis? The Hutus? The freed prisoners and their families? None of them. It's the humanitarian organizations. They are importing forgiveness to Rwanda, and they wrap it lots of dollars to win us over. There is a Forgiveness Plan just as there is an AIDS Plan, with public awareness meetings, poster, petty local presidents, super-polite Whites in all-terrain turbo vehicles. These humanitarian workers lecture our teachers, bring our communal councilors on board. They finance various assistance projects. As for us, we speak of forgiveness to earn their good opinion—and because the subsidies can be lucrative."

Hutu farmer and volunteer deacon in the Catholic Church in Ntarama, Fulgence Bunani, had never killed anyone, until the genocide. He recalls the screaming and remembers striking "without seeing who it was, taking pot luck with the crowd."

Another Hutu man was Alphonse Hitiwork. His job was to search through corpses to find anyone still breathing. Once found, he and his cohorts would work "to finish off everyone conscientiously."

Let the Children Come to Me

Changing family dynamics, social attitudes, and institutional standards are fundamental adjustments the world must make if we want to prevent future tragedies. Men and women, whether as individuals or parents, consciously, or unconsciously, often reinforce negative beliefs about the other and impart those attitudes to children. Liberating men and women from what has prevented a healthy and productive partnership between them means becoming equal partners.

Transforming existing perceptions and archetypal roles is what is needed to help girls learn to convert subordination into strength, and for boys to trade aggression for service toward others. Valuing the other will help both men and women realize their full potential. Family structure will be better served.

Women are the first teachers of their children, so when a mother is educated so will be the children. Humanity is like the two wings of a bird: one male and the other female. If the two wings are not equivalent in strength, the bird is impaired and cannot fly. When wings are equally and fully developed then the bird can achieve further heights and distances.

When gender equality reflects this metaphor it will become a reality. Then extraordinary human development and prosperity will be realized. The women of Rwanda understand how these critical keys will unlock the gender door that has remained a tool of social inequality.

Sensitizing men to respect women often takes innovative measures. Bush theater creator, Bernard Kalume, a Rwandan, travels to Eastern Congo presenting his drama: a couple is being married and during the ceremony a group of armed men kidnap the bride, hold her prisoner in the forest for six months, raping her repeatedly. When she escapes and returns home, her village that rejects and ostracizes her. She is a disgrace to her parents, and she is pregnant. Kalume says, "This play is based on a true story from 2006 in Walungu, North Kivu. My play only reflects the truth."

Kalume is a brave man willing to tell his Rwanda story in the Congo. During the Rwandan genocide he, along with his children, were forced to witness his wife being killed in front of them. He says, "My purpose with this play is to make people start to talk about rape and sensitize men to respect women. Most men in Congo have lost a sense of their obligations, contributing nothing to daily life. The women take care of everything: feeding the children, working in the fields, maintaining the family."

Bringing people together who have been taught to think they should be divided was Rwanda's major challenge. It seems that everything Rwanda does now in response to its genocide is an experiment. In the eyes of the world Rwanda achieved what was thought unachievable: African women serving as powerful role models whose voices had traditionally been suppressed. But these women are speaking loudly and proudly. Rwandan women demonstrated that hope remains alive, even among the gloom of broken spirits. And the men cannot but listen.

Women know how to wage peace. Women sitting in seats of national and local government have achieved great things for their country. Beside the prominent women in Rwanda's parliament and other organizations there are many other heroines. Many are subsistence farmers. Since the genocide they have learned to build their own houses, and paint them, too.

Gender cannot be underestimated. After the genocide a half million women endured the trauma of war, yet they demonstrated a resilience: coping with widowhood; destruction of their families; death of their children and other family members; loss of their homes and possessions; suffering emotional and physical wounds; the rape of their bodies as well as their minds.

The collateral damage of the genocide did not end with the women who lost their children. Children lost mothers, leaving a half million offspring living in orphanages. Rwanda implemented a national campaign; the slogan became "Every home a child, every child a home."

Rwandan women went to orphanages and took dead women's children as their own, whether they were Hutu or Tutsi. Some children were distant relatives, others were strangers, and still others were progeny of genocide perpetrators.

The traditional Rwandan family structure became transformed. Now Rwanda has a high female population (54 percent), of which large proportions are widows and/or single women, with 34 percent of the households headed by women. Most Rwandan women over thirty years old have never attended school. The Office of the UN High Commissioner for Refugees reports that nearly 30,000 households are headed by girls between twelve and eighteen years old.

These daunting statistics illustrate grim conditions that could bring any country to its knees. However, Rwanda's legs are stronger than most.

When a Mountain Is in Your Path Do Not Sit Down at Its Foot and Cry, Get Up and Climb It

Living most of my time in South Africa since its first-ever democratic elections has allowed me to observe that country's reconciliation process. South Africa's process was characterized by unique circumstances that, at times, both succeeded and failed at unifying people. Rwanda has been undoubtedly successful. I believe that this is because of its women.

Christine Tuyisenge, vice president of the National Women's Council, an organ of Rwanda's Ministry for Gender and Family Promotion, is a lawyer and human rights champion in Rwanda. When I asked her how Rwandan women converted the catastrophe of the genocide into the victory of human spirit, she told me, "I learned two *Kinyarwandan* proverbs as a child—'the woman is the heart of the family' and 'to educate a woman is to educate a nation.'"

Tuyisenge was also first vice president of the Pro-Femmes Twese Hamwe, an organization of more than fifty Rwandan groups working for the promotion of the rights of women and children. Eradicating all forms of discrimination against women is an overwhelming challenge, but the organization has made an impact in socioeconomic development as well as the legal rights for women. Their impressive partnerships increase organizational and institutional capacity building and mobilize forums on the role of women. They also support political, economic, social, and cultural development, along with a durable reconciliation and peace process.

Tuyisenge says, "The challenge has been our history—women stayed behind the men. When so many Tutsi men were killed in the genocide, we women were left vulnerable. We had to claim our rights and ensure legal protection. One of the hardest things to do was to change our mindset as women. If I have been told all my life that I am not equal to my brother, it will not be easy to demand my rights when they are violated. So, we also had to change the mentality of men too."

This diminutive woman with long braids and a quick smile, Tuyisenge explained, "In the aftermath of the genocide women shared their painful experiences. They had to find ways to heal from the trauma, and care for the children, and survive. These groups of women became networks for maintaining family needs. With support from government and others donors, women initiated income generating activities, and they were also thrust into participation and decision making at every level of society and government." It was the only direction on our path to progress. It was the only way we could insure there would never be another genocide.

This lawyer and human rights champion explains that the National Women's Council has provided entrepreneurial training for women to change their historically unequal economic status. Until 1999 women in Rwanda did not have legal access to property, bank loans, or inheritance rights. Working with UNIFEM, the National Women's Council has also conducted training for women candidates to strengthen campaigning skills. In 2000 the Minister of Family and Gender Promotion established the Women Guarantee Fund that Tuyisenge describes as an affirmative action plan for women to gain access to credit for a range of new businesses as large as coffee plantations, stores, and beauty salons to traditional basket-making and nontraditional taxi cab companies with women drivers.

Tuyisenge is like many Rwandan women on a mission. She tells me, "There are still at least two hundred thousand children who run households, who have to take care of their younger sisters, brothers, and cousins. They are forced to take charge, their lives will always be difficult. They will never have a childhood. The women of Rwanda are determined to work hard for the development of their families, because life must continue. We have to stand strong in order to achieve the dreams we lost during genocide."

As vice president of the National Commission for the Fight against Genocide, Tuyisenge organized the 2009 annual commemoration at a night vigil at Kigali's Amahoro National Stadium that holds nearly 30,000. As 10,000 people delicately held brightly burning candles, one by one, the flames spelled out the word HOPE—in English, French, and Kinyarwandan. Fifteen years after this tragedy, emotions still run high for genocide survivors everywhere.

It seems that Rwanda likes to break the rules. By all accounts, women in countries that have been economically ravaged and socially divided have a difficult time during reconstruction. Yet the influence of women on Rwanda's reconstruction and reconciliation has been impressive. Women helped draft the constitution, developed guidelines for female parliamentarians, created government policies for the interests of women, and changed laws that once banned women from inheriting property. Women participate in every level of the workforce, in every industry, and especially in politics at the national level.

Rwandan women took action to deal with their experience, and the success of these efforts has been demonstrated in partnerships with many NGOs and humanitarian agencies. A UNIFEM program is strengthening women's organizations to expand capacity to respond to peace building, including training *gacaca* judges. This program also trains women as police officers to remedy the fact that the police force is comprised of only 10 percent women. Logistical and communication facilities are also being implemented to insure rapid response to sexual violence. Rwanda has improved social welfare for vulnerable women who have been sexually violated and infected with HIV/AIDS from gender-based violence.

The Association of Genocide Widows (AVEGA-AGAHOZO) was created by fifty widows, all genocide survivors. Their mission was simple and accomplished—to promote the general welfare of the genocide victims by participating in Rwanda's national reconstruction and reconciliation process at every level. The organization helped women with each need, whether emotional counseling or legal representation.

One of those founders, Chantal Kayitesi, recalls, "Women lost everything all at once, their home, belongings, family, their bodies were stolen. Women needed a way to channel their grief, process their loss, get medical attention, a place to live, food to eat, have a voice in the legal system. In due course AGAHOZO was also able to help women survivors develop their own small businesses and begin a new life."

Rwandan women have seized many opportunities for empowerment and healing. Women own 41 percent of Rwandan businesses. However, some are faced with continuing challenges like repatriation deadlines imposed on U.N. refugee camps in Uganda that pressures Rwanda's exiled women to abandon the vegetables gardens that have sustained them during more than a decade. They have lived on food rations and in camps where they are at the mercy of a neighboring country. Returning to a Rwanda they no longer know could further impoverish as well as *dis*empower these women.

April in Rwanda is a haunting anniversary that continues to see remains reburied. The month also symbolizes the anniversaries of six major modern genocides: Armenia, Bosnia, Cambodia, Darfur, the Holocaust, and Rwanda. In 2009 more than 250 genocide commemorations were held around the world. In the city of Kigali national conferences were held and memorials were observed, setting in motion a 100-day commemoration.

When United Everything Is Possible

In March 2000 Paul Kagame, whose Rwandan Patriotic Front forces overthrew the genocide government in a 1994 triumph over evil, became president of the country. A key powerbroker in the struggle for Rwanda's independence, Kagame is a central figure in its rebirth. The strength of his leadership has been hailed as pivotal in the democratization of Rwanda. As a freedom fighter, Kagame was a soldier for most of his adult life. He is considered an incorruptible teetotaler, a strong disciplinarian, and an intellectual. He refers to himself as Rwandan, and not Tutsi. He has created a successful example of democratic transformative politics and achieved what no one thought was possible.

Kagame notes that Rwanda's gender-sensitive policies were inspired by experience gained during the liberation struggle when women and men together mobilized, managed resources and fought side by side. In February 2007 at the International Conference on "Gender, Nation Building and the Role of Parliaments" in Kigali he addressed a host of women leaders, "African women, in particular, face extraordinary challenges. Key among these is the lack of access to education, healthcare, and economic opportunity...Africa must realize the hidden reserves in its people, especially women...It is painfully evident that gender inequality constrains growth and poverty reduction. Frankly, Africa is missing out on productive potential of more than half its population. Parliamentarians and policymakers have a critical role to play in promoting nationally owned programs for a faster pace of socioeconomic and political transformation. This cannot happen without full participation of women."

In Dakar, Senegal, I witnessed President Kagame accept the well-deserved 2007 African Gender Awards for the substantial gains made in advancing the cause of Rwandan women. Selected by the Women Africa Solidarity and the Committee of the African Women for Peace and Development, Kagame explained, "Prohibiting more than half of a country's population from engaging in productive socioeconomic activity amounts to shortsightedness—and is without question, a waste of human resources...a nation that promotes women is not doing women a favor but, doing the nation itself a favor."

Kagame is proud that 44 percent of the Supreme Court judges are women, including its president, and one-third of Rwanda's parliament members are also women.

Kagame's vision for his nation includes three strategies he says helped the country achieve emancipation for its women: the creation of women advocacy network at all levels; removing gender insensitive laws; and insuring access to education for women and girls. He knows that reconciliation is a healing process that cannot exclude more than half of his nation's population. Martin Luther King, Jr. said, "The ultimate measure of a man is not where he stands in moments of comfort and convenience, but where he stands at times of challenge and controversy."

Despite Kagame's leadership and calls for soul-searching past tragedies many lessons remain to be learned. During April 2008 tensions between genocide survivors and perpetrators became evident when 1,000 mourners gathered at Kigali's Gisozi Genocide Memorial Centre museum to pay respects to slain friends and relatives. Armed men threw a grenade at the building, killed a policeman, and injured others. A car drove through a commemoration procession and killed another. As late as the mourning season of 2009, when again tears would flow within and without, another grenade attack occurred. Kagame will not forget the genocide, but says Rwanda will not be defined by it either.

This is why Paul Kagame stands tall.

ARISE, SHINE RWANDA! WE WILL OVERCOME

After the genocide many victimized, tortured, raped, and traumatized women persisted. It is something women do—everywhere, whether in war or peace. The Rwandan women demonstrated fearlessness and strength when they ensured orphaned children would find new mothers, new families, and new hope for their futures.

The women who initiated and fostered this adoption process became the threads that would weave the very fiber and social fabric of a new nation. The pattern of their design is evident in every aspect of Rwanda's redevelopment today. The women of Rwanda typified the words of Nelson Mandela, "It is what we make of what we have, not what we are given, that separates one person from another."

The lives of Rwanda's women became their message. Living mothers could not allow dead ones to die knowing those children would face an end to their world. They created new beginnings. Motherhood bestows women immeasurable and unbounded power.

So the women of Rwanda began. Insanity gave way to common sense. Maybe it was simple primal survival. For sure it was pure spirit of generosity. Without food or shelter, some covered in blood, most wounded by war and rape, these victims remained valiant. Their bodies may have been destroyed, but the spirit of Rwandan women was not defeated. They would plan the future by correcting the past. They set in motion rebuilding their nation, but that could only happen after they rebuilt families. The women of Rwanda will never again allow another genocide in their land.

Women's organizations such as the Association Des Femmes Chef de Famille, Association for Rwandan Women's Solidarity, Association des Volontaire de la Paix, Federation of African Women Peace Networks, Forum of Women Parliamentarians of Rwanda, Imbabazi z'i Mugongo Orphanage, Pro-Femmes/Twese Hamwe, Reseau des Femmes, Unity Club, and Rwanda Women Leaders Caucus sensitized and encouraged other women to change their traditional views of the world and participate fully in every aspect of society. Women in leadership as well as rural subsistence farmers held public forums and information classes to educate women and students.

First Lady Jeannette Kagame established the Imbuto Foundation and served as an exemplar to others. Under her direction Imbuto created a medical insurance program for more than 230,000 widows, orphans, and those living with AIDS. Other health initiatives included the Protection and Care of Families against HIV/AIDS. Imbuto's education scholarships have been given to nearly 500 academically proficient girls and foster mothers; and its empowerment programs have benefited over 1,500 households, many headed by children. This presidential wife and mother of four also founded the Organization of African First Ladies against HIV/AIDS (OAFLA) that includes the First Ladies of forty African nations.

Rwanda's progress on HIV/AIDS has been remarkable, with less than 3 percent of the population infected. In 2001 the Government of Rwanda established a National Commission to Fight AIDS (CNLS), develop strategies, raise funds, and coordinate programs. The women of Rwanda commanded the attention and assistance of many agencies and NGOs from all over the world. The success of these efforts demonstrated leadership of the Rwandan women. They took action to deal with their experiences and the resulting medical issues.

Rwanda's central bank now offers micro loans to female entrepreneurs. Since the establishment of this women's empowerment credit from the government, international donors, and NGOs, more than 6,500 women have received micro loans worth nearly $1,000,000.

Within a decade of democracy Rwanda became the information technology capital of Africa. Its capital, Kigali, is developing a Technological Center that will rival any in the world. Rwanda is now the number one conference venue on the entire continent. The ecotourism industry is booming, and products like Rwandan handwoven baskets command artistic respect. The country is producing silk, and its world famous gourmet Rwandan coffee and mountain grown tea are considered to be some of the finest in the world.

The success of reconciliation efforts belongs entirely to the Rwandan people, but global support proved to be a key factor in helping to rebuild the country. Institutions such as the United States Agency for International Development (USAID), the United Nations Development Program (UNDP), the World Bank, and the Clinton Foundation all stepped forward to assist Rwanda. This nation is determined to remain sustainable, initiating a fifty-year master plan for its capital and a commitment to democracy for the nation, including a new $155 million international airport.

Rwanda's Government of National Unity has made progress in maintaining the inclusiveness of a broad-based government as an indispensable component of the new political dispensation, and Rwanda's postgenocide economy is fighting the cycle of poverty with a 5.5 percent GDP growth rate (2010). Recently a Free Economic Zone has been established to boost export trade. Rwanda has attracted a host of international investors like the Arab Emirates, which have pumped $300 million into tourist facilities around the country. The nation recently signed a bilateral investment treaty with the United States that enhances Rwanda's national economic vision and environmental orientation.

The political will of the women in this pluralistic democracy has proven that, although Rwanda was once the worst of what Africa can be, it is now the best of what Africa is. The people of Rwanda want to live in peace. They already know what it is like to live in war.

Slowly, Slowly, The Journey Is Completed

"I am a proud African who watched helplessly as my sisters suffered in the genocide. Look at these women now. They lead this nation. They picked themselves up—rich and poor, educated and semiliterate, businesswomen and farmers. Rwandans are exceptional. They moved forward with a fierce determination under horrendous conditions," explains African music icon and UNICEF Goodwill Ambassador for Eastern and Southern Africa, Yvonne Chaka Chaka. Although a South African citizen, she is a frequent visitor to Rwanda. In February 2008 a five-point magnitude earthquake hit the country, killing thirty-seven and injuring more than 600. Nearly 400 were treated for psychological trauma, and 80 percent were women and children. Hospitals, health centers, schools, and more than a thousand homes were damaged or destroyed. Twenty-seven thousand children lost their schools. With a rapid response, UNICEF tents were erected near the demolished structures.

Chaka Chaka recalls, "When the earthquake happened people didn't give in. They picked themselves up, built tents for classrooms, and moved on with their lives. When I saw the disaster sites, especially the temporary classrooms, I had a smile on my face and tears in my eyes because even the children don't give up! It was hot under that plastic, but the teachers carried on and these kids were still learning."

Multi award-winning "Princess of Africa" Chaka Chaka is a beloved humanitarian who has been a tireless campaigner for Africa's women and children. She emphasizes that, "Everyone in this society had a role to play; everyone did something. There is no other country in the world that offers this kind of balance between men and women. They understood that the two wings of a bird have to flutter equally to fly the distance. When you're in Rwanda you feel you belong."

Rwanda offers the world valuable lessons. This small Central African nation may lack many resources found in larger nations on the continent, but what they have are the greatest resources humanity can offer: women and men who understand the Kinyarwandan proverb of Rwanda, "The ruin of a nation begins in the homes of its people."

When the Rwandan genocide occurred the nation was in decay. After it concluded, it appeared the nation was dead. Postgenocide Rwanda is often called a miracle, but it was not a miracle at all—it was the women of this nation that achieved the singular, fundamental, and essential requirement for the continuation of any civilization: they preserved and maintained the family unit, despite its attempted destruction. Family is the core unit of any society; without family there is no sense of caring, no sense of community. What happened in Rwanda has produced improbable, amazing, extraordinary, and unexpected successes.

The world can look to this peaceful, disciplined African country for many lessons. Rwanda rose from the descent of genocide, and it was the women who helped create a nation that is a modern day model of gender equality. The rest of the world would do well to take the same direction.

Rwanda was a profound encounter where part of my heart remained with the people, especially the women in the "land of a thousand hills." They have endured the unimaginable and learned how to transform their horror into hope. Their way of life has become their triumph.

References

Dassié, R. 2009. *Men on men rape cases in DR Congo: The ordeal of bush wives.* (August 13). Available at http://www.en.afrik.com/article16039.html.

Eveleens, I. 2004. Unhappy Anniversary, *Time Magazine* (March 28). Available at http://www.time.com/time/magazine/article/0,9171,605443,00.html.

Gerhart, G. 1996. Not So Innocent: When Women Become Killers, *African Rights* (May 1). Gale Group.

Gjesti, C. 2009. DR Congo: *Drama against Rape*, Action by Churches Together (ACT) International (July 27) Available at http://www.act-intl.org/news.php?uid=714.

Hatzfeld, J. 2005. *Machete Season: The Killers in Rwanda Speak.* Farrar, Straus and Giroux.

House, Robert. 2004. *Culture, Leadership, and Organizations.* The GLOBE Study of 62 Societies. Leadership and Organizational Behavior Effectiveness Research Program. Sage Publications.

Landesman, Peter. 2002. A Woman's Work (September 15). *The New York Times Magazine.* Available at http://www.nytimes.com/2002/09/15/magazine/a-woman-s-work.html.

Prunier, G. 1995. *The Rwanda crisis: History of a Genocide.* New York: Columbia University Press, 231–232.

Sharlach, L. 1999. *Gender and genocide in Rwanda: Women as agents and objects of Genocide.* (November) *Journal of Genocide Research*, Volume 1, Issue 3.

Index

Abortion 51, 62, 220
About-Face 68
Abu Ghraib 127
Accountability viii
Activism/Activist(s) 32, 34–37, 59, 66, 83, 139, 143, 150, 155, 162, 164, 178, 202
Advocacy xiv, 67, 99, 137, 138, 143–149
Afghanistan/Afghani xiii, xvi, 8, 11, 117–134, 206, 207, 216, 222, 224
Africa xiii, 17, 20, 31–44, 60, 75–97, 171–186, 206, 233–254
African American Women in Cinema (AAWiC) 68
Africare 41
Albania(n) 26, 27
Algeria 64, 205
Alliances viii
al Qaeda 121, 213, 216, 228
al-Zarqawi, Abu Musab 213
Amazons 62
American Legion 191, 192, 195, 199, 201
American Refugee Committee International (ARC) 63
Amnesty 85
Amnesty International xi, 33, 47, 60, 66, 118, 124, 127
Angola 64
Apartheid 77, 78, 79, 80, 83, 90
Argentina 40
Armenia 249
Asian-American Justice Center 68

Asian Task Force Against Domestic Violence xi, xiv
Association of Genocide Widows 248
Asylum seekers 45–57

Bangladesh xiii, 20, 64, 132
Baskent University, Turkey xv
Bassa Women's Development Association (BAWODA) 34, 35, 38
Beijing Platform for Action (1995) 66
Belgium 176, 213, 214
Beth Israel Deaconess Medical Center xiv
bin Laden, Osama 118, 119, 206
Black Student Organization (NEU) xi, xii
Bosnia xii, 2, 48, 65, 145, 249
Bosnia-Herzegovina xiii, xvii, 9, 25, 36, 47, 100, 137–154
Boston Area Rape Crisis Center (BARCC) xi, xiii
Boston Care Network xi
Boston Center for Refugee Health and Human Rights xii–xiv, xviii, 46
Boston University School of Medicine xviii
Brandies University xvi, xvii
Brazil 12
Brudnick Center on Conflict and Violence xi
Bush, George W. 119, 121, 122, 127, 220, 221, 223, 224, 225, 228

Cambodia xiv, 4, 41, 249
Canada 40
Censorship 61, 198, 201
Center for Media, Culture and History (at NYU) 68
Center for Media Literacy (CML) 68
Center for New Words 68
Center for Violence Prevention and Recovery xiv
Chad 47, 69
Chandler, Robin M. viii, xi, xv, 1–14, 31–44
Chatham University xv
Chechnya 64, 205, 206, 207, 209–211
China/Chinese xviii, xix, 12, 20, 41, 60, 64
Clark University xv
Class 60, 62, 140, 227
Code Pink 132
Coexistence International xvii
Comics and cartoons 61, 62
Communication 53, 192, 196, 198
Communication for Change 63
Community/communities 18, 21, 23, 24, 25, 26, 28, 32, 34, 36, 43, 47, 48, 49, 51, 52, 53, 54, 55, 64, 65, 76, 117, 178, 201, 202, 215, 226, 236, 244
Community Violence Intervention xiv
Concordia University xvi
Conspiracy of silence 12, 42
Contributors xv–xix, 4–5
Cosar, Simten xv, 9–10, 155–170
Costa Rica 69
Cote d'Ivoire 37, 64
Croatia/Croats 141, 149
Culture 18, 33, 38, 42, 46, 47, 49, 52, 53, 54, 62, 117, 248
Cunningham, Karla J. xv, 10–11, 205–217
Curtis, Robyn xiv

Darfur *see* Sudan
Dean's office of College of Arts and Science (NEU) xi
Democratic Republic of Congo 6, 7, 17, 24, 33, 36, 41, 47, 63, 64, 101, 237, 238
Denmark 41, 214
Development 99
Discrimination 18, 47, 66, 79–82, 138, 247
Disease(s) 37
Domestic violence xii, xiii, xiv, 60, 61, 124, 162, 163, 180
Dorchester People for Peace xvi, 132
Drug(s) 125

East Timor 40, 64, 100
Education 34, 38, 65, 80, 118, 125, 158
El Salvador 205
Enloe, Cynthia vii–ix, xv–xvi, 2, 22, 195, 221, 223
Ensler, Eve 66
Ethics 7, 19, 130
Ethiopia 64
Ethnic cleansing 24, 65, 241
Ethnicity/ethnic struggles 19, 60, 62, 134–189
Ethno-nationalism 20, 23, 27
Europe 12, 143, 144
Exploitation (including sexual exploitation) 31, 46, 79, 106, 107, 108

Fairbank Center for East Asian Studies, Harvard University xix
Family 24, 25, 35, 36, 52, 53, 54, 60, 64, 65, 81, 128, 189–203, 244, 245, 254
Female genital mutilation (FGM) 34, 62
Feminist activism xi, 157
Feminist analyses vii, xvi, 67, 75, 99, 113, 219
Feminist Peace Network 65

Feminist politics viii, 138, 139
Feminist Student Organization (NEU) xi, xii
Films xii
Finland 146, 151
Finley, Meghan xiii
Foreword (Cynthia Enloe) vii–ix
Fuller, Linda K. vii, xii, xvi, 59–72
Funding Exchange xi

Gardiner, Steven L. xvi, 10, 189–203
Gardner-Morkert, Michelle M. xvi, 11, 219–231
Garner, Angie Reed xvi, 10, 189–203
Gay & Lesbian Alliance Against Defamation (GLAAD) 68
The Geena Davis Institute on Gender in Media 68
Gender 18, 21, 31, 33, 50, 53, 59, 60, 61, 62, 66, 67, 68, 99–115, 181, 189
Gender-based violence (GBV) 1–13, 15, 31–44, 50, 52, 59, 62, 63, 64–66, 83, 107, 163, 180, 238, 248
  Literature review 2, 4–5, 61
Gender advisers 100–115
Gender Equity and Equality Project (GEEP) 146, 147, 148
The Geneva Centre for the Democratic Control of Armed Forces (DCAF) 66
Geneva Convention(s) 20
Genocide 2, 11, 18, 22, 47, 64, 171, 172, 173, 235–236, 237, 249
Gerbner, George 60
Germany/Germans xviii, 39, 41, 65, 214
Geula, Marianne Smith xiii
Ghana 40
Global citizenship 2
Global gendered politics vii, 135–186

Gomez, Carol xiv
Gopnik, Melissa xiii
Guatemala 40
Guinea 37, 63
Gurd, Kiri xiii, xvi, 7–8, 75–97

Haiti 36
Hannover University, Germany xix
Hartwick, Lisa xiv
Healing 32, 250
Health (including mental health) 48, 51, 52, 53, 64, 81, 125, 128–129, 241
Hegemony 75–97, 161
History/historical perspective 20, 26, 31, 51, 64, 79–82, 117, 118, 172, 205–207, 210, 226
HIV/AIDS 11, 34, 37, 39, 41, 48, 51, 55, 62, 67, 129, 174, 175, 236, 237, 239, 241, 248, 252
The Holocaust (World War II) 11, 65, 249
Homophobia 198, 227
Honduras xviii
Honor 24, 52, 60, 180
Human rights xiii, 1, 7–8, 13, 33, 42, 55, 64, 67, 75–97, 100, 127, 139, 247
Human Rights Watch (HRW) 66, 120, 235, 236
Humanitarian crisis xiii
Hussein, Saddam 121, 122, 212

Identity 17–18
Ideology 19, 66, 79, 209, 221
Illiteracy xiii, 38, 39, 69, 174
Imam, Hayat xiii, 8, 117–134
Immigration process 51
India xii, 12, 20, 41, 60
Indonesia/Indonesians 12, 64
Information Campaign on Domestic Violence (Zimbabwe) 68
Integrated Regional Information Networks (IRIN) 2, 40

Internally displaced person (IDP) 99
International Committee of the Red Cross (ICRC) 20
International Criminal Court 48
International Monetary Fund 39
International Rescue Committee xvii, 41
International Women's Media Foundation (IWMF) 68
Internet 33, 61, 62, 139
Intifada 208
Iran xii, 4, 205, 206
Iraq xiii, xvii, 8, 10–11, 63, 64, 117–134, 190, 192, 194, 201, 205–217, 224
Islam *see* Muslim(s)
Israel 62, 63, 208
Ivory Coast *see* Cote d'Ivoire

Japan/Japanese 12, 20, 48, 64, 65
Jenichen, Anne xvii, 9, 137–154
Jihad/Jihadis (including the global jihadi movement (GJM/ *Salafi*) 206, 207, 209, 210, 211, 213, 214, 215, 216
Johnson-Sirleaf, Ellen 32–33, 38, 39
Jordan xvi, 212, 213
Justice 1, 11, 41, 200, 242, 243

Karzai, Hamid 119, 120, 124, 125
Kashmir 64
Katz, Jackson 67
Keaney-Mischel, Colleen xiii, xvii, 8, 99–115
Kenya 64, 230
Ki-Moon, Ban 69
King, Martin Luther 12, 250
Koohi-Kamali, Farideh xiv
Korea/Koreans 20, 64, 191
Kosovo 36, 101

Lahore University of Management Science, Pakistan xvi
Lakota/Oglala Nation xviii
Language 52, 141, 194, 197, 199

Lebanon 41, 205
Legal(ities) 37, 38, 42, 54, 64, 80–82, 93, 125, 138, 147, 148–149, 150, 158, 159, 178, 238, 244–253
Liberia/Liberians xviii, 6–7, 31–44, 63, 64, 102

Makeba, Miriam 33
Malawi 69
Mandela, Nelson 233, 251
Manjoo, Rashida xiii, xvii, 7–8, 75–97
Marriage xiii, 47, 52, 60, 63, 80, 124, 125, 175, 227
Masculinity/men 8, 12, 13, 18, 21, 24, 26, 42, 61, 99, 117, 130, 193, 195, 198
Medecins Sans Frontieres (MSF/ Doctors Without Borders) 66
Media 7, 11, 17, 41, 59–72, 119, 196, 220
Media Education Foundation (MEF) 67, 68
Media Monitoring Group (Turkey) 163
Media Monitoring Project (MMP/ South Africa) 68
Medical treatment 52, 64
MERLIN 35
Middle East xv, 117–134, 190, 205–217
Middle East Center for Peace, Culture, and Development xi
Military/militarization vii, 5, 10, 37, 48, 63, 65, 67, 118, 123, 127, 158, 160–162, 165, 189–203, 216, 219–231, 238, 243
Mind on the Media 68
Misogyny 61, 125, 177
Morocco 40
Morrison, Toni 31, 32
Mothers/motherhood 189–203, 219–231, 248
Mozambique 36

Index

Music 61, 62
Muslim(s) 16, 21, 24, 26, 67, 127, 130, 141, 156, 206, 207, 212, 213, 214, 216, 228, 229
Myanmar 64

Namibia xviii
Narratives 75–97, 138, 181, 192
  see also Language, Rhetoric, Stories, Testimonials
National Hispanic Media Coalition 68
National Sexual Violence Resource Center (NSVRC) 66
Nationalism 17–30, 117, 137, 141, 151, 156, 158, 161, 165, 168, 205–217
Neo-liberalism 86, 162
Network of Women in Media, India (NWMI) 68
News 60, 61
New York Women in Film and Television (NYWIFT) 68
Nicaragua 205
Nigeria 34
Northeastern University (NEU) xi, xv, xvi, xvii, 2

Obama, President Barack 131
Oppressed/Oppression 35, 67, 79–82
Organizational reconciliation v, 73–134
Orphans/orphanages 34, 241, 247, 248

Pakistan 20, 36, 119, 214, 236
Palestine 63, 205, 206, 207–209
Patriarchy of war viii, xiii, 13, 19, 22, 25, 61, 187–251
Peace-building/Peace-keeping v, xvii, 11, 15, 76, 99–115, 137–154, 155–170, 179, 242, 245, 249
PeaceWomen 66
Peru 36, 64

Philippines/Filipinas 64, 236
Physicians for Human Rights 47, 129
Piwowarczyk, Linda xiv, xviii, 7, 45–57
Police 37, 99–115
Policy reform vii, 73–134, 137
Political/Politics 19, 25, 26, 31, 36, 37, 46, 65, 67, 78, 79, 90, 100, 138, 141, 142, 143, 144, 155, 156, 157, 158, 160, 171, 175, 177–178, 179, 199–201, 203, 225
Popular culture xii, 61, 62
Pornography 62
Postwar/post-conflict viii, 73–134, 137, 171–186
Poverty/impoverishment 5, 12, 38, 53, 62, 117, 132, 234
Power 17, 18, 21, 25, 33, 37, 47, 53, 75, 76, 182, 190, 192, 221
Preface and acknowledgments xi–xiv
Pregnancy 47, 51, 54, 60, 61, 62, 65, 125, 141, 237, 241
Prevention of war viii
Project for a New American Century (PNAC) 119, 120
Propaganda 6, 173, 215
Prostitution 20, 35, 47, 62, 124, 174, 175, 195, 237
Psychology 51, 52, 53, 60, 130

Quran 125

Racism 77, 83, 93, 198, 228
Radcliffe Institute for Advanced Study 67
Racialicious 68
Rape viii, xiii, xiv, 6, 11, 12, 13, 17–30, 33, 35, 39, 41, 46, 47, 48, 49, 50, 53, 54, 61, 62, 63, 64–66, 67, 83, 118, 124, 125, 127, 130–131, 141, 148, 173, 180, 181, 233–251
Rape Crisis Intervention xiv
Reebok Human Rights Project xi

Rebuilding personal security for girls and women v, 15
Reconciliation 11, 32, 138, 139, 178, 238, 240, 243, 245, 249
Reconstruction 78, 100, 133, 138, 139, 140, 150, 151, 171, 172, 175, 177–179, 181–184, 233–251
Reel Grrls 68
Reframing 21st century feminism 134–186
Refugees (and asylum seekers) xiii, xiv, 7, 45–57, 59, 99, 128, 179
Refugee Immigration Ministry xi
Refugee Women in Development (RefWID) xiii
Refugees International 66
Religion 37, 53, 60, 65, 117, 205–217, 235
Reparations 88
Research 61, 100, 155, 190, 219
Resilience 49
Revolutionary Afghan Women's Association (RAWA) 132
Rhetoric 19, 23, 26, 28, 60, 131, 137, 190
Rice, Tadia xvii–xviii, 11, 233–251
Roskos, Laura xiii
Rotella, Laura xiii
Russia/Russians 65, 210, 230
Rwanda 2, 4, 6, 10, 11, 17, 36, 40, 47, 48, 64, 65, 171–186, 233–251

Safe Transitions xiv
Saudi Arabia 206
Selek, Pinar 155, 161, 164, 165–166, 167, 168
Serbia/Serbs 26, 27, 65, 141, 230
September 11, 2001 49, 119, 121, 219, 226, 228
Sex trafficking xii, xiii, 13, 40, 60, 61, 62, 124
Sexism 19, 77

Sexual violence xii, xiii, 20, 27, 32, 34, 45, 47, 49, 50–51, 60, 88, 106, 118, 124, 138, 173–175
  see also Gender-based Violence, Rape
SheSource.org 68
Sierra Leone 36, 37, 40, 47, 64, 205
16 Days of Activism Against Gender Violence 66
Sjoberg, Laura xviii, 10, 171–186
Slaves/slavery 37, 47, 60, 64, 65, 78, 230
Social awareness xiv
The Solomon Islands 40
Somalia 64
South Africa xiii, xvi, 12, 40, 75–91, 243
South African Truth and Reconciliation Commission xiii, 7, 75–96
Spirituality 13, 32, 54
Sports 61
Sri Lanka 63, 64
Steller, James xiv
Stigma 48, 53, 64, 65, 175, 235
Stories 8, 33, 34, 40, 45, 61, 77, 89, 172, 181, 198, 231, 242
Sub-Saharan Africa xiii
Sudan 4, 6, 17, 24, 36, 41, 64, 65, 69, 230, 246
Suicide(s) xiii, 51, 61, 67, 123, 131, 206, 207, 209, 211, 212, 213, 214, 215, 216, 239
Survivors/survival viii, xvii, 32, 51, 52, 53, 54, 180, 237, 240, 243
Swaziland 39

Taboo(s) 7, 53, 180, 196
Taliban 118, 119, 120, 123, 125, 228
Terrorism 47, 61, 64, 226
Testimonials 3, 32, 40
Theory 139
Torture 46–47, 52, 127, 251

INDEX

Trafficking Victims Outreach and Services Network xi, xiv
Trauma xviii, 3, 7, 11, 32, 34, 46, 50, 51, 52, 53, 54, 55, 65, 117, 238, 243, 248
Traumatic gynecologic fistula (TGF) 34, 46, 237, 240–241
Truth and Reconciliation 32, 40, 75–97
Turkey xv, 9, 12, 64, 155–170, 205, 236

Uganda 64
Unemployment 38
United for Peace with Justice 132
United Nations (UN) vii, xiii, 6, 8, 46, 49, 66
United Nations Commissioner for Refugees (UNHCR) 1, 45, 47, 49, 51
United Nations Convention on Ending Discrimination Against Women (CEDAW) 124, 147
United Nations Declaration on the Elimination of Violence Against Women 13
United Nations Department of Peacekeeping Operations (DPKO) 100
United Nations Development Fund for Women (UNIFEM) 33, 62, 66, 247, 248
United Nations Development Program (UNDP) 180, 252
United Nations High Commission for Refugees 126
United Nations Millennium Development Goals 31
United Nations peacekeeping missions 99–115
United Nations Research Institute for Social Development (UNRISD) xvii
United Nations Resolution 1325 55, 114

United Nations Special Rapporteur xvii
United States xvii, 8, 12, 32, 45, 111, 219–231
United States Agency for International Development (USAID) 249
University of Cape Town xvii
USAID 36

Van Cey xiv
Veteran(s) 189–203
Victim(s) 6, 7, 13, 18, 33, 40, 59, 61, 62, 64, 65, 82, 85, 138, 139, 143, 172, 173–174, 175, 177, 181, 195, 242, 244, 252
Videogames 62
Vienna World Conference on Human Rights (1993) 66
Vietnam xii, xiii, xiv, 3, 36, 191, 205
Violence viii, xi, xiii, xiv, 1, 3, 8, 13, 78, 117, 140, 205–207
Violence against women (VAW) 59, 61, 65, 66, 127, 173–175
Violence by women (VBW) 59, 61, 62, 63, 172, 173, 175–177, 205, 206, 207–209, 212–216, 242–243
see also Domestic Violence
Virginia Polytechnic Institute and State University xviii
Voices 3, 151, 157

Wali, Sima xii–xiii
Wang, Lihua iv, vii, xix, 3
War(s) vii, 3, 4
Wartime violence viii, 123, 126, 141–142, 148, 183, 190, 214
Weapons of mass destruction (WMDs) 121
Web *see* Internet
Webster University xvii

Women xiii
Women at the Forefront (www.womenattheforefront.com) 68
Women combatants and noncombatants 61, 62, 66, 100, 183, 187–251
Women in Film (WIF) 68
Women in the Director's Chair 68
Women for Women International 2, 33, 59
Women Make Movies 68
Women's eNews 68
Women's Media Center 68
Women's rights viii, xiii

Women's Studies xi, xv
Women warriors 62, 159
Worcester State College xv
World Bank 12, 119, 249
World Health Organization (WHO) 1, 42, 47, 50, 60
The World Health Organization Task Force on Violence and Health 66
World Watch 66

Yugoslavia 6, 17, 20, 24, 26, 28, 64, 141, 143

Zabeida, Natalja 6, 17–30

CPSIA information can be obtained
at www.ICGtesting.com
Printed in the USA
LVOW05*0150250817
546313LV00013B/387/P

9 780230 103719